the ANIME CHEF cookbook

75 Iconic Dishes from Your Favorite Anime

NADINE ESTERO

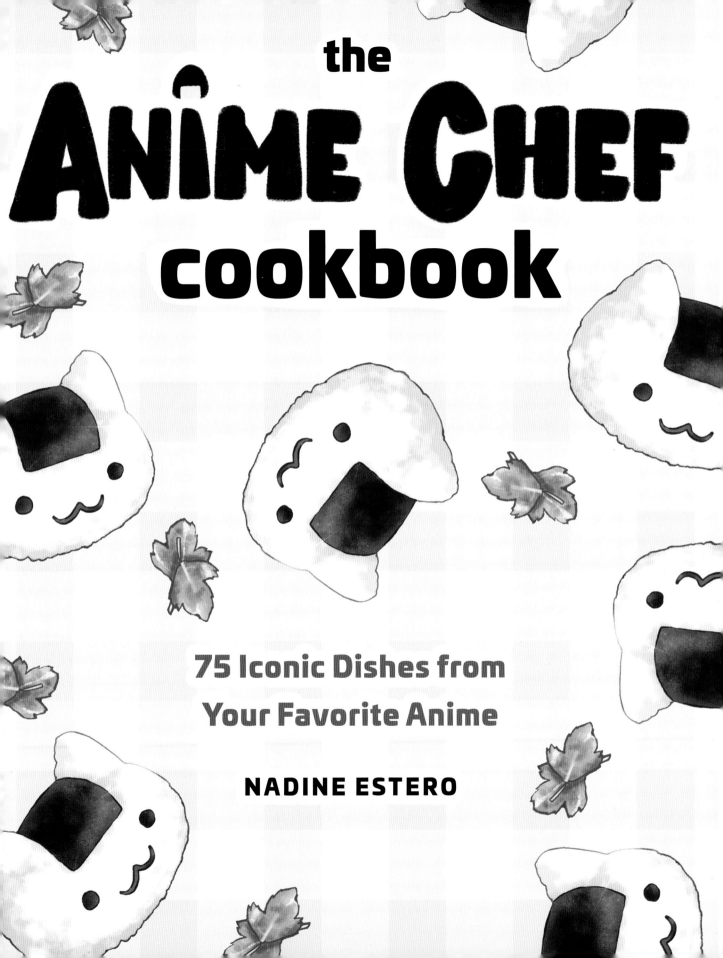

Brimming with creative inspiration, how-to projects, and useful information to enrich your everyday life, quarto.com is a favorite destination for those pursuing their interests and passions.

First published in 2022 by Rock Point, an imprint of The Quarto Group,
142 West 36th Street, 4th Floor, New York, NY 10018, USA
T (212) 779-4972 F (212) 779-6058 www.Quarto.com

Library of Congress Control Number: 2022933759

10 9 8 7 6 5 4 3 2 1

ISBN: 978-1-63106-866-9

Publisher: Rage Kindelsperger
Creative Director: Laura Drew
Managing Editor: Cara Donaldson
Senior Editor: Erin Canning
Interior Design: Chika Azuma
Cover and Interior Illustrations: Jana Paynor
Additional Text: Yashu Pericherla

Printed in China

For my family—Mum, Dad, Kuya, and D—
and my bestest friends—Jesree, Kim, and
Adrian. And to all the people who supported me
to get to this point, thank you so much!

APPETIZERS

MAINS

DESSERTS

DRINKS

CONTENTS

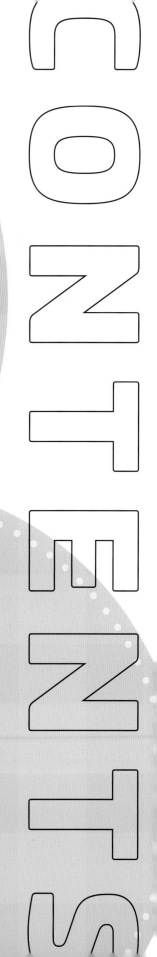

INTRODUCTION

WHO KNEW THAT WHEN YOU SETTLE IN TO WATCH AN ANIME THAT A SIDE EFFECT IS A CRAVING FOR DELICIOUS-LOOKING ANIMATED FOODS?

Just like in our own lives, food plays a huge role in anime, which is one of the many reasons we enjoy watching anime and find it so relatable no matter the subject matter. Food featured in anime can vary from just a flash on the screen to an entire episode devoted to a recipe, from traditional Japanese comfort foods to something completely invented. There are even entire series that are just about cooking and food.

My interest in cooking started while I was at university and would watch cooking videos by self-taught cooks. When I moved into a place of my own, I started cooking for myself, which made me immerse myself even more in the food world. Soon after, I became interested in re-creating foods in anime and video games. I loved the challenge of replicating food artistically, as well as making it appetizing, all while paying respect to the setting of each anime. I've watched anime ever since I can remember, and my favorite series growing up were action anime, such as *Dragon Ball Z* and *YuYu Hakusho*. Now my favorites are in the slice-of-life genre, such as *Laid-Back Camp* and *Fruits Basket*. I started documenting my food re-creations on social media in late 2020, quickly acquiring over two hundred thousand followers. In this book, I wanted to represent a variety of anime (though there a couple of repeats) and dishes, so that there was a nice mix of savory and sweet. A lot of the recipes are common Japanese dishes, but I also created dishes based solely on how they looked or from any hints about flavors that I could glean from the dialogue.

My mission with *The Anime Chef Cookbook* is to share the joy that food, animation, and art bring me with you, and for you to use the recipes in this book to spend time with others creating and eating delicious food. Messages from people describing how I have given them inspiration and how experiences with my food brought their family together fill me with happiness. I also don't want you to feel the need to replicate my recipes exactly. Some of them, especially the desserts, have a lot of bells and whistles, as my goal is to re-create the dishes as they look in the anime, so feel free to do as little or as much as you like. Most importantly, have fun and satisfy that appetite!

THE ANIME KITCHEN

Beyond the basic tools you may already have stocked in your kitchen, these are recommendations for additional items you may want to have on hand that are useful for the recipes throughout the book. For recipes that require more specialized tools, they are listed as Special Tools for that recipe. Regarding the ingredients, use this list as a reference guide because a lot of items are Japanese, which you can find at Japanese and Asian markets or online.

TOOLS

CHOPSTICKS A simple pair of chopsticks comes in handy for stirring, holding, and decorating foods.

COOKING RACK Also called cooling racks, these metal racks have short legs that raise them off a surface. Look for racks that can be used in the oven and for setting items on to cool.

ELECTRIC MIXER A lot of the dessert recipes involve whipping eggs or heavy cream, so a hand mixer with a whisk attachment will make your life easier. For some dough recipes, a stand mixer is recommended, but these are an investment, and you can always knead that dough with your hands and build some muscles.

FINE-MESH STRAINER This strainer with tiny holes is great for rinsing rice and refining purées, jams, and pastes. You can also use cheesecloth.

OFFSET SPATULA This is a thin, metal spatula that works well for frosting cakes and giving them a polished look.

PIPING BAGS AND TIPS To give your desserts that over-the-top anime decoration, piping bags and tips will help. There are disposable and reusable piping bags, and piping tips come in lots of sizes. You can purchase a basic piping bag and tip set online. If you don't have a piping tip, you can also cut a hole at the tip of a piping bag, or even use a resealable plastic bag with a corner cut off if you don't have either.

PASTRY BRUSH This brush is great for brushing egg wash, oil, sauces, and more onto foods.

THERMOMETER I recommend two types of thermometers: an instant-read thermometer for measuring the internal temperature of meat and a candy thermometer for not only candy making but also for measuring oil when deep-frying.

INGREDIENTS

BONITO FLAKES (KATSUOBUSHI) Very thinly shaved pieces of fish that have been dried, smoked, and fermented and used to flavor stocks and top dishes.

BONITO POWDER A finely ground version of bonito flakes.

CHILI OIL A Chinese condiment made with oil infused with chili pepper that adds a little spiciness to a dish.

CHINESE FERMENTED SOYBEANS (DOUBANJIANG) A condiment with a paste-like texture made with fermented soybeans and chili pepper that adds umami and spiciness to a dish.

CHINESE FERMENTED BLACK BEANS (DOUCHI) Whole black beans fermented in salt that add umami to a dish.

CROWN DAISIES Also called chrysanthemum leaves, these greens are eaten both raw and cooked in Asian dishes.

DARK SOY SAUCE Fermented for a longer period of time than regular soy sauce, it results in a product that is thicker and sweeter.

DASHI POWDER An instant soup stock with flavors of bonito flakes (katsuobushi) and dried kelp (kombu) for making dashi, the base for many Japanese soups. Also used to flavor other dishes.

DEEP-FRIED TOFU POCKETS (ABURA-AGE) Golden-brown tofu that has been deep-fried twice. The deep-frying creates a pocket, or pouch.

DRIED KELP (KOMBU) Dried brown kelp that comes in sheets or strips and is used to flavor dashi stock.

DRIED SEAWEED (NORI) A dried seaweed of red algae that comes in sheets and is often used to make sushi rolls and onigiri.

DRIED SEAWEED FLAKES (AONORI) Dried green seaweed that is finely chopped and used to sprinkle on dishes.

DRIED RED BEANS (ADZUKI BEANS) Often cooked and sweetened to make the red bean paste found in many Asian sweets.

FISH CAKE (NARUTOMAKI) Recognizable by its pink swirl when sliced, this cured minced fish paste comes in the shape of a tube with ridges.

JAPANESE MOUNTAIN YAM (NAGAIMO OR YAMAIMO) When grated, this hairy root vegetable is the secret ingredient for fluffy okonomiyaki (savory pancake).

JAPANESE PARSLEY (MITSUBA) This herb used to garnish dishes tastes less like the parsley we know and more like celery.

JAPANESE RADISH (DAIKON) A long, white root vegetable with a slightly bitter taste that can be eaten raw or cooked and is often enjoyed pickled.

KEWPIE MAYO A beloved Japanese mayonnaise that is made with egg yolks instead of whole eggs like other mayonnaise.

MATCHA POWDER A special green tea plant in which the leaves have been ground into a powder. Used in drinks and to flavor and color foods when cooking.

MILK POWDER Also called powdered milk, dry milk, and dried milk, this powder is popular in Asia and gives a concentrated sweet milk flavor to desserts and drinks, such as milk tea.

MIRIN A sweet rice wine similar to sake but with less alcohol and more sugar that plays an important role in Japanese cooking.

MISO A fermented soybean paste that comes in white, yellow, red, and black versions and packs an umami punch.

MUSHROOMS Along with the familiar white button mushroom, some recipes call for shiitake, which have brown caps; enoki, which are long, white, and thin; and king oyster, which are large with thick stems.

NOODLES (RAMEN, UDON, SOBA) Ramen is a thin wheat noodle, udon is a thick wheat noodle, and soba is a thin noodle made with buckwheat. They can be purchased fresh or dried.

OIL Unless a specific type is listed, use a neutral oil (vegetable, canola, peanut, grapeseed, avocado, sunflower, etc.) for the recipes in this book. When frying, use a neutral oil with a high smoke point.

OKONOMIYAKI SAUCE A sauce that is a bit similar to Worcestershire sauce but sweeter for topping okonomiyaki (savory pancake). You can also make your own sauce.

PANKO BREAD CRUMBS Used to give deep-fried Japanese dishes such as tempura and pork cutlet (tonkatsu) a crunchy coating.

PICKLED BAMBOO SHOOTS (MENMA) Seasoned bamboo shoots that are a condiment for topping a bowl of ramen.

RED PICKLED GINGER (BENI SHOGA) Thin, bright red strips of ginger pickled in plum vinegar. It is different from the pickled ginger that comes with sushi.

RICE VINEGAR A vinegar made with fermented rice that is a cooking staple in Japan. Unlike mirin, it is alcohol free.

SESAME OIL An oil made from sesame seeds and used to enhance food flavors.

SHAOXING COOKING WINE A Chinese fermented rice wine used in cooking from the city of Shaoxing. It contains alcohol.

SHISO LEAVES Also called perilla leaves, this versatile, refreshing herb is similar to mint but with its own distinct flavor.

SHORT-GRAIN WHITE RICE Also called sushi rice, it is used for sushi and onigiri, as well as eating on its own.

SOY SAUCE A versatile condiment that has a salty, umami flavor.

STICKY RICE Also called sweet rice and glutinous rice, it is used in savory and sweet dishes. Its low starch content causes it to be sticky.

SWEET RICE FLOUR Also called glutinous rice flour, this gluten-free flour is used for making savory and sweet foods, such as dango and mochi. A popular brand is Mochiko.

TAKOYAKI SAUCE Thicker and sweeter than okonomiyaki sauce, this sauce is used to top takoyaki (balls of fluffy dough with octopus). You can also make your own sauce.

TEMPURA BITS (TENKASU OR AGEDAMA) Crunchy pieces of deep-fried flour used for fillings and toppings. You can substitute with unsweetened crispy rice cereal.

TONKATSU SAUCE A thick sauce comprised of fruits and vegetables and that is savory and sweet for serving with tonkatsu (pork cutlet). You can make your own simplified version of the sauce.

WASABI Japanese horseradish that has a sharp flavor that can clear the sinuses. It usually comes as a bright green paste because real wasabi is hard and expensive to come by.

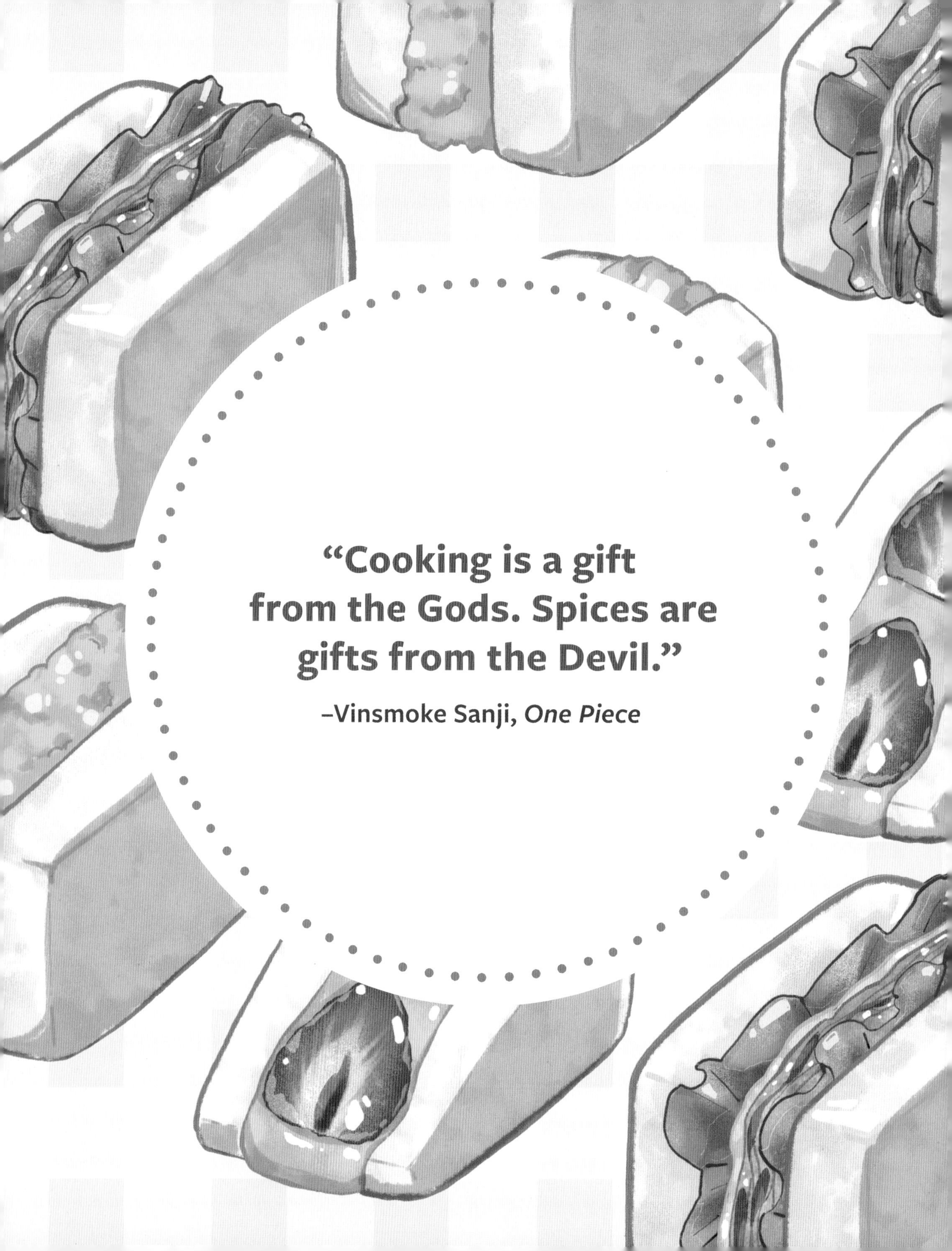

"Cooking is a gift from the Gods. Spices are gifts from the Devil."

–Vinsmoke Sanji, *One Piece*

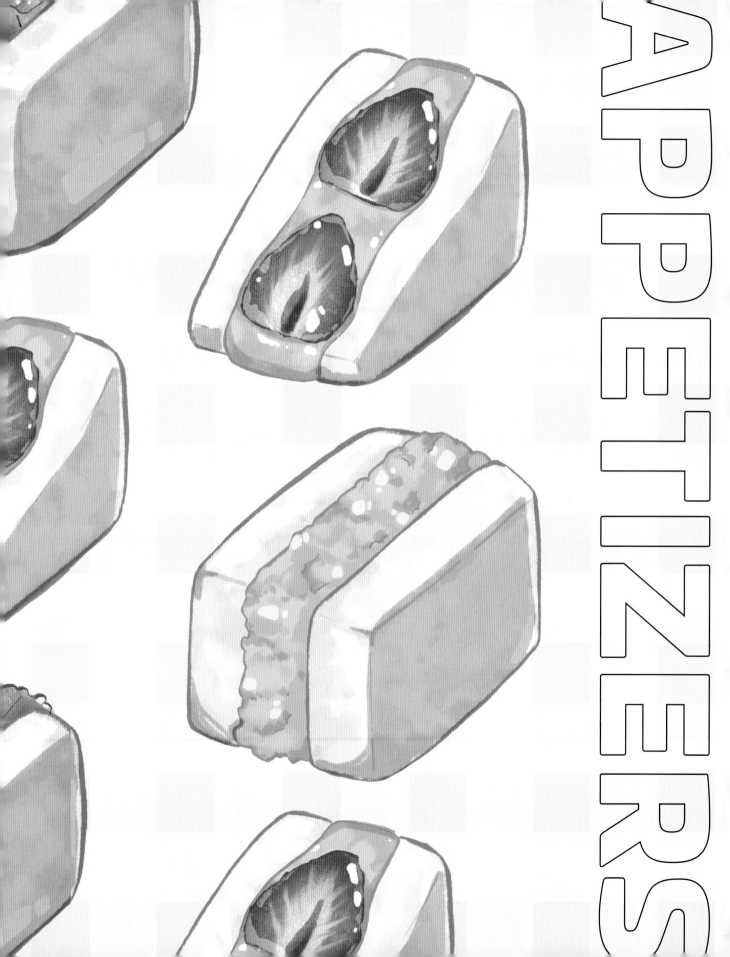

APPETIZERS

AFTER-PRACTICE NIKUMAN

★ ANIME ★
HAIKYUU!!
SEASON 1 | EPISODE 5
A COWARD'S ANXIETY

To teach them to work together, Hinata and Kageyama are forced to play a 3-on-3 match against Tsukishima and Yamaguchi, the two other first years on the team. After Hinata and Kageyama win, the team head to the Sakanoshita Shop convenience store to celebrate. The Karasuno team captain, Daichi, buys everyone nikuman (hot, fluffy pork buns), which becomes a recurring after-practice routine in the anime. Nikuman is a convenience store staple in Japan thanks to its portability and affordability—plus, it's delicious, which doesn't hurt!

YIELD **6** NIKUMAN PREP **45** MINUTES REST **70** MINUTES COOK **15** MINUTES

DOUGH

1 cup (120 g) all-purpose flour, plus more for dusting

½ tablespoon sugar

½ teaspoon active dry yeast

Pinch salt

⅓ cup (80 ml) water

½ tablespoon oil, plus more for greasing

JUICY PORK FILLING

9 ounces (250 g) ground pork

1 tablespoon soy sauce

1 tablespoon sake

1½ tablespoons cornstarch

2 scallions, white parts minced

2 tablespoons minced onion

3 cloves garlic, minced

½ teaspoon minced ginger root

2 teaspoons sugar

½ teaspoon salt

3 dashes white pepper

For Serving

Mustard and/or soy sauce

《 CONTINUED 》

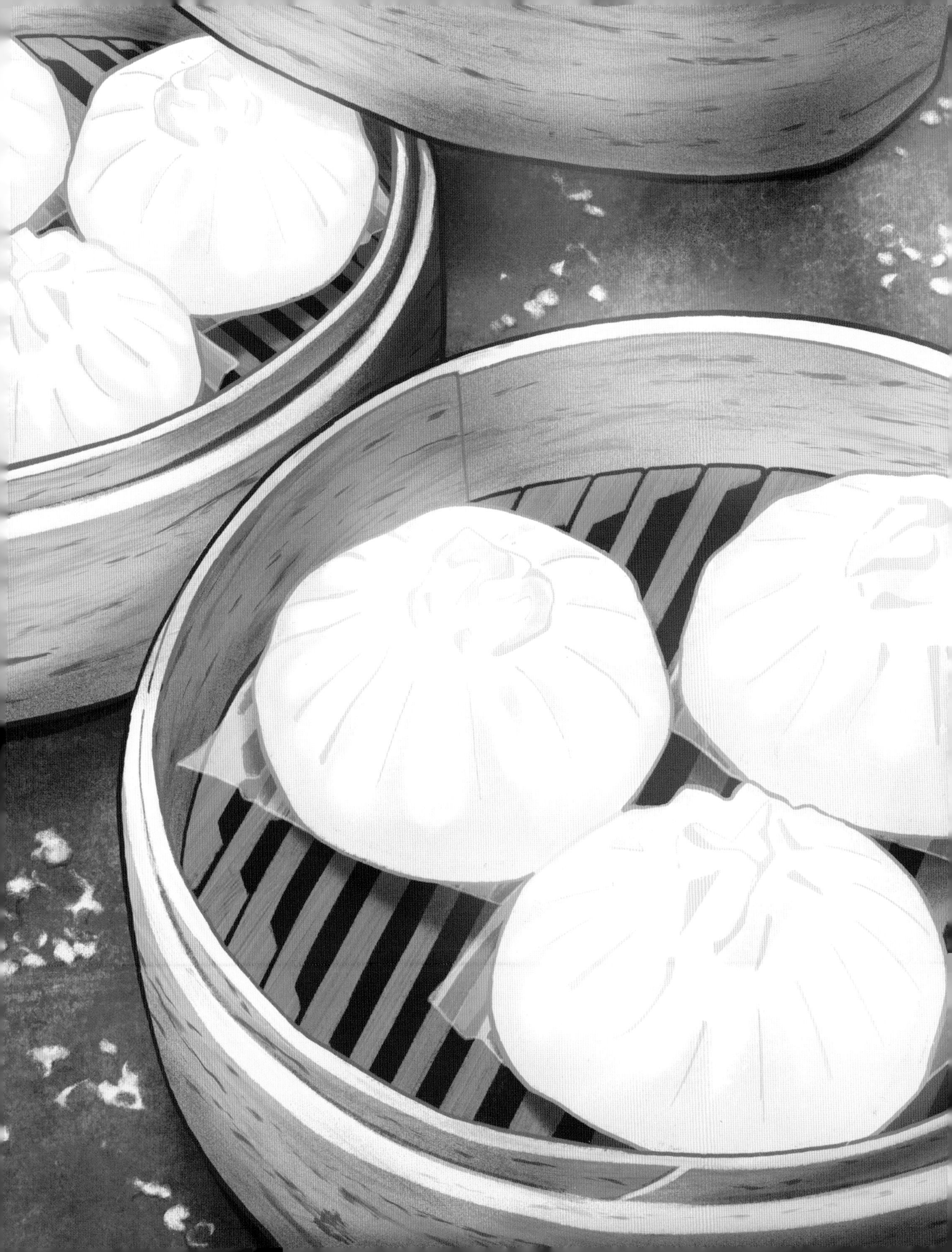

AFTER-PRACTICE NIKUMAN STEPS

1 To make the dough: In a medium bowl or bowl of a stand mixer, stir together the flour, ½ tablespoon sugar, yeast, and pinch of salt. In a separate small bowl, stir together the water and oil, then slowly drizzle the liquid into the flour mixture while stirring with a wooden spoon.

2 If using a stand mixer, mix on medium speed with a dough hook attachment for 7 minutes. If mixing by hand, knead in the bowl until it comes together, then tip out the dough and knead it on a lightly floured surface for 8 to 10 minutes, or until the dough is soft, smooth, and elastic. Lightly oil a large bowl and place the dough inside. Wrap the bowl with plastic wrap or a damp cloth and leave the dough to rise in a warm area until doubled in size, around 1 hour.

3 To make the juicy pork filling: In a medium bowl, combine the ground pork, soy sauce, and sake and stir in one direction for 3 minutes to achieve a sticky, paste-like consistency. Add the cornstarch, scallions, onion, garlic, ginger, 1 teaspoon sugar, and salt and pepper and mix until well combined. (You may test the flavor by frying a small piece of the mixture and adjusting the seasonings as you see fit.) Set aside.

4 Once the dough has risen, degas the dough by punching it in the center. Place the dough on a lightly floured surface, roll it out with a rolling pin as thin as possible, and fold it in half and roll it out again. Repeat this four times; this will help to create a smooth final product, free from air bubbles.

5 Roll the dough into a log, cut it into 6 equal-size pieces, and shape each piece into a ball. Work with one dough ball at a time and cover the rest with a damp tea towel to avoid them drying out. Flatten each ball with a rolling pin to a circle with a 5-inch (12.5 cm) diameter. Roll over the edges to make the ends thinner than the center. Place one-sixth of the juicy pork filling in the center and pleat the dough closed by pinching with your dominant hand while pushing the filling inside with the other. Place the finished nikuman on individual pieces of parchment paper and continue working on the rest of the dough.

6 Once you have finished making all your nikuman, let them rest for 10 minutes under a cloth, or until the dough slowly bounces back when poked gently.

7 Steam the nikuman on the pieces of parchment paper in the bamboo steamer or large pot with a steamer insert for 16 to 18 minutes, until firm to the touch and the internal temperature of the filling reaches 145°F (62°C) on an instant-read thermometer. If using the pot with a steamer insert, leave the lid open and slightly tilted to allow the water to run off the sides and not onto the nikuman, which may cause a bumpy effect on the surface of the buns. Do not open the steamer lid until the 16-minute mark, as changes in temperature can also ruin the appearance of the buns.

8 Serve warm with mustard and/or soy sauce for dipping.

SOUFFLÉ OMELET

★ ANIME ★

FOOD WARS! SHOKUGEKI NO SOMA

SEASON 1 EPISODE 13
EGGS BEFORE DAWN

SEASON 1 EPISODE 14
METAMORPHOSIS

While Soma Yukihira's father spends the next three years traveling and cooking around the world, he sends Soma to the Totsuki Culinary Academy. The program is cutthroat (pun intended), and the students participate in shokugeki (food competitions) to prove themselves as culinary experts. In this two-episode challenge, Soma and his fellow classmates are tasked to prepare a buffet-style egg dish "with a fresh sense of wonder" to serve at breakfast the following morning for a large, discerning crowd. Soma's soufflé omelets give him some grief, but I added a special ingredient to help stabilize the omelets so that they don't deflate: sugar!

YIELD 2 SERVINGS **PREP** 15 MINUTES **COOK** 30 MINUTES

TOMATO SAUCE

2 large hothouse tomatoes

1 tablespoon olive oil

1 shallot, minced

2 cloves garlic, minced

1 tablespoon tomato paste

1 teaspoon dried oregano

¼ teaspoon sugar

Salt and black pepper, to taste

SOUFFLÉ OMELETS

6 large eggs, separated into yolks and whites

½ teaspoon sugar

2 tablespoons heavy whipping cream

Pinch each salt and black pepper

1 tablespoon butter, divided, for cooking

Dried parsley, to taste, for serving

((CONTINUED))

1 To make the tomato sauce: Place the tomatoes on a cutting board and draw an X with a sharp knife on the skin at the top and bottom of each one for easy peeling. Transfer the tomatoes to a heatproof bowl, pour over some boiling water to cover, and let sit for 2 minutes, or until the skin starts to peel. Remove the tomatoes from the water using a slotted spoon and set on a cutting board to cool. Once cool to the touch, peel and discard the skin and chop the flesh into small dice.

2 In a medium saucepan, heat the olive oil over medium heat, then add the shallots and cook until translucent, about 2 minutes. Add the garlic and cook until fragrant, about 2 minutes more, then stir in the tomato paste and cook for another 2 minutes, or until red oils release. Stir in the diced tomatoes, oregano, and ¼ teaspoon sugar and season with salt and pepper. Simmer for 8 minutes, or until the tomatoes have softened and the sauce has slightly thickened.

3 To make the soufflé omelets: In a medium bowl, using a hand mixer with a whisk attachment, mix the egg whites and ½ teaspoon sugar until stiff peaks form.

4 In a large bowl, whisk together the egg yolks, heavy cream, and pinch each of salt and pepper. Gradually add the egg white mixture to the yolk mixture in three additions, gently folding in with a spatula until fully combined after each addition.

5 In a medium nonstick skillet (with a lid), heat ½ tablespoon of the butter over medium heat. Add half of the egg batter and spread it into a circle 1 inch (2.5 cm) thick. Cover with the lid and reduce the heat to medium-low. Cook for 3 minutes, then add a splash of water around the omelet directly onto the pan to create steam. Cover with the lid again and cook for another 3 minutes, or until the surface has set and the omelet is lightly browned and has a slight wiggle when the pan is shook. Transfer the soufflé omelet to a plate and fold in half immediately. Repeat this step with the remaining ½ tablespoon butter and the egg batter.

6 Top the soufflé omelets with the tomato sauce, sprinkle with dried parsley, and serve.

"Don't think of unnecessary things, just make a dish that suits you!"

—Soma Yukihira, *Food Wars! Shokugeki no Soma*

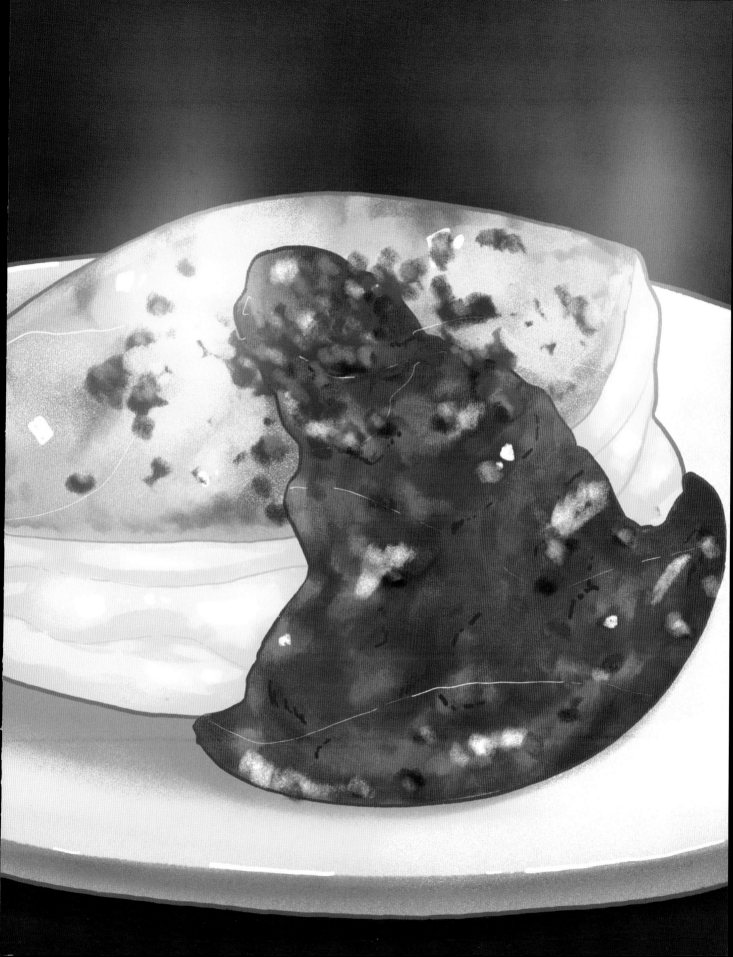

TUNA MEATBALLS IN ORANGE SAUCE

★ ANIME ★
ONE PIECE
SEASON 7 | EPISODE 2
SANJI THE COOK! SHOWING HIS REAL WORTH AT THE MARINE DINING-ROOM!

The Straw Hats are forced to abandon their ship in the hostile G-8 marine base to escape enemy marines, getting separated from one another in the process. Sanji and Luffy disguise themselves as kitchen staff and are, fortunately, confused for expected arrivals from headquarters. Sanji has to prove himself in the kitchen to the beautiful but icy head chef, Jessica, so he whips up his delicious tuna meatballs using the "wasted" parts of the fish—heads, bones, and guts. Because these parts aren't exactly available at your local grocery store, I used a tuna steak and made sure not to leave any scraps, just like Sanji would want. I also added an orange sauce for some vitamin C, since we don't want any seafarers to keel over from scurvy!

YIELD **10** MEATBALLS PREP **15** MINUTES REST **30** MINUTES COOK **20** MINUTES

TUNA MEATBALLS

1 tuna steak (about 1 pound, or 454 g)

1 teaspoon grated orange zest

¼ teaspoon sesame oil

½ teaspoon grated ginger root

1 tablespoon mirin

1 tablespoon sake

1 tablespoon soy sauce

1 large egg, beaten

¼ cup (20 g) panko bread crumbs

Salt and black pepper, to taste

Oil, for deep-frying

ORANGE SAUCE

½ tablespoon oil

¼ small onion, sliced

¼ red bell pepper, seeded and sliced

¼ green bell pepper, seeded and sliced

½ cup (120 ml) fresh orange juice, squeezed from 1 large navel orange

1 teaspoon dashi powder

1 tablespoon cornstarch

⅓ cup (80 ml) rice vinegar

½ cup (110 g) packed brown sugar

2 tablespoons soy sauce

3 tablespoons ketchup

Salt and black pepper, to taste

1 To make the meatballs: Chop the tuna steak into very fine pieces, then place in a large bowl. Add the orange zest, sesame oil, ginger, mirin, sake, 1 tablespoon soy sauce, beaten egg, bread crumbs, and salt and pepper and fully incorporate. Shape the mixture into 10 equal-size meatballs. Transfer the meatballs to a plate and put the plate in the freezer for 30 minutes

2 Meanwhile, make the orange sauce: In a medium skillet, heat the ½ tablespoon oil over medium heat. Add the onions and cook until translucent, about 2 minutes. Add the red and green peppers and cook for another 2 minutes, or until softened.

3 In a small bowl, combine the orange juice, dashi powder, and cornstarch for a slurry, stirring to dissolve the cornstarch. Pour this slurry into the skillet along with the rice vinegar, brown sugar, 2 tablespoons soy sauce, and ketchup and stir to combine. Season with salt and pepper, then simmer until thick, stirring occasionally, around 3 minutes. Reduce the heat to low and keep the sauce warming while you deep-fry the meatballs.

4 In a medium heavy-bottomed pot, heat 3 inches (7.5 cm) of oil over medium heat to 350°F (175°C), measuring with a thermometer, or a small piece of the meatball mixture sizzles when it hits the hot oil. Line a plate with paper towels. Deep-fry the meatballs for no more than 3 minutes, or until golden. Transfer to the prepared plate. You may need to do this in batches, depending on the size of your pan.

5 Add the fried tuna meatballs to the skillet with the orange sauce, toss to coat, and serve.

"Great food comes from a special place in all our hearts."

—Jessica, *One Piece*

MITARASHI DANGO

✳ ANIME ✳
SAMURAI CHAMPLOO
SEASON 1 | EPISODE 20
ELEGY OF
ENTRAPMENT, VERSE 1

While on their journey, Fuu—a waitress in search of the mysterious "samurai who smells of sunflowers"—and her two samurai companions, Mugen and Jin, seek shelter from the rain at a restaurant. Here, they meet a blind musician named Sara, who asks them to travel with her and pays for their board and food, including a generous amount of dango (skewered sweet rice dumplings). I've included a recipe for mitarashi syrup for drizzling.

YIELD **12** DANGO   PREP **15** MINUTES   COOK **20** MINUTES

SPECIAL TOOLS

4 (6-inch, or 15-cm) bamboo skewers

DANGO

4 ounces (113 g) silken tofu

1 cup (160 g) sweet rice flour

Pinch salt

MITARASHI SYRUP

2 tablespoons soy sauce

1 tablespoon brown sugar

1 teaspoon cornstarch

½ cup (120 ml) water

《 STEPS 》

1 To make the dango: In a medium bowl, combine the tofu, flour, and salt. Mix and knead to form a ball of dough, about 2 minutes

2 Divide the dough into 12 equal-size pieces, then form each piece into a ball. Gently push 3 dango balls onto each bamboo skewer, trying to keep their shape and leaving space at the bottom of the stick for holding them.

3 In a pot large enough to hold the skewers, bring enough water to a boil over medium-high heat to submerge the skewers. Once boiling, add the skewers and boil until they float and the dango are cooked through, about 4 minutes. Remove from the pot and transfer to a plate.

4 Heat a nonstick skillet large enough to fit the skewers over medium heat, then toast the dango with no oil, 1 to 2 minutes per side. Alternatively, you can torch them over a direct flame. Transfer the toasted dango to a serving plate.

5 To make the mitarashi syrup: In a small pot, combine the soy sauce, brown sugar, cornstarch, and water over medium heat and stir until the cornstarch is dissolved. Simmer the sauce until syrupy, about 5 minutes.

6 Drizzle the toasted dango with the mitarashi syrup.

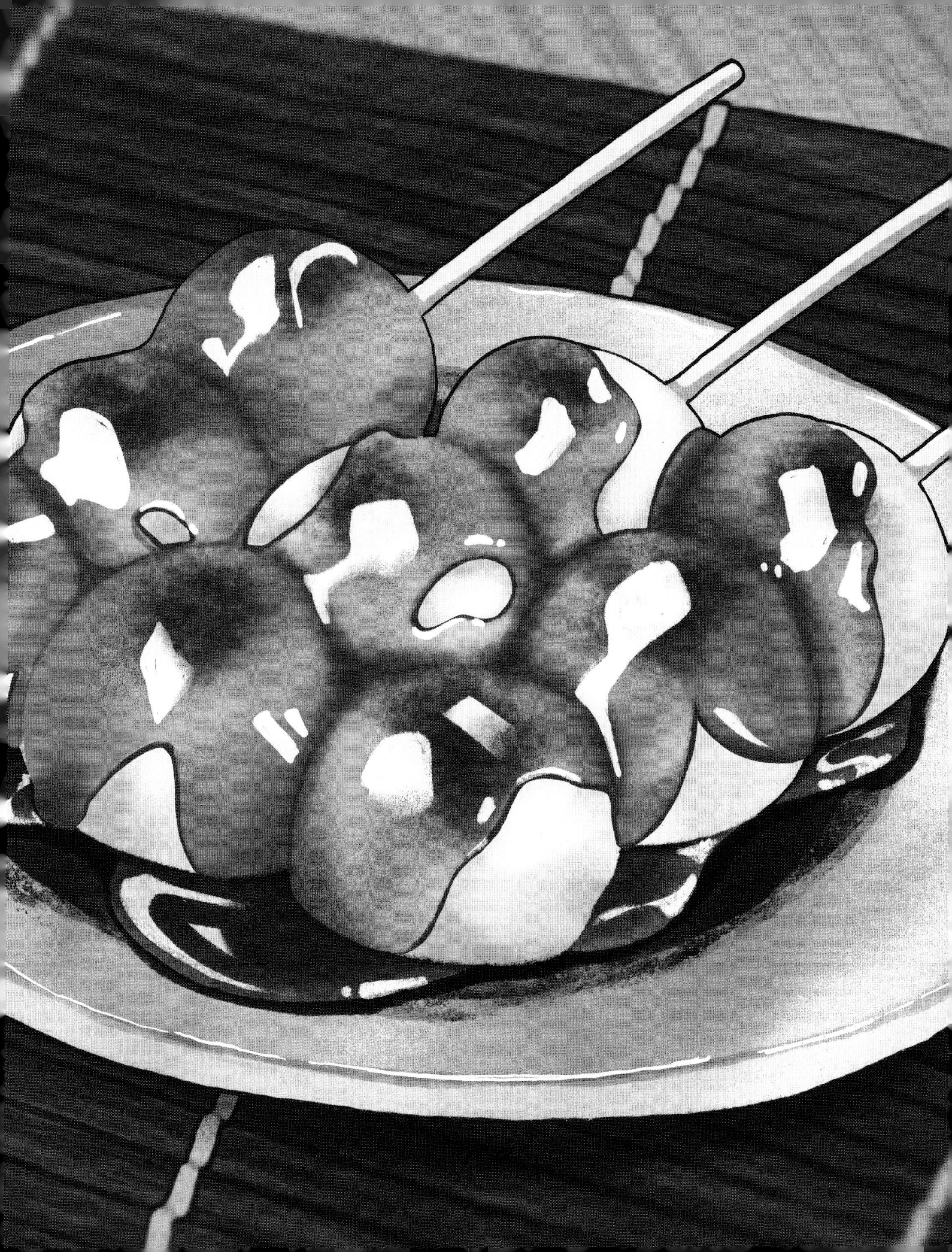

PAPRIKA SEAFOOD CAESAR SALAD

ANIME

MISS KOBAYASHI'S DRAGON MAID

SEASON 1 EPISODE 8

NEW DRAGON, ELMA! (SHE'S FINALLY APPEARING, HUH?)

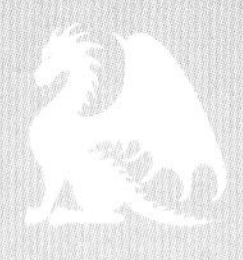

Kobayashi and Tohru compete in a three-round match to see who will make Kanna's bento (lunch) for the school field trip. In the salad round, Kobayashi offers a couple of cherry tomatoes while Tohru makes an extravagant "seafood and paprika Caesar salad." Though Tohru's salad is magnificent, the judges end up choosing Kobayashi's cherry tomatoes because the Caesar salad is much too large to fit in a bento box. Though Tohru lost, we're the true winners who get to enjoy this unique, delicious dish!

YIELD 8 SERVINGS · PREP 15 MINUTES · MARINATE 15 MINUTES · COOK 25 MINUTES

SPECIAL TOOLS

Spice grinder

CRISPY GARLIC PARMESAN CROUTONS

1 medium-size Italian crusty bread loaf, chopped into ½-inch (12 mm) cubes

¼ cup (25 g) grated Parmesan

3 tablespoons olive oil

½ tablespoon garlic powder

¼ teaspoon salt

¼ teaspoon black pepper

PAPRIKA SEAFOOD SEASONING

1½ tablespoons salt

4 bay leaves

1 tablespoon sweet paprika

½ tablespoon smoked paprika

½ tablespoon celery seed

½ tablespoon garlic powder

2 teaspoons onion powder

1 teaspoon black pepper

½ teaspoon crushed red pepper flakes (optional)

SMOKY PAPRIKA SEAFOOD

1 pound (454 g) black tiger shrimp, peeled and deveined

½ pound (227 g) calamari, cut into ¼-inch-thick (6 mm) rings

2 tablespoons olive oil

½ to 1 lemon, for squeezing

CAESAR DRESSING

3 anchovies in oil, rinsed if salted (see Harlot Spaghetti on page 103 to use the rest of the anchovies)

3 cloves garlic

½ teaspoon salt

2 tablespoons fresh lemon juice

1 teaspoon Dijon mustard

2 egg yolks (from pasteurized eggs)

¼ teaspoon black pepper

1 cup (240 ml) extra-virgin olive oil

¼ cup (25 g) grated Parmesan

((CONTINUED))

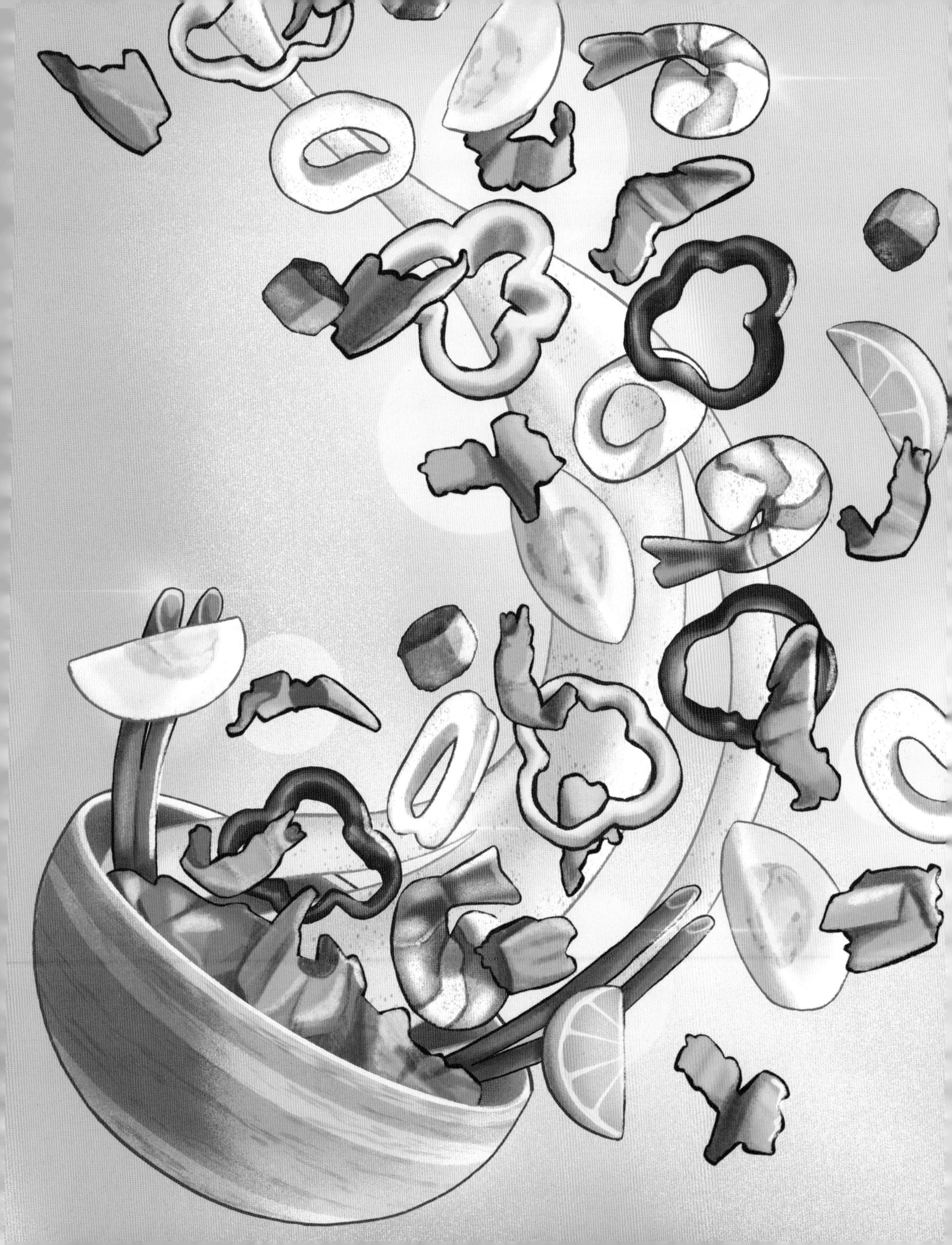

FOR ASSEMBLY

2 large heads Romaine lettuce, chopped into 1-inch (2.5 cm) pieces

Grated Parmesan, to taste

1 small red bell pepper, sliced into ¼-inch-thick (6 mm) rings

1 small yellow bell pepper, sliced into ¼-inch-thick (6 mm) rings

4 hard-boiled eggs, cut into wedges

1 lemon, cut into wedges

2 scallions, trimmed and sliced in half lengthwise

)) PAPRIKA SEAFOOD CAESAR SALAD STEPS))

1 To make the crispy garlic Parmesan croutons: Preheat the oven to 450°F (230°C; gas mark 8). Line a baking tray with foil.

2 In a medium bowl, mix all the crouton ingredients together to evenly coat the bread cubes and spread the cubes on the prepared tray. Bake for 10 to 15 minutes, until golden and crisp, flipping the croutons halfway through the baking time. Remove from the oven and let cool on the pan.

3 Meanwhile, make the paprika seafood seasoning: Add all the seasoning ingredients to a spice grinder and blend until finely ground.

4 To make the smoky paprika seafood: In a medium bowl, combine the shrimp, calamari rings, and 2 tablespoons of the paprika seafood seasoning. Toss to coat the seafood and let marinate for 15 minutes.

5 In a medium skillet, heat the olive oil over medium-high heat, then cook the shrimp and calamari for 2 to 3 minutes per side. Transfer to a plate and squeeze some fresh lemon juice to taste on top. Set aside.

6 To make the Caesar dressing: In a medium bowl, crush the anchovies, garlic, and salt together with a fork to make a paste. Using a whisk, incorporate the lemon juice and Dijon mustard to loosen the paste. Add the egg yolks and whisk until incorporated, then add the black pepper. Drizzle in the extra-virgin olive oil in a slow, steady stream with one hand and whisk vigorously with the other to emulsify the dressing until it is creamy, thick, and pale yellow. Lastly, add the Parmesan and stir.

7 To assemble: In a large salad bowl, toss the lettuce with the Caesar dressing to taste (don't use all of it, as you will add more in the next step) and sprinkle with Parmesan. Top with the pepper rings, smoky paprika seafood, hard-boiled-egg wedges, and crispy garlic Parmesan croutons.

8 Set the lemon wedges around the inside of the bowl. Place 2 scallion halves sticking out of the top left of the bowl and the other 2 scallion halves sticking out of the top right to resemble Tohru's horns. Drizzle with more Caesar dressing to taste and serve immediately.

NOTE

The dressing for this recipe calls for 2 raw egg yolks, which may contain Salmonella (1 in 20,000 pasteurized eggs contain it) and make you ill. Make sure to use only pasteurized eggs and that you understand the risk of eating raw egg yolks.

RUSSIAN ROULETTE TAKOYAKI

× ANIME ×
DRAGON BALL SUPER

SEASON 1 EPISODE 6
DON'T ANGER
THE GOD OF
DESTRUCTION!
THE HEART-POUNDING
BIRTHDAY PARTY

Beerus, a powerful being that can destroy worlds (and authorized the destruction of Vegeta's home planet), has come to Earth searching for the last Saiyan. Bulma, Vegeta's wife, invites them to her birthday party thinking they are a friend of her husband, but Vegeta spends the rest of the party hoping nobody angers the god. Meanwhile, Krillin offers Beerus this dish, identical takoyaki (balls of fluffy dough with octopus), except that one is filled with wasabi. Luckily, Krillin's little prank doesn't jeopardize the planet, but it does backfire on Krillin! You may want to have a cold drink at the ready for the unlucky person.

YIELD 30 TAKOYAKI · **PREP** 15 MINUTES · **COOK** 30 MINUTES

SPECIAL TOOLS

Takoyaki pan

TAKOYAKI BATTER

1½ cups (360 ml) cold water

1 teaspoon dashi powder

1 large egg, beaten

1 teaspoon soy sauce

1 cup (130 g) cake flour (or substitute with 1 cup, or 120 g, all-purpose flour)

½ tablespoon cornstarch

Pinch salt

Oil, for cooking

STANDARD FILLINGS

1 piece (9 inches, or 23 cm, long) boiled tender octopus, finely diced

2 teaspoons bonito powder

2 teaspoons red pickled ginger (beni shoga)

1 scallion, thinly sliced

¼ cup (5 g) tempura bits (tenkasu or agedama; you can substitute with unsweetened crispy rice cereal)

OPTIONAL FILLINGS

¼ cup (35 g) finely diced cheese (such as cheddar or mozzarella)

¼ cup (50 g) finely diced sausage

¼ cup (25 g) finely diced peeled and deveined shrimp

¼ cup (38 g) finely diced kimchi

Wasabi, to taste

FOR SERVING

Kewpie mayo, to taste

Takoyaki sauce, to taste

Dried bonito flakes (katsuobushi), to taste

Dried seaweed flakes (aonori), to taste

((CONTINUED))

RUSSIAN ROULETTE TAKOYAKI STEPS

1. To make the takoyaki batter: In a medium bowl, stir together the cold water and dashi powder until dissolved, then add the beaten egg, soy sauce, flour, cornstarch, and salt. The batter should be a loose and fluid consistency. Transfer the batter to a pouring vessel for easier assembly on the grill.

2. Set out the standard and optional fillings you are using beside the takoyaki pan. (Takoyaki cooks quickly, so I recommend laying out all the ingredients and having them at hand before you start cooking.)

3. Place the takoyaki pan over medium heat. Once hot, brush oil over the entire takoyaki pan, including the molds, then pour the batter into the molds, filling them all the way to the brim. Sprinkle a small amount of the standard fillings in each mold, then add some optional fillings (if using) with one or a few having wasabi!

4. Cook until the top of the batter is almost set, 2 to 3 minutes. Using chopsticks or bamboo skewers, loosen each takoyaki by scraping around the edges of the batter, then turn each ball ninety degrees to its side. Add more batter to each mold and shove cooked extra batter from the takoyaki's perimeter to fill any holes. Turn another ninety degrees to expose the crispy bottom half to the top. Add more batter to fill any holes. Continue cooking until all sides are crispy, 10 to 12 minutes total. Remove the pan from the heat and the takoyaki from the pan. Repeat step 3 and this step with any remaining batter and fillings, brushing additional oil over the pan if needed.

5. To serve: Place 6 takoyaki on each plate while hot, drizzle with Kewpie mayo and takoyaki sauce, and sprinkle with a few pinches each of bonito and seaweed flakes.

NOTE

It's easy to buy everything at an Asian supermarket to make takoyaki in a jiffy. Check the open refrigerator aisles for precooked octopus (*tako* in takoyaki means "octopus"), or you may discover other ingredients you would like to add as fillings. Some stores even sell takoyaki pans, but they are also available to buy online.

"Inside a warm and fluffy ball of powdered grain lurks the chewy sensation of an eight-armed earth mollusk!" —Beerus, *Dragon Ball Super*

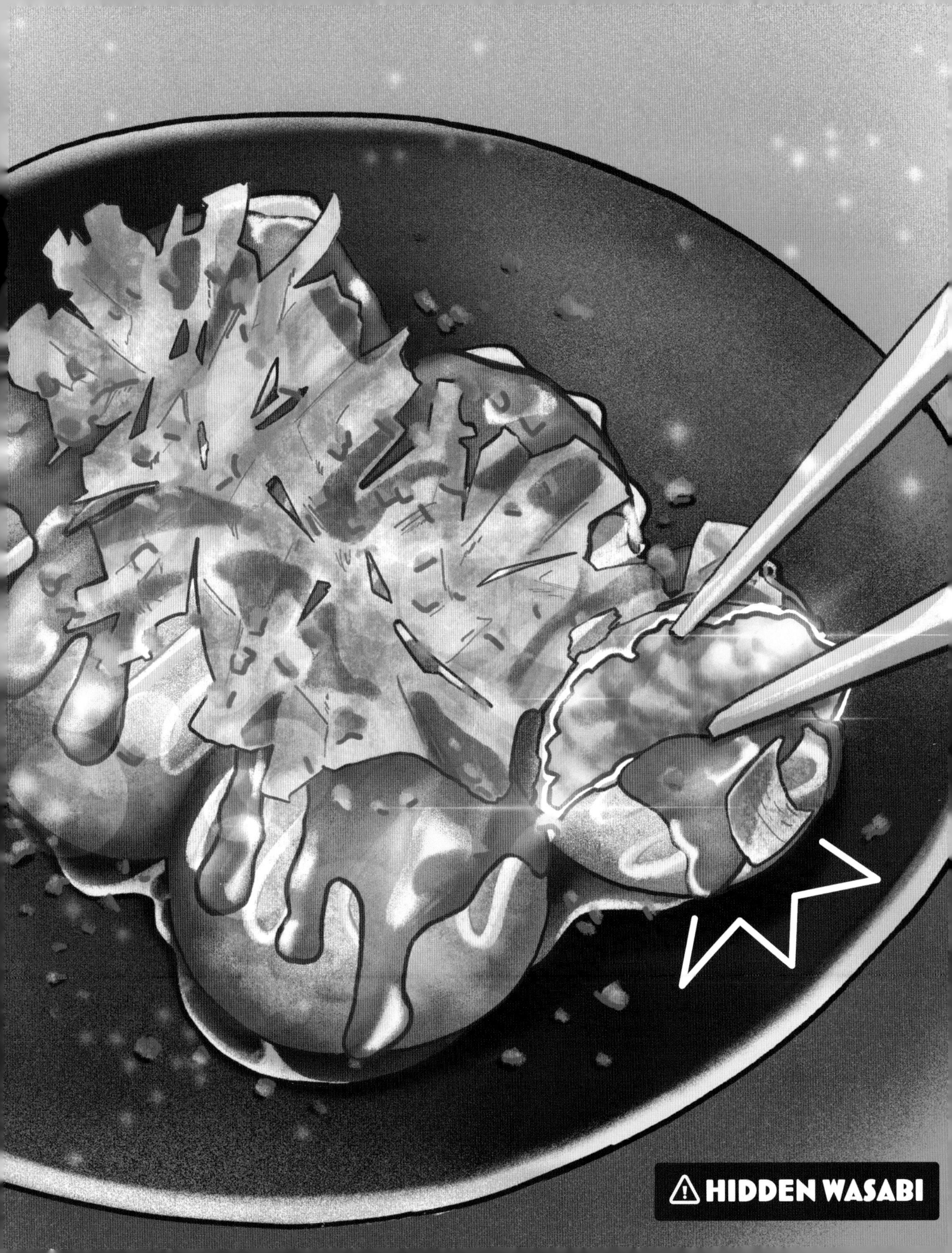
HIDDEN WASABI

CAT ONIGIRI

★ ANIME ★
FRUITS BASKET

SEASON 1 EPISODE 6
PERHAPS WE
SHOULD INVITE
OURSELVES OVER

Fruits Basket is a cute shoujo (rom-com) anime in which the female protagonist, Tohru Honda, moves in with the reclusive Sohma family. The kicker is that the family is cursed—when hugged by someone of the opposite sex, the members of the family turn into animals from the Chinese zodiac. In this episode, Tohru makes cat-shaped onigiri (rice balls with savory fillings) to sell at the school's festival day, giving one to Kyo Sohma, who is cursed to turn into a cat (the cat just missed out on being part of the zodiac when it was tricked by the rat). This scene gives us one of the most iconic lines in the show from Kyo, who wonders if eating the onigiri is considered "cannibalism." While you can make any filling you want, I chose my favorite fish flavors to go with the cat theme. You can make one or both fillings!

YIELD **4** ONIGIRI PREP **15** MINUTES MARINATE **1** HOUR COOK **10** MINUTES DECORATE **20** MINUTES

HONEY GINGER SALMON FILLING

½ teaspoon garlic powder

Pinch red chili flakes (optional)

1 teaspoon sesame oil

1 teaspoon freshly grated ginger root

Zest and juice of ½ lemon

½ tablespoon honey

1 tablespoon soy sauce

Salt and black pepper, to taste

1 salmon fillet
(about 7 ounces, or 198 g),
skin on

Oil, for cooking

1 scallion, thinly sliced

½ teaspoon sesame seeds

¼ cup (60 g) Kewpie mayo

½ tablespoon oil, for cooking

TUNA MAYO FILLING

1 tablespoon finely chopped cucumber

Pinch salt, plus more to taste

1 cup (154 g) drained tuna, flaked

1 scallion, thinly sliced

1 tablespoon soy sauce

3 tablespoons Kewpie mayo

Black pepper, to taste

ASSEMBLY

Salt, for dusting

5 cups (1 kg) freshly cooked, warm short-grain white rice

2 sheets dried seaweed (nori)

Pinch salt and black pepper

1 To make the honey ginger salmon filling: In a medium bowl, combine the garlic powder, chili flakes, sesame oil, ginger, lemon zest and juice, honey, and 1 tablespoon soy sauce, and salt and pepper and stir together. Add the salmon to the bowl and coat it with the mixture. Cover the bowl and let marinate in the refrigerator for at least an hour, or overnight.

2 Meanwhile, make the tuna mayo filling: In a small bowl, toss the cucumber with the pinch of salt, then tip into a colander to allow the water to drain from the cucumbers. After 10 minutes, pat them dry with paper towels.

3 Put the cucumbers in a separate medium bowl and add the tuna, scallion, 1 tablespoon soy sauce, and 3 tablespoons mayo. Season with pepper and stir to combine. Set aside. (If not using immediately, place in the refrigerator until ready to assemble.)

4 When the salmon is ready to cook, in a medium skillet, heat the oil over medium heat. Place the salmon, skin side down, in the pan, reserving the marinade, and cook for 4 minutes. Flip the salmon, pour over the reserved marinade, and cook for another 3 to 4 minutes.

5 Transfer the cooked salmon to a clean medium bowl. Using two forks, break the salmon into small pieces and discard the skin, then add the scallion, sesame seeds, and ¼ cup (60 g) mayo. Combine well and set aside.

6 To assemble the cat onigiri: Line a work surface with plastic wrap, about 12 inches (30 cm) long. To make the cat head, wet your hands with water to prevent sticking, then dust them with a touch of salt. Grab half a handful of warm rice and form it into a flat oval, then place it on the prepared surface. Place a tablespoon of salmon or tuna filling on the center of the flattened rice. Add another half a handful of rice to cover the filling, then press down with your fingertips to seal. Place the rice ball between both hands and compress to solidify. Place the rice ball back onto the plastic wrap and gently refine the shape into an oval if it was altered while compressing the rice.

7 To make a cat ear, grab 1 tablespoon of warm rice and, using the tips of your fingers, compress it into a pyramid shape. Repeat for the second ear. Connect the ears to the cat head by carefully pushing them to squish the rice together and act as glue.

8 To make the face details, cut a nori sheet into a rectangle that will fit between the ears, two small circles for the eyes, and a small, horizontal number-three (3) shape for the mouth. Place the nori shapes onto the cat onigiri; they will adhere naturally. Repeat steps 6, 7, and this one to make the remaining cat onigiri. Serve at room temperature.

> **"When we're born, all we have are desires for food and material things."**
>
> —Tohru Honda, *Fruits Basket*

BENTO INSPIRATION

ANIME
SCHOOL BABYSITTERS
SEASON 1 | EPISODE 2

When Ryuu takes the toddlers from the daycare on a field trip to the zoo, they enjoy a bento. Bentos (lunch boxes) are common in Japan and can be comprised of lots of different foods for adults and children. The bento I made here is inspired by the toddlers in the anime and includes kawaii elements and easy-to-eat handheld foods.

YIELD 2 SERVINGS | PREP 15 MINUTES | COOK 25 MINUTES | DECORATE 25 MINUTES

OCTOPUS HOT DOGS WITH SCRAMBLED EGGS

6 cocktail wieners (or 3 small hot dogs, cut in half horizontally)

1 tablespoon oil, divided, for cooking

2 large eggs, beaten

Salt and black pepper, to taste

1 sheet dried seaweed (nori)

SHIBA INU ONIGIRI

3 cups (615 g) freshly cooked, warm short-grain white rice

Ketchup

1 sheet dried seaweed (nori)

PIG ONIGIRI

3 cups (615 g) freshly cooked, warm short-grain white rice

Ketchup

2 slices ham

1 sheet dried seaweed (nori)

1 slice white cheddar cheese

MINI MEATBALLS

½ recipe Hamburg Steak (from Mystery Sizzling Steak on page 100; make only the meat mixture in step 4 and form it into 12 mini meatballs)

½ tablespoon oil, for cooking

Ketchup

2 leaves lettuce

KARAAGE

½ recipe Karaage To-Go (page 42)

4 leaves lettuce

4 cherry tomatoes

STEPS

1 To make the octopus hotdogs with scrambled eggs: Slice half of each hot dog lengthwise four times to make 8 legs. In a medium skillet, heat ½ tablespoon of the oil over medium heat. Add the hot dogs and panfry for 5 minutes, or until warmed through and the legs have opened. Transfer from the pan to a plate. Heat the remaining ½ tablespoon in the same pan over medium or medium-low heat. Add the beaten eggs, season with salt and pepper, and scramble for 2 minutes, or until desired firmness, stirring every 30 seconds with a spatula. Assemble by topping the scrambled eggs with the hotdogs. For the octopus eyes, use kitchen shears to cut out 12 small circles from the nori sheet, then place them on the hotdogs.

CONTINUED

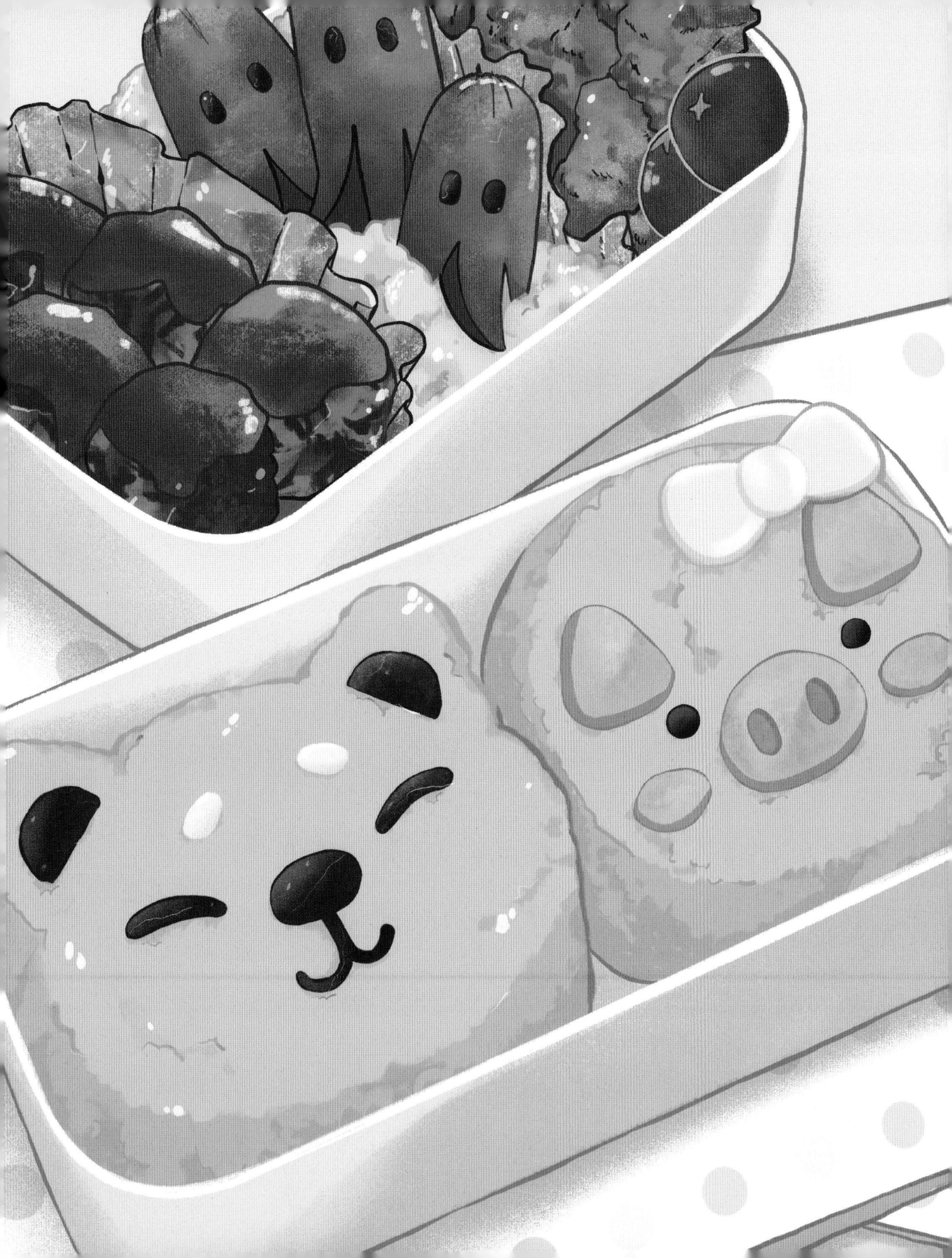

2 To make the Shiba Inu onigiri: Reserve 4 grains of the cooked rice for decorating, then add enough ketchup to the rest of the rice to make an orange-pink color. Form a rice ball and ears with your hands (use the same method as steps 6 and 7 for Cat Onigiri on page 28). Use kitchen shears to cut out details from the nori sheet: 4 semicircles for the ears, 4 upside-down U shapes for the eyes, 2 ovals for the noses, and 2 horizontal number-three (3) shapes for the mouths. Stick half of these details onto the onigiri. Lastly, place 2 reserved rice grains for the eyebrows. Repeat the shaping of the onigiri and placing the face details for the second Shiba Inu onigiri.

3 To make the pig onigiri: Add enough ketchup to the cooked rice to make an orange-pink color. Form a rice ball and ears with your hands (use the same method as steps 6 and 7 for Cat Onigiri on page 28). Use kitchen shears to cut out details from the ham: 4 triangles with softened corners for the ears and 4 ovals for the cheek blush. For each nose, overlap 2 pieces of ham and cut out 2 identical oval shapes, larger than the blush ovals, through the layers. Cut out 2 smaller vertical ovals in the middle of one of the larger ovals for the nose holes. Layer the 2 nose shapes again with the one with the nose holes on top. For the eyes, cut out 4 small circles from the nori sheet. Place half of the ham and nori details on the onigiri. Lastly, for the bows, cut out 4 triangles with softened corners as big as the ham ears and 2 small circles from the cheese. Place 2 triangles, with one of their edges touching on top of the right ham ear, then place a small cheese circle on the center of the bow. Repeat the shaping of the onigiri and placing of the face and bow details for the second pig onigiri

4 To make the mini meatballs: In a medium skillet, heat the ½ tablespoon oil over medium heat, then panfry the 12 mini meatballs until browned on all sides, about 8 minutes, or until the internal temperature on an instant-read thermometer reaches 160°F (71°C).

5 To assemble: Place a Shiba Inu and pig together in one compartment of each bento. In a separate compartment(s), place 6 meatballs on a lettuce leaf and squirt ketchup on top of the meatballs; 3 octopus hotdogs on top of scrambled eggs; and half of the karaage on a lettuce leaf with a side of 2 cherry tomatoes.

"They're not just cute. They're delicious too!"

—Umi Mamizuka, *School Babysitters*

CHEESY POTATO PAVE

★ ANIME ★

**GODZILLA
SINGULAR
POINT**

SEASON 1 | EPISODE 10
ENCIPHER/PRINCIPLES
OF MECHANICS

While Mei is in India waiting for BB to take her to the SHIVA Consortium—a mysterious multinational organization which includes a research facility that is studying the "singular point"—she recalls a conversation she had with Li, a SHIVA researcher, at a swanky upscale restaurant. They talked about time travel and sending information across time, heavy philosophical topics, but all Nakagawa, Li's bodyguard, could focus on was the delicious-looking potato pave and edible origami garnish that they were served. This meal looked good enough for Godzilla to stop his rampage for a moment!

YIELD 6 SERVINGS	PREP 20 MINUTES	REST 6 HOURS	COOK 2 HOURS

SPECIAL TOOLS

7 × 4-inch (18 × 10 cm) loaf pan

6 unicorn origamis (optional)

CHEESY POTATO PAVE

Nonstick cooking spray

1 cup (240 ml) heavy whipping cream

2 tablespoons minced garlic (6 cloves)

Zest of 1 lemon

1 teaspoon salt

1 teaspoon onion powder

¼ teaspoon celery seed

⅛ teaspoon white pepper

3 russet potatoes, peeled

¾ cup (85 g) shredded aged white cheddar, divided

1 tablespoon vegetable oil

SIDES

1½ cups (225 g) frozen fava beans

2 tablespoons unsalted butter, divided

Salt and black pepper, to taste

12 stalks asparagus, trimmed and sliced in half lengthwise

((CONTINUED))

CHEESY POTATO PAVE STEPS

1 To make the cheesy potato pave: Preheat the oven to 350°F (175°C; gas mark 4). Spray the baking dish with nonstick cooking spray and set aside.

2 In a large bowl, stir together the heavy whipping cream, garlic, lemon zest, salt, onion powder, celery seed, and white pepper. Thinly slice the russet potatoes with a mandolin to ⅛-inch (3 mm) thickness, then submerge the sliced potatoes in the bowl of cream to cover them.

3 Remove the potato slices from the cream, one at a time, and stack them in the baking dish, overlapping the slices and creating layers. When the layers reach halfway up the baking dish, sprinkle ½ cup (55 g) of the shredded cheddar in a thin layer. Continue to layer the potatoes, leaving 1 inch (2.5 cm) of space at the top of the dish. Place the dish on a baking tray in case of spills.

4 Bake for 1 hour 15 minutes, or until the potatoes are fully cooked and soft when a sharp knife is inserted. Remove from the oven, place a layer of aluminum foil on top of the potatoes, and set a similar-size pan with weights, such as cans of soup, on top to flatten the potatoes. Let the mixture cool to room temperature, then refrigerate for at least 6 hours, or overnight for best results, to firm up the pave.

5 Remove the pan with weights and foil, cover the baking dish with a cutting board, and flip it over to release the potatoes. With a knife, trim the edges and slice the potatoes into 6 equal-size pieces.

6 In a large skillet, heat the vegetable oil over medium heat. Panfry in batches, 3 pieces at a time, for about 2 minutes on each side (top, bottom, and all sides), or until golden. Remove from the heat and place on a baking tray. Add the remaining ¼ cup (30 g) shredded cheddar on top of the potato pieces and broil or toast in the oven or a toaster oven for 2 minutes, or until the cheese becomes bubbly and browned.

7 To make the sides: In a medium pot, bring enough water to a boil over medium heat to cover the fava beans. Once boiling, submerge the fava beans and boil until the outer shell is peeling away, about 2 minutes, then drain immediately in a colander. Place the blanched fava beans in a medium bowl and cover with cold water to cool. Peel away the outer shells, then dry the beans with paper towels.

8 In a medium skillet, melt 1 tablespoon of the butter over medium heat. Add the fava beans and salt and pepper and cook for 3 minutes, or until tender. Remove the fava beans from the skillet, then melt the remaining tablespoon butter and panfry the asparagus until tender, 4 to 5 minutes.

9 To serve: Place 4 asparagus halves on the center of each plate and balance a warm potato piece on top. Add 2 spoonfuls of fava beans on the side and serve with an (inedible) origami (if using)

NOTE

You can make most of the pave a day in advance. Follow steps 1 through 4, then refrigerate overnight and follow steps 5 and 6 right before your dinner party.

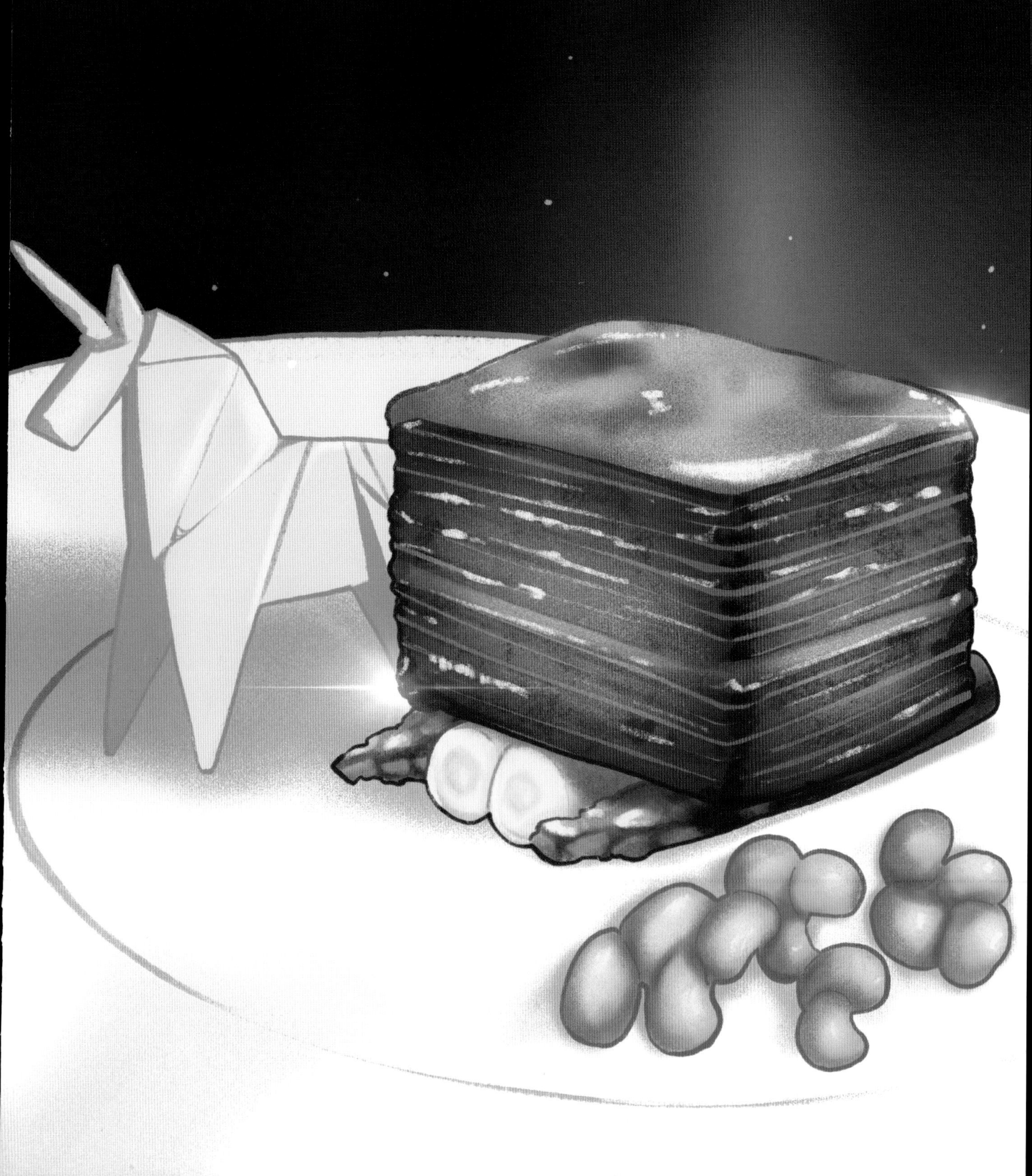

PEANUT BUTTER SQUID

★ ANIME ★
**FOOD WARS!
SHOKUGEKI
NO SOMA**
SEASON 1   EPISODE 1
AN ENDLESS
WASTELAND

Protagonist Soma Yukihira challenges his father—professional chef and owner of Restaurant Yukihira—yet again to a cooking duel, which he loses for the 489th time in a row. Before the duel, Soma is seen grilling squid with peanut butter, something even he deems "disgusting." This is a dish that he continues to develop and perfect throughout the manga and is special to fans because it bookends the series, appearing in the first episode of the anime and the last chapter of the manga. While Soma's recipe achieves a comic level of inedibility, I used Thai flavors and elevated the dish to make an edible—and enjoyable—version.

YIELD **4** SERVINGS   PREP **20** MINUTES   COOK **6** MINUTES

SPECIAL TOOLS

Outdoor grill

Charcoal, for grilling (optional)

Grilling skewers (optional; if using wooden skewers, soak for an hour in cold water before placing on the grill)

INGREDIENTS

1 pound (454 g) medium-size squid tentacles

2 tablespoons peanut butter

1 tablespoon lime juice

½ tablespoon fish sauce

4 cloves garlic, grated

1 teaspoon yellow curry powder

1 tablespoon soy sauce

¼ cup (60 ml) full-fat coconut milk

Chili garlic sauce, to taste, plus more for serving

Salt and black pepper, to taste

1 Preheat the grill.

2 In a medium bowl, clean the squid tentacles with lightly salted water, making sure to scrub all the suckers to release any dirt. Rinse and repeat twice. Pat the squid tentacles dry with paper towels and transfer them to a clean medium bowl.

3 Add the peanut butter, lime juice, fish sauce, garlic, curry powder, soy sauce, coconut milk, chili garlic sauce, and salt and pepper to the bowl. Toss to coat the squid.

4 If your grill has large gaps, you may prefer to place the squid on skewers to grill them. Grill the tentacles for 6 minutes total, turning halfway through the cooking time and basting them with the leftover marinade, until lightly charred and firm but tender..

5 Remove from the grill and serve with more chili garlic sauce for dipping.

NOTE
You can also cook this recipe on the stovetop. Heat ½ tablespoon of oil in a medium skillet over medium heat. When a drop of marinade added to the pan sizzles, panfry the squid, stirring occasionally, for 6 to 7 minutes total, until firm but tender. Turn them halfway through the cooking time and baste with the leftover marinade.

"Repeating trial and error
and failing many times
. . . it's that process
which makes the dishes shine."

—Soma Yukihira, *Food Wars! Shokugeki no Soma*

TOMATO MUSHROOM SOUP

ANIME
TALES FROM EARTHSEA

In this Studio Ghibli film, Arren is a young, disgraced prince who is on the run after killing his father. Ged, an archmage, saves him from wolves and the two travel together as companions. Their journey takes them down many paths, one of which brings them to seek shelter in Tenar's home, where they recall their moments together while enjoying Tenar's tomato mushroom soup by the fire.

YIELD 4 SERVINGS | PREP 15 MINUTES | COOK 45 MINUTES

INGREDIENTS

7 ounces (198 g) small yellow potatoes

2 tablespoons olive oil, divided

Salt and pepper, to taste

½ large red onion, sliced

¼ cup (20 g) sliced leek

4 cloves garlic, minced

1 can (28 ounces, or 794 g) whole peeled tomatoes

½ teaspoon cayenne pepper

½ tablespoon sugar

5½ ounces (155 g) mixed mushrooms (shiitake, button, oyster, and shimeji), trimmed as necessary

1½ cups (360 ml) vegetable stock

4 sprigs fresh parsley, plus more chopped for garnishing

3 sprigs fresh dill, plus more chopped for garnishing

Heavy whipping cream (or coconut milk), to taste, for drizzling

STEPS

1 Preheat the oven to 450°F (230°C; gas mark 8). Scatter the small yellow potatoes on a baking tray, drizzle with 1 tablespoon of the olive oil, and season with salt and pepper. Shake the pan until all the potatoes are seasoned and oiled. Bake for 20 minutes, flipping the potatoes halfway through the baking time.

2 Meanwhile, in a medium pot, heat the remaining 1 tablespoon olive oil over medium heat. Add the onions and leeks and cook until translucent, 2 to 3 minutes. Add the garlic and cook until fragrant, about 2 minutes, then add the tomatoes, cayenne, sugar, and salt and pepper. Stir together. Let simmer for 15 minutes, stirring occasionally.

3 Carefully transfer the hot contents of the pot (or let cool first) to a food processor or blender, or use an immersion blender, and blend until smooth. Strain the liquid back into the pot through a fine-mesh strainer.

4 Add the roasted potatoes, mushrooms, vegetable stock, parsley, and dill to the pot and cook, stirring occasionally, until the mushrooms are tender, 10 to 15 minutes. Remove and discard the herb sprigs.

5 Ladle the soup into bowls, drizzle with heavy cream, and garnish with chopped parsley and dill.

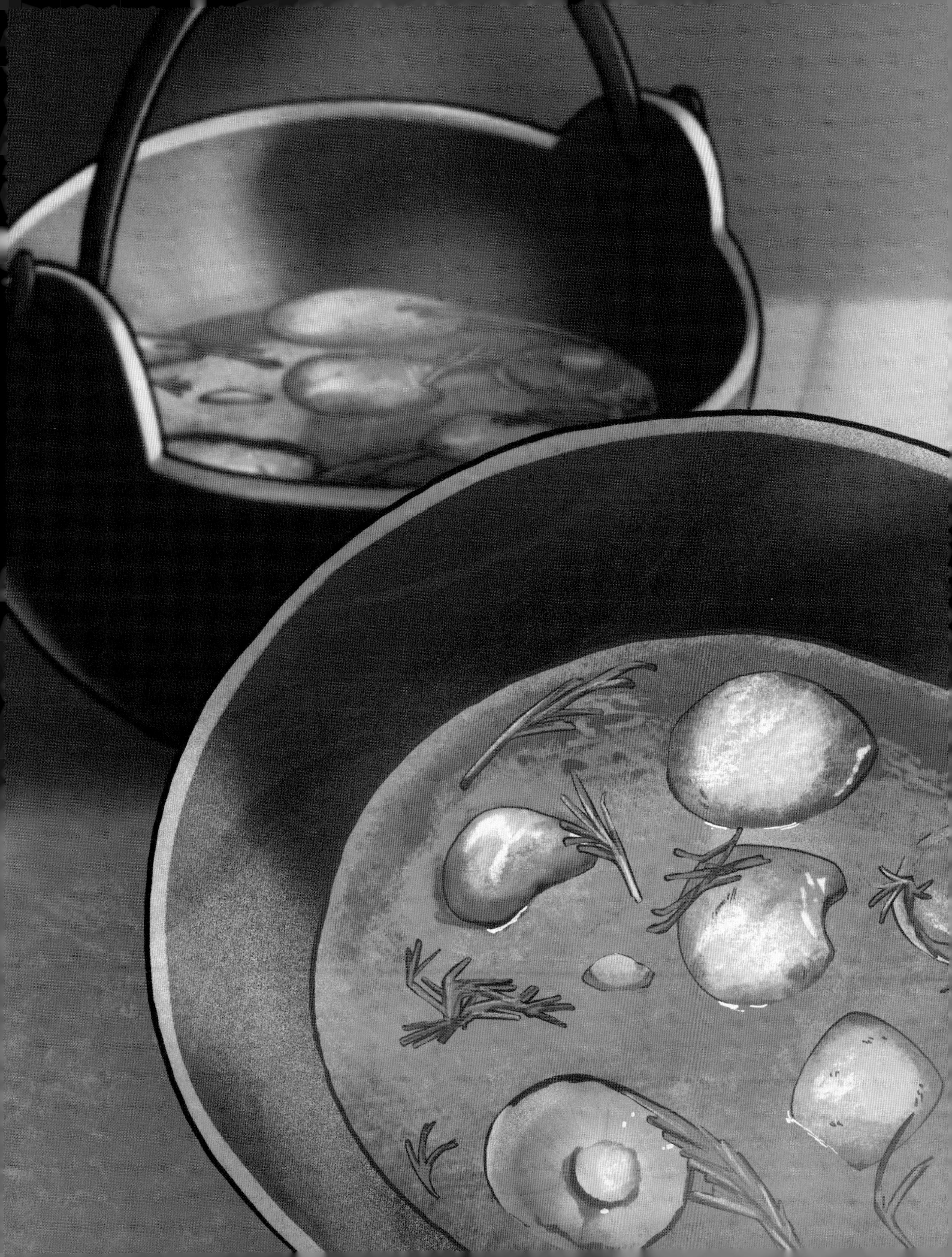

SHRIMP "EBI" KATSU SANDWICH

ANIME
GOURMET GIRL GRAFFITI
SEASON 1 | EPISODE 12
SOAK UP AND SQUEEZE

Gourmet Girl Graffiti is such a sweet and heartwarming anime/manga that feels like a love letter to family—found and related—as well as food. Shiina makes Kirin and Ryō this shrimp katsu sandwich after they pass their high school entrance exams, as a sign of victory and to "win ev'ry (ebi) day." It's a play on words because *ebi* is the Japanese word for "shrimp" and *katsu* means "fried cutlet" as well as "victory." This sandwich is sure to be as tasty as it is satisfying to eat!

YIELD **4** SANDWICHES · PREP **20** MINUTES · FREEZE **30** MINUTES · COOK **25** MINUTES

SHRIMP PATTIES

20 large black tiger shrimp, peeled and deveined

1 large egg white

1 tablespoon potato starch

1 tablespoon sake

Salt and black pepper, to taste

Oil, for deep-frying

SHRIMP BATTER

2 large eggs, beaten

½ cup (65 g) cornstarch

1½ cups (120 g) panko bread crumbs

EGG SALAD FILLING

4 large eggs

4 tablespoons Kewpie mayo

¼ teaspoon sugar

⅛ teaspoon salt

FOR ASSEMBLY

8 slices white bread

Butter, to taste

8 leaves Romaine lettuce

1 To make the shrimp patties: On a cutting board, mince 13 or 14 shrimp into a paste with a sharp knife and chop the remaining 6 or 7 shrimp into small pieces.

2 Place the shrimp paste and chopped shrimp in a medium bowl, then add the egg white, 1 tablespoon potato starch, sake, and salt and pepper. Combine well, then divide the mixture into 4 pieces. Form each piece into a 2½ × 2-inch (6 × 5 cm) patty, then place each patty on an individual piece of parchment paper. Place the patties in the freezer until frozen, about 30 minutes, for easier handling.

3 To make the shrimp batter: Place the 2 beaten eggs and cornstarch in a medium shallow bowl and combine until paste-like. Put the panko bread crumbs in a separate medium shallow bowl.

4 Remove the frozen patties from the freezer and dip and cover with the egg mixture, then coat in the panko. (You can freeze the panko-covered shrimp patties for up to 1 week; defrost to room temperature before frying.)

5 In a medium heavy-bottomed pot, heat at least 2½ inches (6 cm) of oil over medium heat to 350°F (175°C), measuring with a thermometer, or a few bread crumbs sizzling when they hit the hot oil. Once the shrimp patties are close to room temperature, place them on a spatula and slowly and carefully slide them into the oil. Deep-fry in batches, 2 patties at a time, for 4½ minutes, or until golden. Remove from the oil and place on a wire rack. Season each patty with a pinch of salt immediately.

6 To make the egg filling: In a separate medium pot, bring enough water to a boil over medium-high heat to cover the 4 eggs. Once boiling, carefully submerge the eggs using a spoon and boil for 12 minutes. Remove from the pot using a slotted spoon and transfer to a bowl of cold water. When cool enough to handle, remove the shells.

7 Place the peeled eggs in a medium bowl, mash them with a fork, and then add the mayo, sugar, and ⅛ teaspoon salt.

8 To assemble: Lightly toast the bread slices for 1 minute, then spread the bottom slices with butter. Add a layer of egg filling to the bottom bread slice of each sandwich, then top with a shrimp patty, 2 lettuce leaves, and a top bread slice. Slice off the crusts and cut the sandwiches in half. Serve hot or cold.

"Just touch it. Just give it a feeling . . . and the food will respond by being delicious."

—Ryō Machiko, *Gourmet Girl Graffiti*

KARAAGE TO-GO

★ ANIME ★

ODD TAXI

SEASON 1 EPISODE 5

DON'T CALL
ME AN IDOL

Yamamoto, the manager of the up-and-coming girl group Mystery Kiss, picks up one of the members, Mitsuya Yuki, in the taxi. He has brought along her favorite food, karaage (Japanese fried chicken), which she declares is her "soul food." This recipe has apple in the marinade and is double-fried for extra crispiness, which helps it last longer while you're out and about!

YIELD 4 SERVINGS

PREP 15 MINUTES

MARINATE 2 HOURS

COOK 20 MINUTES

SPECIAL TOOLS

To-go containers

Wooden food picks

INGREDIENTS

1 Fuji apple, grated

2 tablespoons grated onion

4 cloves garlic, grated

1 teaspoon grated ginger root

3 tablespoons soy sauce

3 tablespoons mirin

Pinch black pepper, plus more to taste

8 boneless, skin-on chicken thighs, sliced into 1-inch (2.5 cm) pieces

Canola oil, for deep-frying

¼ cup (40 g) potato starch, for dredging

Salt, to taste

((STEPS))

1 In a large bowl, stir together the grated apple, onion, garlic, ginger, soy sauce, mirin, and pinch of black pepper. Add the chicken to the bowl and coat with the apple mixture. Cover the bowl and let marinate in the refrigerator for at least 2 hours, or overnight for best results.

2 When ready to deep-fry the chicken, in a large heavy-bottomed pot, heat 3 to 4 inches (7.5 to 10 cm) of canola oil over medium heat to 350°F (175°C), measuring with a thermometer. Line a baking tray with a wire rack and set aside.

3 Add the potato starch to a shallow bowl. Dredge the chicken pieces in the potato starch and discard the marinade.

4 Cooking in two batches, carefully drop the chicken pieces into the hot oil and cook for 7 to 8 minutes, until lightly browned and cooked all the way through. Remove the chicken from the oil using a slotted spoon and transfer to the wire rack. Let the oil heat to 375°F (190°C), then double-fry the chicken by reintroducing it in one batch to the hot oil and cooking until golden, 3 to 5 minutes. Transfer the chicken to the wire rack and sprinkle with salt while hot.

5 Once cooled a little, transfer the karaage into to-go containers and stick some of the pieces with food picks for easy eating.

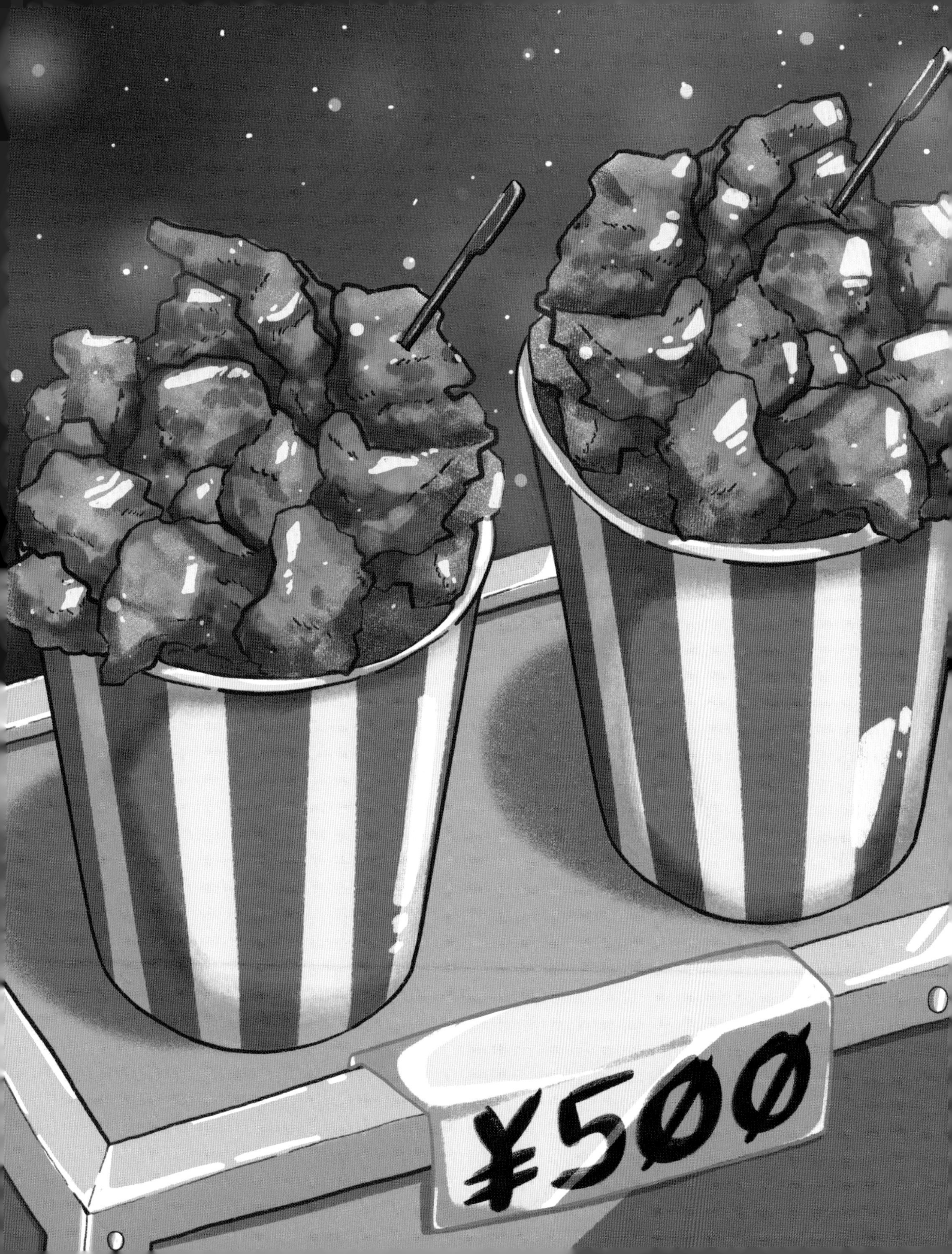
¥500

SHINOBU'S HIREKATSU SANDWICH

★ANIME★
ISEKAI IZAKAYA: JAPANESE FOOD FROM ANOTHER WORLD

SEASON 1 | EPISODE 10
UNINVITED GUESTS

Izakaya Nobu's front door opens to a parallel world, the ancient city of Aitheria. In this episode, Baron Brentano reserves the entire restaurant and asks for schnitzel. Nobuyuki Yazawa, the owner and chef of the izakaya, has no idea how to make this, so he leaves the restaurant to ask about it at the palace guard barracks. Shinobu Senke, the waitress, is left behind, and as the baron becomes agitated, he asks her to make something to fill his stomach. She makes hirekatsu (*hire* means "tenderloin" and *katsu* means "fried cutlet"), which is essentially a pork cutlet, and turns it into a sandwich. The baron has never had a pork cutlet sandwich before and is pleasantly surprised by the crunchiness of the fried cutlet, rich sauce, and the soft bread holding all the flavors together.

YIELD **6** SANDWICHES · PREP **15** MINUTES · COOK **15** MINUTES

PORK CUTLETS

1½ pounds (700 g) pork tenderloin, cut into 12 slices (½ inch, or 12 mm, thick)

Salt and black pepper, to taste

1 cup (120 g) all-purpose flour

2 large eggs, beaten

3 cups (240 g) panko bread crumbs

Canola or vegetable oil, for deep-frying

KARASHI MAYO

6 tablespoons Kewpie mayo

2 teaspoons Japanese karashi mustard (or 4 teaspoons Dijon mustard)

¼ teaspoon sugar

ASSEMBLY

8 slices white bread

Tonkatsu sauce, to taste

1 To make the pork cutlets: Season the pork slices with salt and pepper on both sides.

2 Prepare a dredging station with three medium shallow bowls, placing the flour mixed with a pinch of the salt in one, the beaten eggs in another, and the panko in the remaining one. Dip the pork slices into the flour, then the eggs, and then the panko, shaking off any excess, and set on a plate.

3 In a medium heavy-bottomed pot, heat 3 inches (7.5 cm) of oil over medium heat to 350°F (175°C), measuring with a thermometer, or a few bread crumbs sizzling when they hit the hot oil. Cooking in batches, deep-fry the pork for 5 to 6 minutes, until golden brown. Transfer the pork slices to a wire rack and immediately season each slice with a pinch of salt.

4 To make the karashi mayo: In a small bowl, stir together the mayo, karashi mustard, and sugar until well combined.

5 To assemble: Thinly spread the karashi mayo on one side of each slice of bread, then add 2 fried pork cutlets to the bottom bread slice of each sandwich, generously drizzle with tonkatsu sauce, and top with a top bread slice. Slice off the crusts and cut in half. Serve while hot.

NOTES

• Japanese karashi hot mustard is spicier than Dijon mustard and comparable to Chinese mustard. Use an amount that suits your palate—I suggest starting with 1½ teaspoons, especially if you cannot handle spice, but do not omit it altogether, as it has an aromatic, wasabi-like flavor that complements the dish.

• If you do not have store-bought tonkatsu sauce, mix 6 tablespoons A1 steak sauce, 2 tablespoons soy sauce, and 2 teaspoons honey together for a mock version.

"It seems there are many delicacies in the world that I do not know yet."

—Baron Brentano, *Isekai Izakaya: Japanese Food from Another World*

ASUNA'S STEAK SANDWICH

★ ANIME ★

SWORD ART ONLINE

SEASON 1   EPISODE 6

ILLUSIONARY AVENGER

Asuna hands Kirito a steak sandwich that she reveals she made herself. While the two aren't exactly enemies anymore—instead unwitting allies on their way to becoming friends—when Kirito makes a joke about Asuna being able to cook, she gets mad and Kirito accidentally drops the sandwich, which then disintegrates. She makes him another sandwich in episode 9 with the addition of homemade special sauces. For this recipe, I also took inspiration from the light novel for episode 9 (volume 1, episode 10), as Kirito describes in it that "the thick, sweet-and-salty taste reminded me of the Japanese-style fast food." For my version, I used steak dressed in a sweet-and-salty homemade teriyaki sauce.

YIELD 2 SANDWICHES

PREP 15 MINUTES

MARINATE 1 HOUR

COOK 25 MINUTES

STEAK

2 cloves garlic, grated

¼ teaspoon ginger, grated

½ tablespoon olive oil

Salt and pepper, to taste

2 hanger or skirt steaks (10½ ounces, or 300 g, total), membranes removed

TERIYAKI SAUCE

¼ cup (60 ml) soy sauce

¼ cup (60 ml) sake

¼ cup (60 ml) mirin

2 tablespoons sugar

OMELETS

4 large eggs, beaten, divided

Salt and pepper, to taste

1 tablespoon butter, divided

ASSEMBLY

2 loaves (6 inches, or 15 cm, long each) French bread (or ½ recipe Sasha's Stolen Bread on page 95)

Mayonnaise, to taste

1 cup (25 g) microgreens (or 4 leaves lettuce)

8 white edible flowers

2 tablespoons pomegranate seeds

《 CONTINUED 》

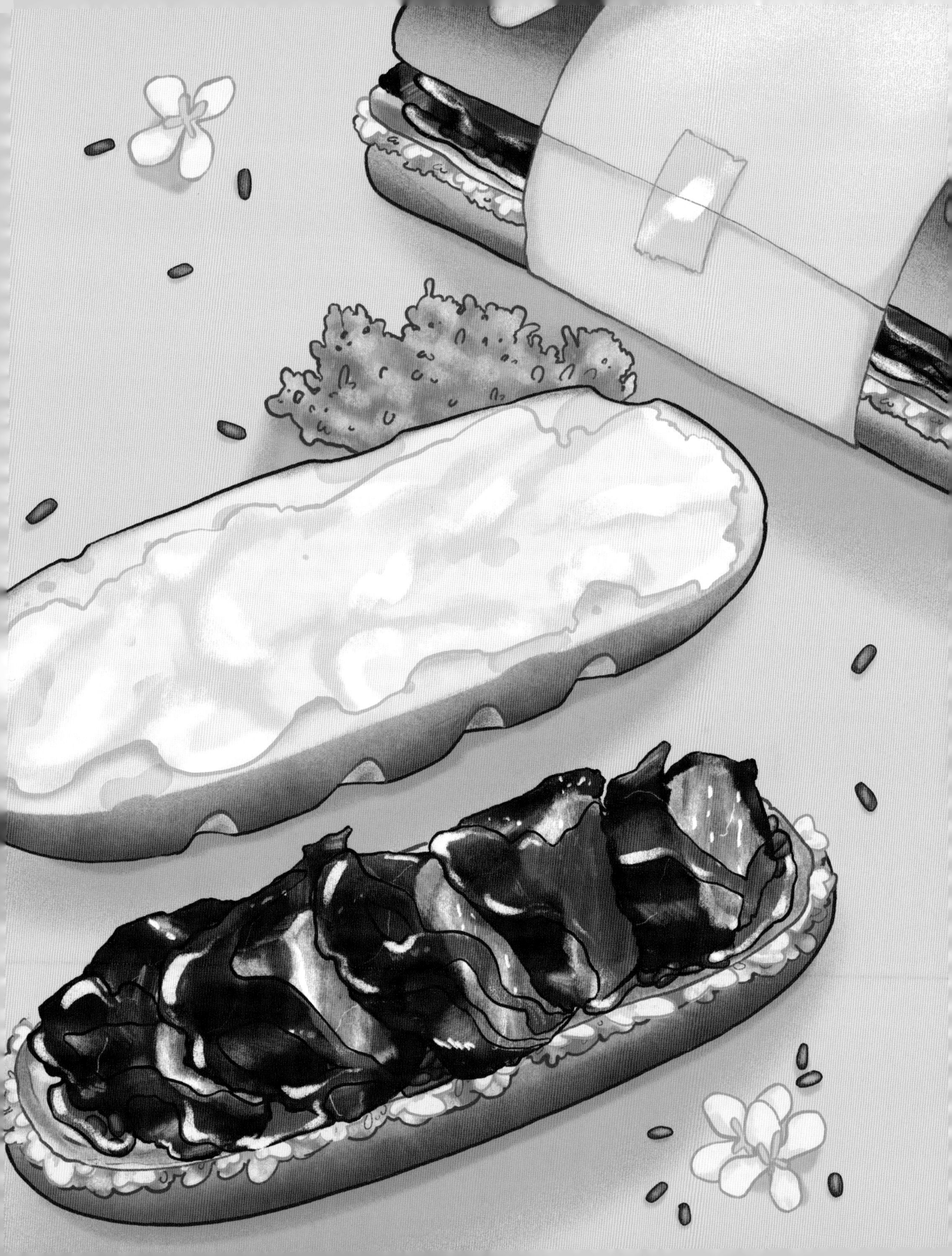

ASUNA'S STEAK SANDWICH STEPS

1 To make the steak: In a medium bowl, stir together the garlic, ginger, olive oil, and salt and pepper. Add the steaks and turn to coat in the marinade. Cover the bowl and let marinate in the refrigerator for at least 1 hour, or up to overnight.

2 Meanwhile, make the teriyaki sauce: Add all the sauce ingredients to a medium saucepan over medium heat and bring to a boil. Reduce the heat to medium-low and let the sauce reduce until thickened and glossy, stirring occasionally, 2 to 3 minutes. Transfer the sauce to a heatproof container and let cool to room temperature.

3 Remove the steaks from the refrigerator and let come to room temperature. Heat a large skillet over medium-high heat. Cook the steaks for 3 minutes on one side, or until browned and crusted, then flip and cook for another 2 minutes, or until desired doneness (for medium, cook to an internal temperature of 135°F, or 57°C). In the last minute of cooking, drizzle 3 tablespoons of the teriyaki sauce onto the steaks and flip to cover each surface thoroughly. Place the steaks on a cutting board, let rest for 10 minutes, and then slice against the grain at a forty-five degree angle into thick pieces.

4 To make the omelets: In a medium bowl, stir together the beaten eggs and salt and pepper. In a medium nonstick skillet, melt ½ tablespoon of the butter over medium heat, then add half of the beaten eggs. Cook to the desired doneness and, using a spatula, fold the edges into the middle from both sides of the pan to form a rectangle the width of the French bread. Transfer the omelet to a plate, then make a second omelet in the same pan with the remaining ½ tablespoon butter and beaten egg mixture.

5 To assemble: Slice the French bread loaves in half lengthwise and toast the cut sides. Smear mayonnaise on the inside of the top half of each loaf. On the bottom half of each loaf, layer the ingredients in this order: microgreens or lettuce, 4 edible flowers, an omelet, 1 tablespoon pomegranate seeds, 5 or 6 slices of steak, more teriyaki sauce, and the top half of the loaf. Wrap the sandwiches in parchment paper, cut in half, and serve.

NOTES

- **You can buy edible flowers at the grocery store. They are commonly found near the packaged fresh herbs.**
- **If you love the taste of teriyaki sauce, double or triple the recipe for this homemade version for quick stir-fries. It can be stored in an airtight container in the refrigerator for up to 1 week.**

SANDO INSPIRATION

★ ANIME ★
K-ON!
SEASON 1 EPISODE 7
CHRISTMAS

There are a lot of memorable foods in *K-On!*, thanks to Mugi—one of the four members of the girl band—who brings the girls various pastries and snacks to enjoy during their teatime breaks, when they bond with one another and talk about what's going on in their lives. Mini sandwiches, also called mini sandos, are a common teatime snack, and these particular sandwiches are special because Li serves them in the Christmas episode, when she and her older sister, Yui, host their friends to celebrate and exchange gifts. Mini sandos are super easy to make for any age group and are a quintessential component of the slice-of-life genre of anime.

YIELD **6** SANDWICHES PREP **20** MINUTES

STRAWBERRY

1 cup (240 ml)
heavy whipping cream

2 tablespoons freeze-dried strawberries, pulverized into powder

1 tablespoon confectioners' sugar

Pink gel food coloring (optional)

4 slices white bread
(or milk bread)

2 tablespoons condensed milk

4 strawberries, stems removed

CLASSIC

Kewpie mayo, to taste

4 slices white bread

4 slices ham

4 leaves lettuce

EGG SALAD

1 recipe Egg Salad Filling
(see Shrimp "Ebi" Katsu Sandwich on page 40)

4 slices white bread

《 CONTINUED 》

SANDO INSPIRATION STEPS

1 To make the strawberry sandos: In a medium bowl, using a hand mixer with a whisk attachment, whip the heavy cream on high speed until medium-stiff peaks form, about 2 minutes. Add the freeze-dried strawberry powder, confectioners' sugar, and 1 drop of pink food coloring and whip until stiff peaks form, about 1 minute.

2 To assemble: Spread ½ tablespoon of condensed milk on one side of all the bread slices. Spread 2 bread slices each with a dollop of strawberry whip, then top with 2 strawberries, another dollop of strawberry whip to fully cover the strawberries, and a top bread slice with the condensed-milk side facing down.

3 Tightly cover each sandwich with plastic wrap to hold its shape and place in the refrigerator for 15 minutes. Cut in half diagonally and enjoy cold.

4 To make the classic sandos: Smear mayonnaise on one side of all the bread slices, then top 2 bread slices each with a lettuce leaf, 2 ham slices, another lettuce leaf, and a top bread slice. Slice off the crusts, cut in half, and serve.

5 To make the egg salad sandos: Smear the egg salad filling on the bottom bread slice of each sandwich and top with the top bread slice. Slice off the crusts, cut in half, and serve.

NOTE

You can make the classic and egg salad sandos a couple of hours ahead of time. Slice off the crusts, then tightly cover each sandwich with plastic wrap and refrigerate. When ready to serve, remove the plastic wrap and cut the sandwiches in half.

"I wish we'll get better."
"I wish we will have fun."
"I wish I can eat more of the delicious cakes that Mugi-chan brings."

—Members of Ho-kago Tea Time, *K-On!*

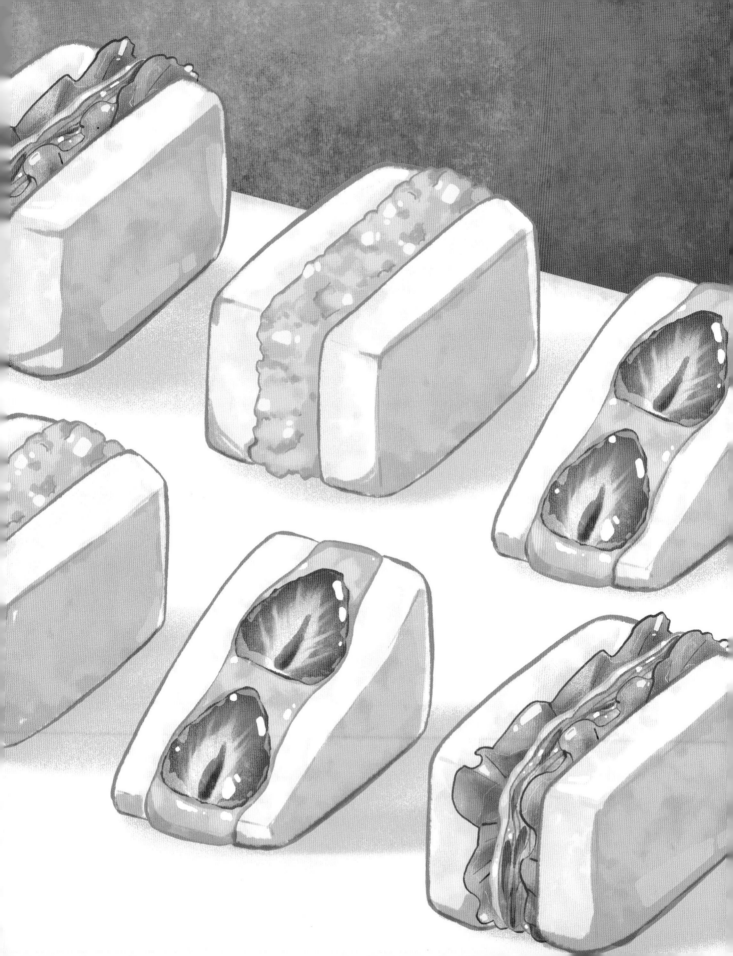

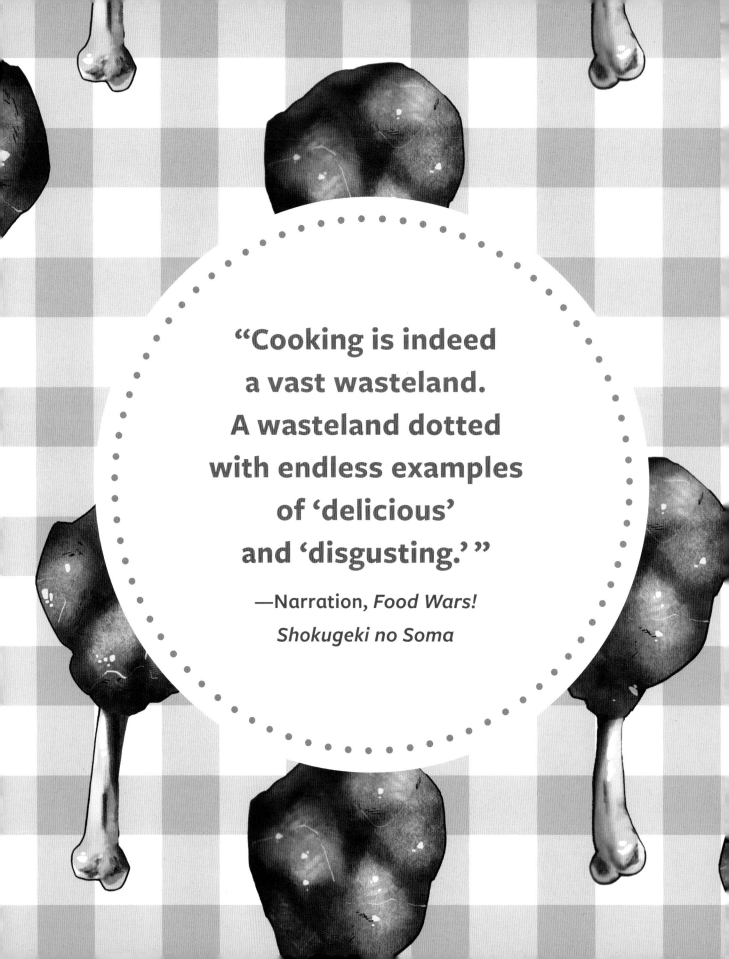

"Cooking is indeed
a vast wasteland.
A wasteland dotted
with endless examples
of 'delicious'
and 'disgusting.'"

—Narration, *Food Wars!*
Shokugeki no Soma

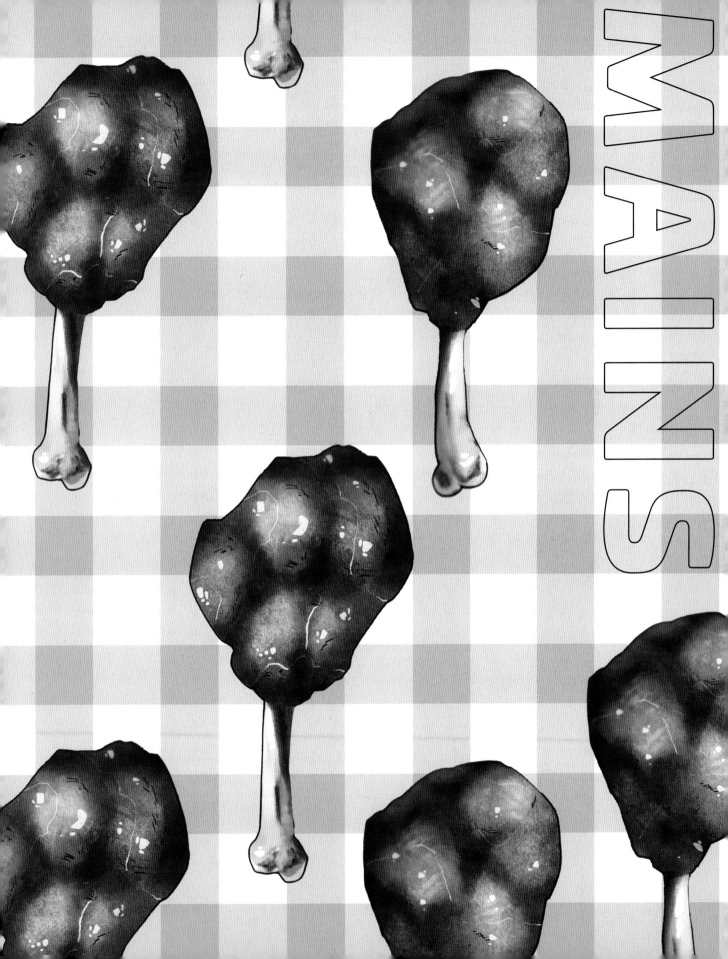

MAINS

HOWL'S BREAKFAST PLATE

★ANIME★
HOWL'S MOVING CASTLE

This hearty breakfast is quite easily one of the most memorable dishes from the Studio Ghibli movies and is often referred to when people talk about foods from those films. When Sophie tries to make breakfast in the castle that she is not yet familiar with, Howl steps in and takes over with a casual grace. To stay authentic to the anime, I suggest cooking this over a fire.

YIELD **3** SERVINGS | PREP **15** MINUTES | COOK **10** MINUTES

SPECIAL TOOLS

Firewood and starter for outdoor campfire

Cooking grate for campfire

Large cast-iron pan

Heavy-duty oven mitts

Tongs

INGREDIENTS

3 slices thick-cut bacon

6 large eggs

Pinch salt (optional)

3 large slices bread

3 thick slices Swiss cheese, cut from a wedge

Prepared hot hibiscus tea

((STEPS))

1 Prepare a campfire. Place the grate over the fire and set the cast-iron pan on it over direct heat. Heat until the pan is smoking, then, using the heavy-duty oven mitts, move the pan over indirect heat.

2 Place the bacon in a single layer in the pan and cook until the underside is crispy, 3 to 4 minutes. Using a pair of tongs, flip over the bacon, then push it to one side of the pan to make room for the eggs. Crack the eggs into the free space and feed Calcifer the eggshells. Sprinkle the pinch of salt over the eggs—this is optional as the bacon has already salted the dish.

Cook for 3 to 4 minutes, until the egg whites set. Using the heavy-duty oven mitts, remove the cast-iron pan from the heat.

3 With a spatula, equally divide the eggs and bacon among three plates. Serve each plate with a large slice of bread, a thick slice of Swiss cheese, and a mug of hibiscus tea.

NOTE
You can also make this dish on the stovetop. Heat the cast-iron skillet over medium heat, then follow steps 2 and 3.

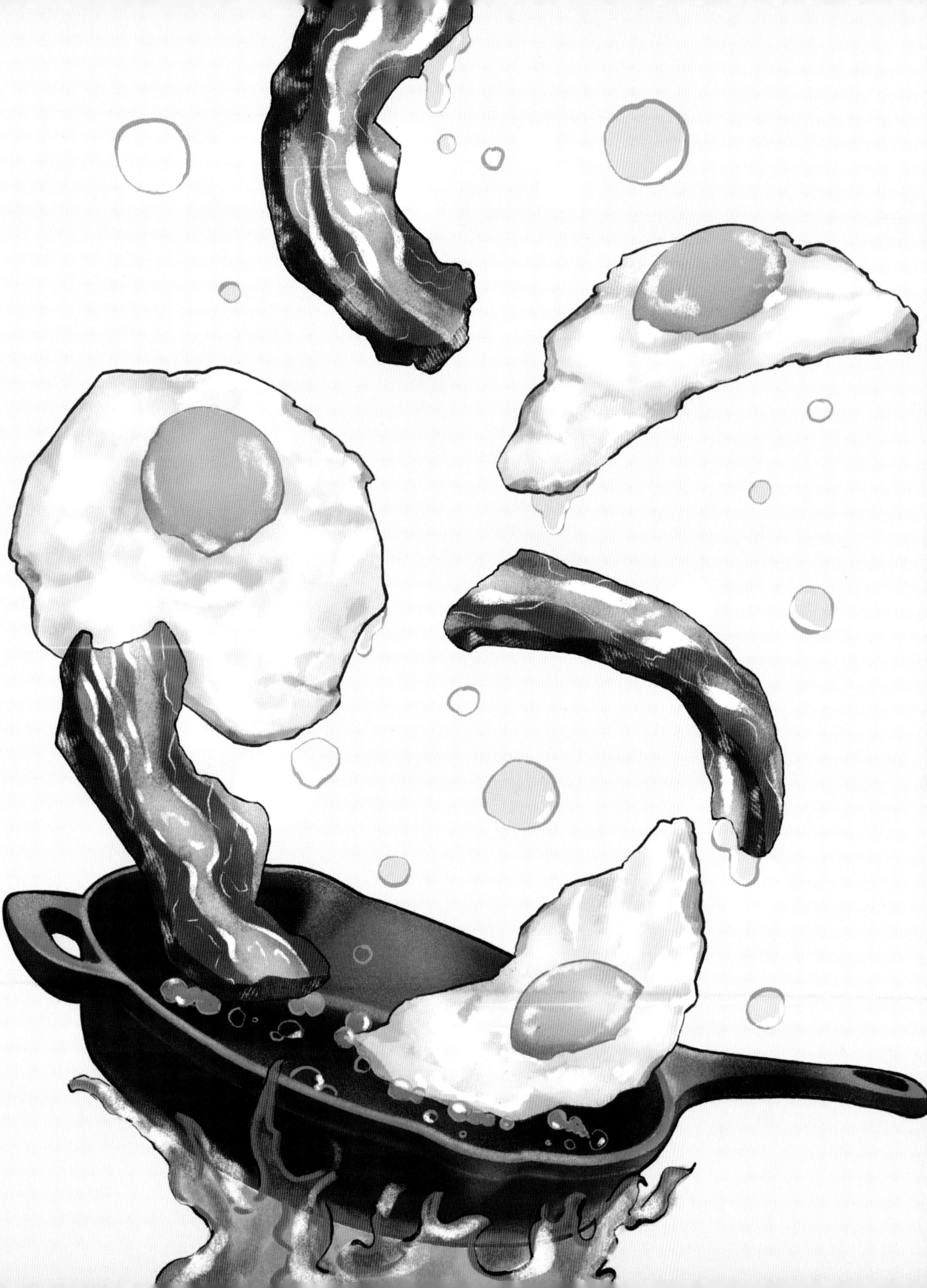

PAMPERED UDON

ANIME

MARCH COMES IN LIKE A LION

SEASON 2 EPISODE 20
SUMMER VACATION (PART 2)/NEW YEAR

While Rei tutors his younger friend Hinata for her high school entrance exams, Akari, Hinata's sister and Rei's friend, makes them "pampered udon" just like their mother made when Akari was young and studying for her entrance exams. When Akari couldn't choose between shrimp tempura topping and fried tofu, her mother "pampered" her by making both. This scene is quite sweet and shows how Akari has taken on the motherly role after their mother died. I hope you can also find some comfort in these delicious noodles!

YIELD 4 SERVINGS

PREP 15 MINUTES

COOK 30 MINUTES

FRIED TOFU (INARI AGE)

2 deep-fried tofu pouches (abura-age)

2 tablespoons soy sauce

3 tablespoons sugar

SHRIMP TEMPURA

Vegetable oil, for frying

4 large prawns or shrimp, peeled and deveined, leaving the tails on

½ cup (60 g) all-purpose flour

½ teaspoon baking soda

¼ cup (40 g) plus 1 teaspoon potato starch, divided

2 pinches salt, divided, plus more to taste

1 large egg

½ cup (120 ml) ice-cold water with ice cubes

4 wedges lemon (optional)

UDON SOUP

5 cups (1.1 L) water

2 tablespoons mirin

2 tablespoons soy sauce

2 teaspoons dashi powder

1 piece (2 inches, or 5 cm, square) dried kelp (kombu)

1 teaspoon sugar

4 single-serving packages (8.8 ounces, or 250 g, each) udon noodles

FOR ASSEMBLY

8 slices (⅛ inch, or 3 mm, thick) fish cake (narutomaki)

2 scallions, thinly sliced

1 To make the inari age: Bring a medium pot of water to a boil. On a cutting board, slice each abura-age in half diagonally for 4 triangles. Add the abura-age to the boiling water and boil for 2 minutes to remove any excess oil. Remove from the water with a slotted spoon and place in between some sheets of paper towel. Use a rolling pin to squeeze out extra water by applying pressure.

2 Discard the water from the pot and rinse, then add the drained abura-age, ¼ cup (60 ml) clean water, 2 tablespoons soy sauce, and 3 tablespoons sugar. Simmer over medium heat until the liquids are almost evaporated and soaked into the tofu, about 8 minutes. Remove from the heat and set aside.

3 To make the shrimp tempura: Make a few shallow slices across the undersides of the shrimp, then flip them over and gently push down on their backs to straighten them.

4 To make the tempura batter, in a medium bowl, whisk together the flour, baking soda, 1 teaspoon of the potato starch, and a pinch of the salt. In a small bowl, beat the egg, then combine with the ice-cold water and ice cubes. Pour and whisk the egg-water mixture into the flour mixture, just enough to get a batter consistency that lightly coats a spoon. Do not overmix; lumps are okay. Spread the remaining ¼ cup (40 g) potato starch on a tray and scatter over the remaining pinch of salt.

5 In a medium heavy-bottomed pot, heat 2½ inches (6 cm) of the vegetable oil over medium heat to 350°F (175°C), measuring with a thermometer, or a little tempura batter sizzling when it hits the hot oil. Once the oil is hot enough, lightly coat the shrimp with the potato starch in the tray, then dip into the tempura batter, shaking off any excess, and carefully submerge in the oil. Cook for 2 minutes, or until the shrimp become orange in color and the batter turns golden. Remove from the oil using a slotted spoon and let cool on a rack. Lightly salt the cooked tempura. Squeeze over some juice from the lemon wedges (if using) right before serving.

6 To make the udon soup: In a separate medium pot, add the water, mirin, 2 tablespoons soy sauce, dashi powder, kombu, and 1 teaspoon sugar. Bring to a boil over medium-high heat, then reduce the heat to a low simmer while the udon noodles cook. Cook the udon noodles in a large pot according to the package instructions.

7 To assemble: Place the udon noodles into serving bowls and ladle in some broth. Top with the inari age, shrimp tempura, and sliced fish cakes. Sprinkle with scallions and serve.

TOFU STEAK

ANIME

RESTAURANT TO ANOTHER WORLD

SEASON 1 EPISODE 4

OMELET RICE /TOFU STEAK

The Western Restaurant Nekoya is a regular restaurant six days of the week, but on Saturdays it opens a doorway to a fantastical world, welcoming all kinds of patrons, from elves to dragons. On one occasion, Fardania, an elf, comes in searching for something delicious to commemorate the anniversary of her mother's death. Not seeing anything to satisfy her vegan diet, the owner offers her a grilled tofu steak with ponzu sauce and kelp. Ponzu sauce is comprised of mostly soy sauce and yuzu (citrus) and can be quite salty and tangy. I made a sauce with sweet-and-savory flavors.

YIELD 2 SERVINGS **PREP** 15 MINUTES **COOK** 30 MINUTES

SPECIAL TOOLS

Nonstick grill pan

2 sizzling (or fajita) plates with wooden bases

HONEY-ROASTED VEGETABLES

4 small carrots

4 baby potatoes

1 tablespoon olive oil

1½ tablespoons honey

1 teaspoon garlic powder

½ teaspoon onion powder

½ tablespoon finely chopped Italian flat-leaf parsley

½ teaspoon salt

¼ teaspoon black pepper

BLANCHED SPINACH

½ bunch spinach

Salt, for boiling water

Ice cubes, for ice bath

GRILLED TOFU

1 block (12 ounces, or 340 g) medium or firm tofu, cut in half crosswise

¼ teaspoon salt

¼ cup (40 g) potato starch

1 tablespoon oil, plus more if needed, for grilling.

PONZU SAUCE

2½ tablespoons soy sauce

2 tablespoons mirin

2 tablespoons sugar

1 clove garlic, grated

1 scallion, trimmed and sliced in half lengthwise

1 tablespoon lemon juice

½ teaspoon lemon zest

1 piece (1 inch, or 2.5 cm, square) dried kelp (kombu)

FOR ASSEMBLY

1 piece (½ inch, or 12 mm, long) Japanese radish (daikon), finely grated

2 shiso leaves, thinly sliced

« CONTINUED »

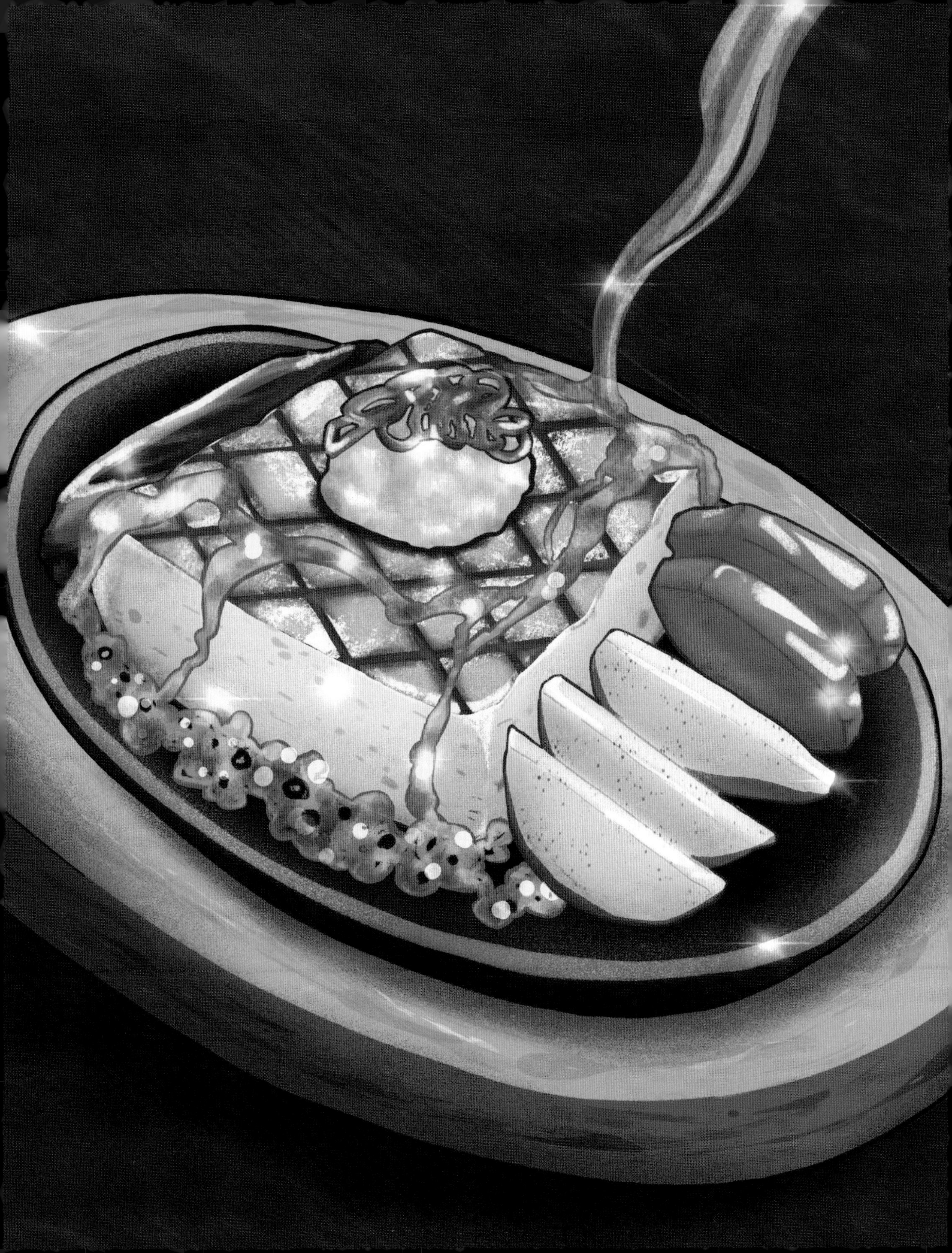

1 To make the honey-roasted vegetables: Preheat the oven to 350°F (174°C; gas mark 4). Line a baking tray with parchment paper and set aside.

2 Trim the carrots, then slice them into 2-inch (5 cm) lengths. Use a tournée cut to shape each piece or trim the carrots into football shapes. Place the carrots on the prepared tray. Slice the potatoes into wedges, about the same size as the carrots, then place them on the prepared tray.

3 Drizzle the veggies with the olive oil and season with the honey, garlic powder, onion powder, parsley, ½ teaspoon salt, and pepper. Mix and coat the veggies.

4 Cover the tray with foil and bake for 15 minutes, or until the veggies are fork-tender.

5 Meanwhile, make the blanched spinach: In a medium pot, bring enough water to a boil over medium-high heat to submerge the spinach bunch. In a medium bowl, prepare an ice bath with cold water and ice cubes and set aside.

6 Once boiling, salt the water, then submerge the spinach bunch and boil for 30 seconds, or until bright green. Remove from the water using a slotted spoon and transfer to the ice bath until cool and to stop the cooking process, about 30 seconds. Remove, drain, and pat dry with paper towels. Trim the roots or stems, if necessary, and slice the bunch neatly in half lengthwise. Set aside.

7 To make the grilled tofu: Cover the tofu in paper towels, place in a microwave-safe bowl, and microwave for 2 minutes. Drain the moisture that has seeped out and pat the tofu dry with paper towels

8 In the grill pan, heat the oil over medium heat. In a small shallow bowl, mix the potato starch and ¼ teaspoon salt, then dredge the tofu halves in the mixture. Add the tofu to the pan immediately and grill for 3 minutes on each side, or until darkened with grill marks, adding more oil if needed. Remove the tofu from the grill pan to a plate and wipe away any oil residue with a paper towel. At this point, preheat the sizzling plates.

9 Reduce the stovetop heat to low, then add all the ponzu sauce ingredients to the grill pan the tofu was cooked in. Let simmer until the sugar has dissolved, then pour the sauce into a heatproof bowl and discard the scallions and kombu.

10 To assemble: Place the heated sizzling plates on their bases, then neatly stack half of the spinach on the left side of each plate, half of the roasted veggies on the right side, and a grilled tofu half in the middle. Top the tofu with the grated radish and thinly sliced shiso leaves. Just before serving, drizzle the ponzu sauce over the tofu.

SKYTREE PORK BOWL

★ANIME★
SILVER SPOON
SEASON 1 | EPISODE 10
HACHIKEN SAYS GOODBYE TO PORK BOWL

Hachiken is a city kid who enrolls in an agricultural school in the countryside to distance himself from his strained relationship with his family. He quickly grows attached to one of the smaller piglets, affectionately naming them Pork Bowl, before he learns that in a few months Pork Bowl will be going to the slaughterhouse. When that unfortunately happens, Hachiken buys Pork Bowl's meat to honor them and makes the vertically impressive Skytree pork bowl, named after Tokyo Skytree, the tallest building in Japan. I made this dish with pork tenderloin, a prized cut of meat. Stack as high as you like!

YIELD 2-4 SERVINGS | **PREP** 15 MINUTES | **CHILL** 30 MINUTES | **MARINATE** 30 MINUTES | **COOK** 25 MINUTES

SPECIAL TOOLS

Outdoor grill

Charcoal (optional)

INGREDIENTS

¼ cup (60 ml) soy sauce

¼ cup (60 ml) mirin

2 tablespoons rice vinegar

2 tablespoons brown sugar

3 large cloves garlic, grated

¼ teaspoon grated ginger root

3 scallions, trimmed and sliced in half lengthwise

Black pepper, to taste

1 Fuji apple, peeled and grated

1 teaspoon white miso

1 tablespoon canola oil, for greasing

1 pound (454 g) pork tenderloin, sliced ¼ inch (6 mm) thick

Cooked short-grain white rice, for serving

《 CONTINUED 》

SKYTREE PORK BOWL STEPS

1 In a medium pot, combine the soy sauce, mirin, rice vinegar, brown sugar, garlic, ginger, scallions, and pepper. Bring to a rapid simmer over medium heat until the brown sugar dissolves and the sauce slightly reduces, about 10 minutes. Remove from the heat and add the grated apple and miso, stirring to dissolve it. Transfer the marinade to a heatproof container, cover, and refrigerate until it cools to room temperature.

2 Place the sliced pork tenderloin in a large bowl. Pour half of the cooled marinade over the pork. Mix to coat the meat, then cover and marinate in the refrigerator for 30 minutes.

3 Meanwhile, grease the outdoor grill grates with the canola oil, then preheat the grill.

4 Grill the pork tenderloin until the internal temperature reaches 145°F (62°C) on a meat thermometer, about 12 minutes, turning and basting it with the remaining marinade every 3 minutes.

5 Serve the pork stacked on the cooked white rice.

NOTE

You can also make this dish on the stovetop. Follow steps 1 and 2, then coat a medium skillet with ½ tablespoon oil and heat over medium heat. Cook the pork in two batches until browned and the internal temperature reads 145°F (62°C) on an instant-read thermometer, about 4 minutes per side. Serve the pork stacked on the cooked white rice.

"Making bacon out of tenderloin? That would be an insult to Pork Bowl."

—Tamako Inada, *Silver Spoon*

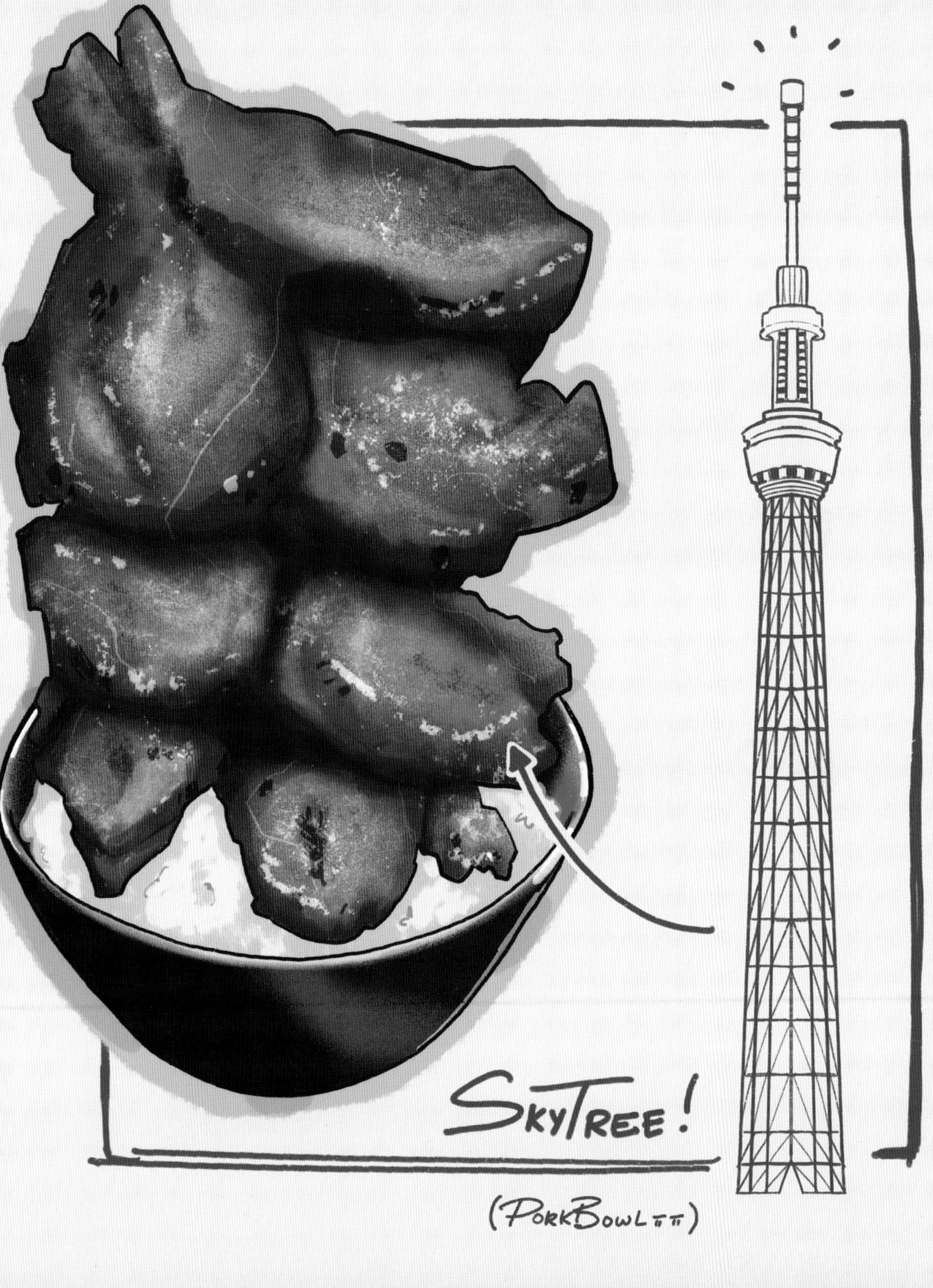
SKYTREE!
(PORKBOWL π π)

MISO CHASHU RAMEN

★ ANIME ★
BORUTO: NARUTO NEXT GENERATIONS

SEASON 1 EPISODE 18

A DAY IN THE LIFE OF THE UZUMAKI FAMILY

Even if you've never watched a single anime, it's unlikely you haven't at least heard of *Naruto*. Well, the sequel series, *Boruto*, follows Naruto's son . . . Boruto. Yeah, kinda saw that one coming, huh? And, well, you can't make an anime cookbook without including Naruto's ramen! When Hinata, Boruto's mom and Naruto's wife, kicks them out to fend for themselves, nobody is surprised to see them go to Ichiraku Ramen, where Naruto has an all-you-can-eat gift certificate, gifted to him by the owner for a wedding present. In previous episodes, Naruto reveals that his favorite ramen is miso pork ramen, often ordered with extra noodles, so I decided to pay homage to the franchise with this delicious recipe!

YIELD 6 SERVINGS • PREP 30 MINUTES • REST 2.5 HOURS • COOK 3 HOURS

SPECIAL TOOLS

Pressure cooker

Kitchen twine

Kitchen torch (optional)

PORK BONE BROTH

3½ pounds (1.6 kg) pork bones

8 cups (1.9 L) water

1 piece (2 inches, or 5 cm, square) dried kelp (kombu)

Dried bonito flakes (katsuobushi), to taste

TENDER CHASHU (BRAISED PORK)

1½ pounds (680 g) pork belly

2 teaspoons each salt and black pepper

2 tablespoons oil, for cooking

2½ cups (600 ml) soy sauce

2 cups (480 ml) sake

1¼ cups (300 ml) mirin

1 cup (220 g) packed brown sugar

MISO TARE

1½ cups (360 ml) white miso

½ cup (120 ml) soy sauce

½ cup (100 g) sugar

¼ cup (60 ml) sesame oil

1 cup (150 g) sesame seeds, puréed (or 1 cup, or 240 g, tahini)

10 medium cloves garlic (3½ ounces, or 100 g), minced

1 piece (1½ inches, or 4 cm, long) ginger root, minced

INFUSED AROMA OIL

1 cup (240 ml) canola oil

2 scallions, trimmed and sliced in half lengthwise

1 piece (1 inch, or 2.5 cm, long) ginger root, thinly sliced lengthwise

FOR ASSEMBLY

6 single-serving packs fresh ramen noodles (5 to 6 ounces, or 142 to 170 g, each) or dried ramen noodles (3 ounces, or 85 g, each)

6 soft-boiled eggs (see Ponyo's Ham Ramen on page 80, steps 1 and 2)

2 sheets dried seaweed (nori), cut into 6 squares each

Pickled bamboo shoots (menma), to taste

12 slices (⅛inch, or 3 mm, thick) fish cake (narutomaki)

2 scallions, thinly sliced

((STEPS))

1 To make the pork bone broth: In a large pot, place the pork bones and add enough water to cover them. Boil the bones for 10 minutes, then strain and scrub them in running water to remove any shards and impurities.

2 Add the bones to a pressure cooker with the 8 cups (1.9 L) water and pressure-cook for 1½ hours. You may also boil the bones in a pot on the stovetop over medium-high heat for 12 to 18 hours, making sure to replenish the water throughout to keep the bones covered and skimming the scum occasionally.

3 Once finished cooking and the broth is milky white and slightly thickened, open the pressure cooker, add the dried kelp and a handful of bonito flakes, turn off the heat, and let steep for 30 minutes. Strain the broth through a fine-mesh strainer, discarding the bones, and set aside.

4 To make the tender chashu: Place the pork belly on a cutting board and trim and discard the skin layer. Rub the pork belly all over with the salt and pepper, then roll it tight and tie it closed with kitchen twine: Equally space four pieces of twine across the width of the pork belly and tie each one around it. Then, using one piece of long twine, tie it along the length of the pork belly to secure the roll

5 In a large skillet, heat the oil over medium heat just until smoking, then panfry all sides of the pork belly until a deep golden brown.

6 Transfer the pork to a clean large pot and add the soy sauce, sake, mirin, brown sugar, and enough water to almost submerge the meat. Place a piece of parchment paper over the chashu mixture to cover, then cook without a lid. Bring the contents of the pot to a boil over medium-high heat, then reduce the temperature to a simmer and cook for 1 hour, turning the chashu every 10 minutes to achieve beautiful color throughout. After 1 hour, remove from the sauce and let the meat rest for 2 hours before slicing. (Do not discard the chashu sauce; see Notes below for use for the sauce.)

7 To make the miso tare: In a large bowl, mix all the miso tare ingredients until homogenous.

8 To make the infused aroma oil: In a small pot, heat the canola oil over medium heat, then add the scallions and ginger and cook until browned, about 2 minutes. Remove from the heat and discard the scallions and ginger. Set aside.

9 To assemble the ramen. Cook the fresh ramen noodles according to the package instructions. Warm the pork bone broth over medium-high heat.

((CONTINUED))

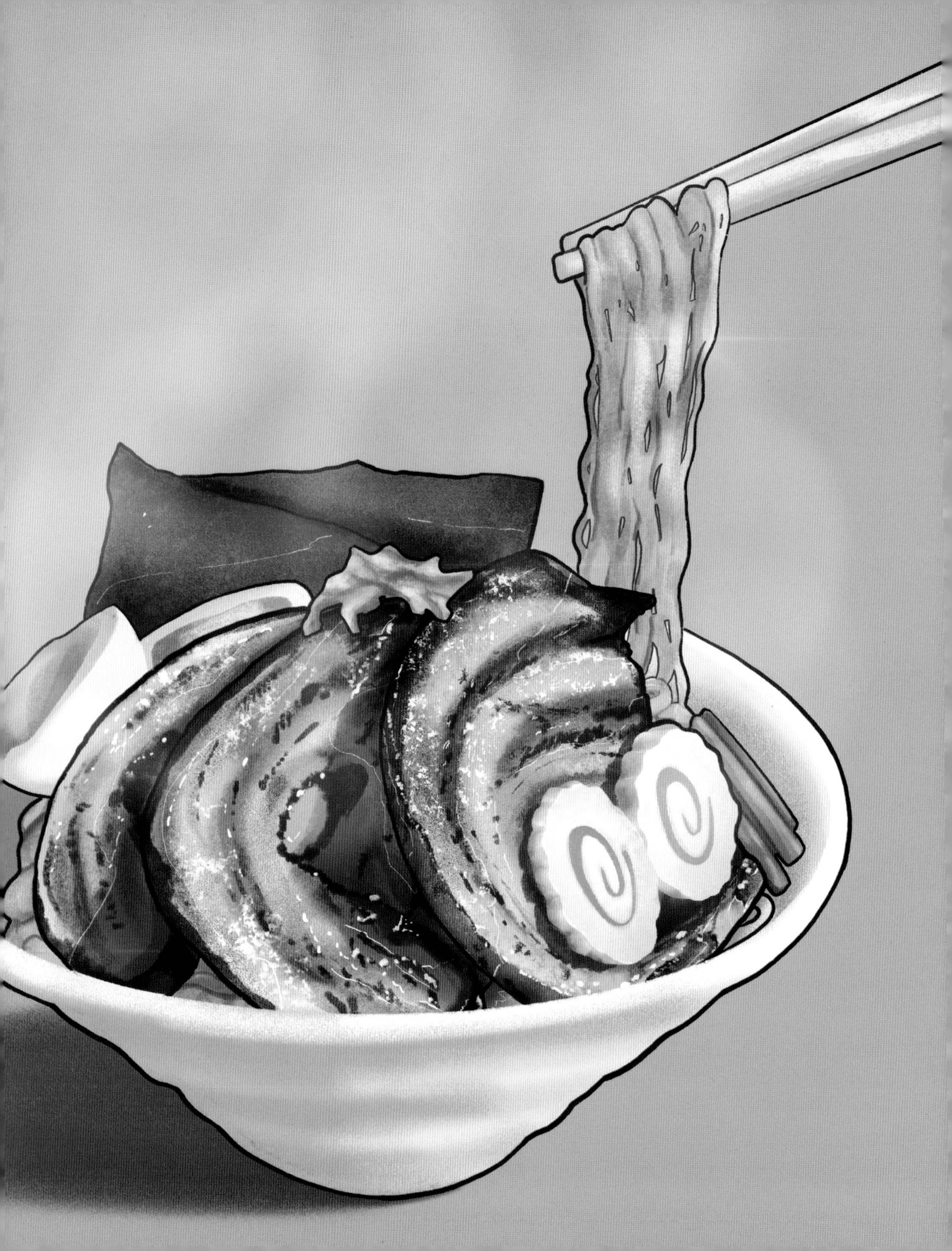

10 Cut the chashu into ¼-inch-thick (6 mm) slices. Torch the chashu surface until browned over a direct flame or using a kitchen torch (this is optional but recommended).

11 Assemble the ramen in this order: In each ramen bowl, add 2 teaspoons of infused aroma oil, ¼ cup (72 g) of miso tare, and ¼ cup (60 ml) of pork broth. Dissolve the miso tare in the broth, then add more broth to taste. Gently place the ramen noodles in the broth. Lastly, add the toppings, in generous amounts: chashu slices, 2 soft-boiled-egg halves, 2 nori sheets, some pickled bamboo shoots, 2 sliced fish cakes, and a sprinkle of sliced scallions

NOTES

• The pork bone broth, chashu sauce, miso tare, and infused aroma oil can be refrigerated in airtight containers for up to 1 week, so you can make them in advance or save the leftovers for later.

• Use the leftover chashu sauce to make soy sauce eggs for ramen. Let the sauce cool to room temperature, transfer to a bowl, and submerge the peeled soft-boiled eggs. Cover and refrigerate for 2 days for perfectly seasoned eggs.

"This smell brings back memories. Everything's shiny and new now, but this is where your mom and I went to eat on our first date."

—Naruto Uzumaki, *Boruto: Naruto Next Generations*

STUFFED HARD CRAB

★ ANIME ★
TORIKO

SEASON 1 | EPISODE 130

LIVE OR DIE? DEATH
IN THE BALANCE
COOKING!!

Zero-waste cooking is a recurring theme in this book, and in this episode, Komatsu enters the Cooking Festival competition to cook with leftover ingredients. He boils a hard crab with a shell that is "diamond-hard" for 9 minutes and 6.2 seconds, and then fries it in oil at a temperature of 96.2°C, or 205°F. (Spoiler alert: This wouldn't work in real life, so don't try it at home!) He also stuffs it with "beach fried rice," which looks to be comprised of peas, corn, shrimp, mushrooms, crab meat, and red bell peppers. If this sounds mouthwatering to you, then you are thinking just like the judges, because Komatsu passed this first round with flying colors!

YIELD 4 SERVINGS | **PREP** 10 MINUTES | **COOK** 15 MINUTES

BEACH FRIED RICE

4 cups (665 g)
day-old fried rice

2 egg yolks

1½ tablespoons vegetable oil,
divided, for cooking

½ small onion, finely chopped

¼ teaspoon grated ginger root

4 cloves garlic, minced

¼ cup (20 g) finely
chopped cabbage

¼ red bell pepper, seeded and
finely chopped

2 white button mushrooms,
thinly sliced

12 small-size shrimp, peeled
and deveined

2 scallions, finely chopped

¼ cup (34 g) frozen
peas, thawed

¼ cup (34 g)
frozen corn kernels, thawed

½ teaspoon sesame oil

1 tablespoon soy sauce

½ teaspoon salt

⅛ teaspoon pepper

STUFFED HARD CRAB

8 large soft-shell crabs

Oil, for shallow-frying

¾ cup (90 g) all-purpose flour

1 teaspoon paprika

1 teaspoon garlic powder

¼ teaspoon salt, plus
more to season

2 eggs, beaten

LEMON GARLIC DIP

½ cup (120 g) Kewpie mayo

Zest and juice of 1 lemon

1 clove garlic, grated

FOR SERVING

1 scallion, finely chopped

4 wedges lemon

1 To make the beach fried rice: In a medium bowl, combine the day-old rice and egg yolks and mix until the rice is separated into grains and turns yellow from the egg yolk.

2 Heat 1 tablespoon of the vegetable oil in a large nonstick skillet or wok, then add the rice and continuously cook for 1 to 2 minutes. Push the rice aside and add the onions, ginger, and minced garlic with the remaining ½ tablespoon vegetable oil. Cook until fragrant, about 2 minutes. Mix the onions, ginger, and minced garlic with the rice, then add the cabbage, red bell peppers, and mushrooms. Cook for 2 minutes, then add the shrimp, scallions, peas, corn, sesame oil, soy sauce, ½ teaspoon salt, and pepper. Cook until the shrimp turns pink on both sides, 3 to 4 minutes. Remove from the heat.

3 To make the stuffed hard crab: Carefully open the top shells of the crabs, without fully removing them, and discard the gills. (The gills are the long, triangular filaments on both sides of a crab, usually dark or light gray in color. Simply tear them off using your fingers, then discard.) Flip the crabs over and remove the aprons. (The apron is a flap that is either rounded for a female or pointed in shape for a male. Simply tug to tear it off, then discard.) Thoroughly wash the crabs and pat dry with paper towels.

4 In a medium deep skillet, heat ½ inch (12 mm) of oil to 350°F (175°C), measuring with a thermometer. Prepare a dredging station with two medium shallow bowls, combining the flour, paprika, garlic powder, and ¼ teaspoon salt in one and adding the beaten eggs to the other. Carefully open the top shell of a crab and stuff it with some of the beach fried rice. Fully coat the crab in the flour-paprika mixture, dip it into the beaten egg, and then coat again in the flour-paprika mixture. Repeat this step for the remaining crabs.

5 Once the oil is hot, slide a crab with a spatula into the oil, bottom side down. Cook for 2 to 3 minutes, then carefully flip and cook for another 2 to 3 minutes. Remove from the pan with the spatula and tongs to help hold the crab, transfer to a wire rack, and then lightly season with a pinch of salt. Repeat this step for the remaining crabs.

6 To make the lemon garlic dip: In a small bowl, mix all the dip ingredients until well combined.

7 To serve: Place 2 stuffed hard crabs on each plate with a dollop of lemon garlic dip, 2 lemon wedges, and a sprinkle of scallions.

KATSUDON

★ANIME★

YURI!!! ON ICE

SEASON 1 EPISODE 1
EASY AS PIROZHKI!!
THE GRAND PRIX
FINAL OF TEARS

❄

It's established in the first episode of the anime that protagonist Yuri (Katsuki) loves katsudon (pork cutlet bowl). When he returns home to Japan after five years, and a year after his devastating loss at his first ice skating Grand Prix Final, his mom immediately offers him the dish, which is served at his family's hot springs resort, Yu-topia Katsuki. Later in the series, Yuri is teased often by Viktor Nikiforov—his love interest and coach—and Yuri (Plisetsky)—his competitor and namesake—when they give him the nickname "Katsudon." The dish appears multiple times in the show, either in a scene, by mention, or in the commercial bumper.

YIELD **4** SERVINGS · PREP **10** MINUTES · COOK **15** MINUTES

TONKATSU

4 pork loin cutlets or boneless pork chops (½ inch, or 12 mm, thick)

¼ teaspoon each salt and black pepper, plus more to taste

¼ cup (30 g) all-purpose flour

2 eggs, beaten

2 cups (160 g) panko bread crumbs

Oil, for deep-frying

KATSUDON

½ tablespoon oil, for cooking

1 small onion, thinly sliced

¼ cup (60 ml) soy sauce

¼ cup (60 ml) mirin

1 tablespoon sugar

1 teaspoon dashi powder dissolved in 1 cup (240 ml) water

4 eggs, beaten

FOR SERVING

8 cups (1.6 kg) cooked short-grain white rice

¼ cup (15 g) Japanese parsley leaves (mitsuba) or thinly sliced scallions

《 CONTINUED 》

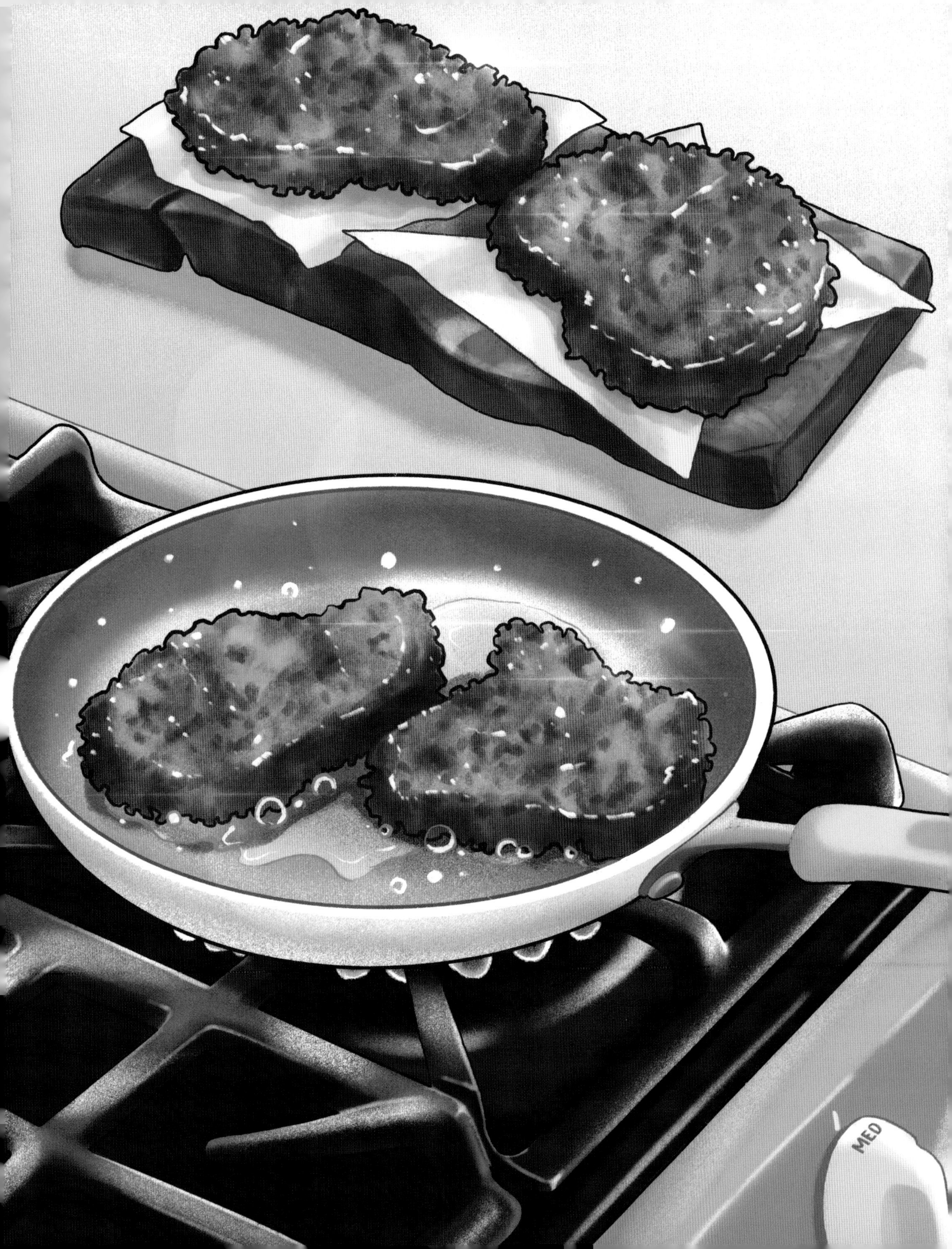
MED

1. To make the tonkatsu: Place a piece of plastic wrap on a cutting board and put the pork cutlets on top. Cover with another piece of plastic wrap and pound with a rolling pin until the pork is an even ¼-inch (6 mm) thickness.

2. Season the pork with salt and pepper on both sides. Prepare a dredging station with three medium shallow bowls, placing the flour mixed with the ¼ teaspoon each of salt and pepper in one, the 2 beaten eggs in another, and the panko in the last. Dredge the cutlets in the flour, then the egg, and then the panko, pressing them into the flour and panko to coat well.

3. Fill a medium heavy-bottomed pot with 3 inches (7.5 cm) of oil and heat over medium heat to 350°F (175°C), measuring with a thermometer, or a few bread crumbs sizzling when they hit the hot oil. Deep-fry each pork cutlet for 5 to 6 minutes—you may need to do this in batches. Once golden brown throughout, remove from the heat to a cutting board lined with paper towels. Sprinkle each tonkatsu with a pinch of salt while still hot. Wait 2 minutes, or until the tonkatsu are warm to the touch, then slice each one crosswise into ½-inch-thick (12 mm) pieces.

4. To make the katsudon: In a large skillet (with a lid), heat the oil over medium heat. Add the onions and cook until translucent, about 2 minutes, then add the soy sauce, mirin, sugar, and dashi powder liquid. Cover with the lid and cook for 2 minutes.

5. Remove the lid and add the tonkatsu slices to the skillet in a single layer, making sure to keep the slices in the shape of the tonkatsu before you sliced them. Pour the 4 beaten eggs around them. Place the lid and cook the eggs, until set, about 2 minutes.

6. To serve: Portion each tonkatsu and egg into a bowl filled with cooked rice and sprinkle with the Japanese parsley leaves.

> "Vkusno! Delicious, too good for words! Is this what God eats?!"
>
> —Viktor Nikiforov, *Yuri!!! on Ice*

COLD SOBA NOODLES

★ ANIME ★
MY HERO ACADEMIA
SEASON 2   EPISODE 34
GEAR UP FOR FINAL EXAMS

Todoroki, one of the main characters, mentions that his favorite food is cold soba noodles and is seen eating the dish in this episode. It's also noted on his info card, which occasionally shows up during the commercial bumper (the show cycles through all the main and side characters' quirk cards). Even though this is a simple Japanese dish, it's delicious!

YIELD 4 SERVINGS   **PREP** 10 MINUTES   **COOK** 10 MINUTES

SPECIAL TOOLS

4 bamboo zaru (optional)

INGREDIENTS

½ cup (120 ml) soy sauce

½ cup (120 ml) mirin

¼ cup (60 ml) sake

1 cup (12 g) dried bonito flakes (katsuobushi)

1 teaspoon dashi powder

14 ounces (397 g) soba (buckwheat) noodles

Ice cubes, for ice bath

1 sheet dried seaweed (nori), shredded into thin strips

3 scallions, thinly sliced

Wasabi, to taste (optional)

‹‹ STEPS ››

1 In a medium pot, combine the soy sauce, mirin, sake, bonito flakes, and dashi powder for a mentsuyu sauce. Bring to a boil over medium-high heat, and then boil for 5 minutes. Strain into a heatproof glass container, cover, and let cool in the refrigerator.

2 Cook the soba noodles according to the package instructions. Tip the noodles into a colander, then rinse under cold running water for 20 seconds while gently tossing. Transfer the noodles to a medium bowl, add the ice cubes and enough cold water to submerge the noodles, and let sit for 5 minutes. Drain and serve on plates or bamboo zaru.

3 Top the soba noodles with the shredded nori and serve alongside small bowls of the cold mentsuyu sauce topped with scallions and wasabi (if using). Dip the soba noodles into the mentsuyu sauce and enjoy.

NOTE
Mentsuyu sauce is a flavorful, all-purpose sauce that can be used for dipping tempura and takoyaki into or as a base for stir-fries. It can be stored in an airtight container in the refrigerator for up to 1 week.

GYUDON

ANIME
DEMON SLAYER: MUGEN TRAIN

Bullet train ekiben (*eki* means "train" and *ben* is short for "bento") are packaged meals commonly available at train stations in Japan to be eaten on the train. They can be sweet or savory, come in a variety of flavors, and be cold or warm. In the movie, Rengoku eats several ekiben, specifically gyudon (beef bowl), which he seems to really enjoy with his multiple exclamations of "UMAI!" (DELICIOUS!).

YIELD 2 SERVINGS · PREP 10 MINUTES · COOK 15 MINUTES

SAUCE

2 tablespoons sake

2 tablespoons mirin

2 tablespoons soy sauce

2 tablespoons brown sugar

BEEF

4 scallions, white parts only, trimmed

1 tablespoon beef fat or vegetable oil

4 ounces (113 g) medium-firm tofu, cut in half crosswise and then sliced into 1 × 2-inch (2.5 × 5 cm) rectangles

Salt and black pepper, to taste

1 small onion, thinly sliced

10 ounces (283 g) thinly sliced rib-eye, at room temperature

FOR ASSEMBLY

1 soft-boiled egg, sliced in half lengthwise (see Ponyo's Ham Ramen on page 80, steps 1 and 2)

Cooked short-grain white rice

Red pickled ginger (beni shoga)

STEPS

1 To make the sauce: In a small pot, combine all the sauce ingredients over medium heat, stirring until the sugar is completely dissolved. Remove from the heat and set aside.

2 To make the beef: Heat a medium skillet over medium heat, then add the scallions and cook until charred, 3 to 4 minutes. Remove the scallions from the pan, then melt the beef fat or heat the oil and cook the tofu until golden on both sides, about 5 minutes total. Season with salt and pepper. Remove the tofu from the pan, then add the onions and cook until translucent, about 2 minutes.

3 Add the sliced rib-eye to the pan in a single layer. Pour in the sauce, toss to coat the beef, and then remove from the heat. (Thinly sliced rib-eye should not take more than 2 minutes to cook to preserve its tenderness.)

4 To assemble: Add the cooked rice to each bowl as the base and top with some sweet-and-savory beef, then arrange the toppings of a sliced soft-boiled-egg half, 2 charred scallions, panfried tofu, and pickled ginger. Serve hot or cold.

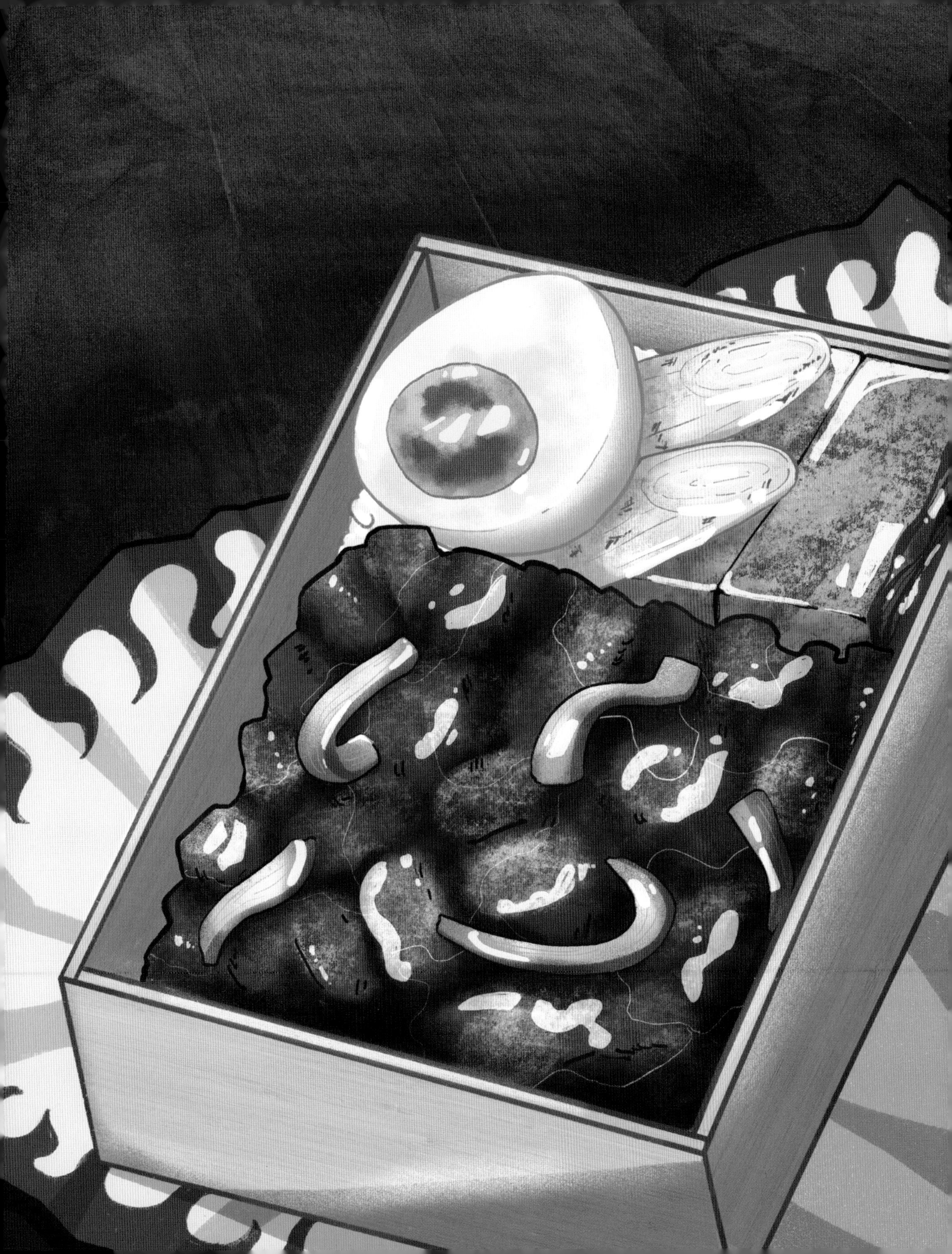

LOBSTER AND SHRIMP RISOTTO

★ANIME★

LAID-BACK CAMP

SEASON 2 EPISODE 12

IZU CAMPING!!!
BIRTHDAYS!

The group, which consists of protagonists Rin and Nadeshiko and their friends, are continuing their camping trip in the Izu Peninsula, visiting Dogashima, the Darumayama Highlands, and Cape Mihama, among other sights. Using the leftover shell of a spiny lobster and some ingredients they bought at the market, the group enjoys a filling "shrimp and tomato risotto" for dinner, highlighting quality Parmesan cheese, rich tomato flavors, and the rich shrimp stock ladled over the hot risotto. The shrimp flavor is so intense that they even turn into shrimp for a moment! This is a recipe that utilizes the zero-waste concept, which I focused on when creating it.

YIELD 4 SERVINGS   **PREP** 15 MINUTES   **COOK** 1 HOUR

SPECIAL TOOLS

Outdoor Grill

Charcoal (optional)

3 grill-safe pots (optional)

GRILLED LOBSTER

1 spiny (rock) lobster
(about 2 pounds, or 907 g)

2 pinches each salt and
black pepper

¼ cup (55 g) unsalted butter,
at room temperature

½ teaspoon paprika

½ teaspoon chili powder

3 cloves garlic, crushed

Zest of ½ lemon, reserving
the lemon half for squeezing

½ tablespoon canola oil,
for greasing

PANFRIED VEGETABLES

5 white button mushrooms,
thinly sliced

2 stalks asparagus, cut into
¼-inch (6 mm) pieces

½ medium red bell pepper,
seeded and sliced into strips

1 tablespoon olive oil, divided,
for cooking

3 pinches each salt and black
pepper, divided

SHRIMP STOCK

12 medium-size shrimp with
heads and shells
(about 1 pound, or 454 g)

SEAFOOD RISOTTO

1 tablespoon olive oil

1 medium onion,
finely chopped

5 cloves garlic, minced

2 cups (380 g) arborio rice

¼ cup (66 g) tomato paste

½ cup (68 g) frozen vegetable
medley (corn, peas, carrots,
green beans)

½ cup (50 g) grated quality
Parmesan

Salt and black pepper, to taste

1 lemon, cut into wedges

1 To make the grilled lobster: Split the lobster in half lengthwise from head to tail and carefully loosen the meat from the shell by pushing it with your fingers. (Don't remove the meat from the shell.) Be careful not to break up the meat. Season each half with a pinch of salt and pepper.

2 In a medium bowl, mix the butter, paprika, chili powder, garlic, and lemon zest until well combined. Set aside.

3 Grease the outdoor grill grates with the canola oil, then preheat the grill to high, around 425°F (220°C). Place the lobsters in their shells, meat sides down, over direct heat for 2 to 3 minutes, until charred. Flip the lobsters, shell sides down, and place over indirect heat. Using a spoon or spatula, spread 1 tablespoon of the seasoned butter over the lobster meat of each half and continue to grill for another 3 to 5 minutes, until tender or the internal temperature reaches 140°F (62°C). Remove from the heat and squeeze fresh lemon juice onto the lobsters. Immediately enjoy the lobster meat as an appetizer! Reserve the lobster shells for the lobster stock and the leftover seasoned butter for the shrimp stock.

4 To make the lobster stock: Add the reserved lobster shells to a medium pot (with a lid) and add enough water to submerge the shells. Cover with the lid and let simmer for 30 minutes over medium heat. Remove the shells and set aside.

5 Meanwhile, prep the vegetables for the panfried vegetables, reserving trimmings and cuttings (scraps) for the shrimp stock.

6 To make the shrimp stock: Peel and devein the shrimp and remove the heads. Put only the shrimp heads and shells in a separate medium pot, reserving the shrimp meat for the seafood risotto. Add the reserved seasoned butter from the grilled lobster and the scraps from the vegetable prep to the pot.

7 Cook over a medium heat until the shells turn orange, about 3 minutes, then add enough water to cover the ingredients and simmer for 7 minutes. Strain into a heatproof container and extract extra liquid by pushing the ingredients on the strainer. Set aside.

8 To make the panfried vegetables: In a medium skillet, heat ½ tablespoon of the olive oil over medium heat. Add the mushrooms and a pinch each of salt and pepper and cook for 3 minutes, or until soft, then remove from the pan. Heat the remaining ½ tablespoon olive oil, then add the asparagus and another pinch each of salt and pepper. Cook until tender, about 8 minutes, then remove from the pan. Lastly, add the bell peppers and the remaining pinch each of salt and pepper and cook until tender, about 4 minutes, then remove from the pan.

9 To make the seafood risotto: Bring the lobster and shrimp stocks to a simmer over medium heat. Meanwhile, in a large pot, heat the ½ tablespoon olive oil over medium heat. Add the onions and cook until translucent, about 2 minutes, then add the garlic and cook until fragrant, about 1 minute. Add the rice and toast it by stirring with a wooden spoon for about 2 minutes. Add the tomato paste, combine with the rice, and cook for 2 minutes, or until the paste darkens.

•••••••••••••••••••••••••••••••••••••• ((**CONTINUED**)) ••••••••••••••••••••••••••••••••••••••

LOBSTER AND SHRIMP RISOTTO STEPS (CONTINUED)

10 Ladle in 1 cup (240 ml) of the hot lobster stock. Stir the stock and rice to combine. From here you must stir to scrape the bottom of the pot to prevent the rice from sticking and burning, once every 1 to 2 minutes. Continue to ladle in 1 cup (240 ml) of the lobster stock every time the rice absorbs the stock. Do this until all the lobster stock is used, then do the same with the shrimp stock, stirring every 1 to 2 minutes to prevent the rice from sticking to the bottom of the pan, until the rice is almost al dente. This entire process takes about 20 minutes, and you should have leftover shrimp stock to pour over when serving.

11 At the 20-minute mark, add the reserved shrimp meat. Once the shrimp turn orange, gently fold in the panfried vegetables and frozen vegetable medley. The rice should be al dente around the 25-minute mark. Check the rice by tasting it—it should be tender yet firm.

12 Remove the risotto from the heat, gently fold in the quality Parmesan, and season with salt and pepper. Serve hot with a small ladleful of shrimp stock for extra "shrimpy" flavor.

"Shrimp!"
"The shrimpiness is so strong!"
"My whole mouth is shrimpy!"
"Shrimp everywhere!"

—Nadeshiko Kagamihara, Aoi Inuyama, and Akari Inuyama, *Laid-Back Camp*

MEAT LOVER'S MEAT FEAST

ANIME
DRAGON BALL Z: KAKAROT

Food is abundantly represented in the world of *Dragon Ball Z*, so for this recipe, I took inspiration from the video game *Kakarot*. Even if you aren't familiar with this video game, fans of the anime should not be surprised that a Super Saiyan like Goku needs to keep up his physique and energy with a massive amount of protein. This recipe has the same name as the meal in the game and makes enough to feed two Super Saiyans or four regular humans.

YIELD **2-4** SERVINGS   PREP **5** MINUTES   COOK **15** MINUTES

SPECIAL TOOLS

Nonstick grill pan

INGREDIENTS

1 can (12 ounces, or 340 g) 25% Less Sodium Spam, sliced ¼ inch (6 mm) thick

½ cup (120 ml) less-sodium soy sauce

½ cup (110 g) brown sugar

2 tablespoons oyster sauce

1 tablespoon unsalted butter

12 cups (2.5 kg) cooked short-grain white rice

2 scallions, thinly sliced

STEPS

1 Heat the grill pan over medium heat.

2 Cook the Spam slices until grill marks form, about 3 minutes per side.

3 In a medium pan, heat the soy sauce, brown sugar, and oyster sauce and heat over medium heat, stirring occasionally, until the sugar is dissolved, about 8 minutes. Add the butter to melt.

4 Add the grilled Spam to the pan and cook until the sauce is thickened, 4 to 5 minutes, flipping halfway through to cover the other side with sauce.

5 Set out ramen bowls and divide the cooked rice among them. Scoop out the Spam and place on top of the rice, drizzle over the sauce from the pan, and sprinkle with a generous amount of scallions.

PONYO'S HAM RAMEN

★ ANIME ★
PONYO

Ponyo is another beloved Studio Ghibli film, which, of course, features mouthwatering food. This dish is made by Lisa for her son, Sosuke, and his friend Ponyo, as they wait for Koichi, her fisherman husband, to return after a mighty storm has passed. Like many Studio Ghibli dishes, this ramen is a fan favorite and a comfort food in both taste and nostalgia!

YIELD **2** SERVINGS   PREP **5** MINUTES   COOK **15** MINUTES

INGREDIENTS

1 egg

Ice cubes, for ice bath

2 packs chicken-flavored instant ramen (or flavor of choice)

Boiling water, to cook the ramen noodles

4 slices ham

2 scallions, thinly chopped

((STEPS))

1 To make a soft-boiled egg, bring a small pot of water to a boil with enough water to submerge the egg. Once boiling, reduce the heat to medium, place the egg on a spoon with a long handle and carefully place it in the water onto the bottom of the pot. Set a timer for 6 minutes and 30 seconds. Using the same spoon, carefully turn the egg by pushing it gently. Turn the egg every minute to make sure the egg yolk is centered when sliced open.

2 In a small bowl, prepare an ice bath with some cold water and the ice cubes. When the timer beeps, transfer the egg to the ice bath to stop the cooking process. Peel the eggshell within the first 5 minutes to make it easier to remove. Start by cracking the egg at its base, the wider side, then start peeling. Place the peeled egg on a cutting board and slice in half lengthwise with a sharp knife.

3 To assemble: Set out two ramen bowls and empty a package of instant ramen and its seasoning packet into each bowl. Slightly crush the noodles if you want your ramen to be like Ponyo's version. Add just enough boiling water to submerge the noodles in each bowl, then cover the bowls with a larger plate or bowl for 3 minutes. Remove the covers, stir, and add the toppings to each bowl: 2 slices of ham, a sprinkle of scallions, and half of a soft-boiled egg. Serve hot.

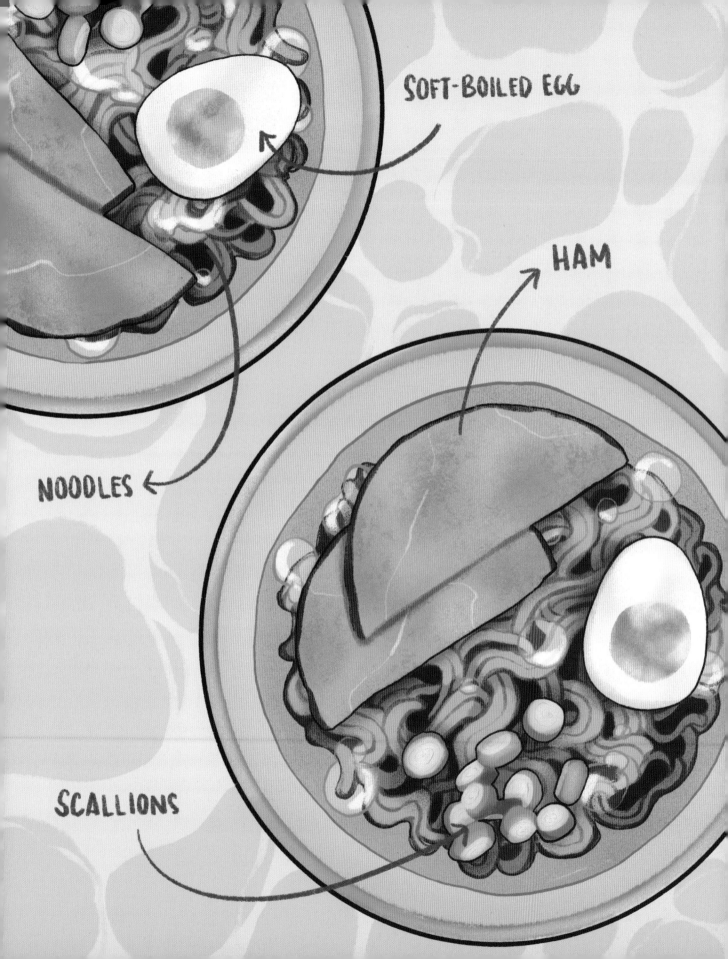

SOFT-BOILED EGG

HAM

NOODLES

SCALLIONS

GRILLED WHOLE FISH

★ ANIME ★
VIOLET EVERGARDEN

SEASON 1 EPISODE 1
'I LOVE YOU'
AND AUTO
MEMORY DOLLS

Protagonist Violet Evergarden is a Great War veteran, recently discharged because of a major injury in which she lost both of her arms. This first episode focuses on her reacclimating to daily life and integrating back into society with her robotic prosthetics made of "adamant silver." A poignant scene shows her struggling to cut fish at a restaurant, which mirrors one of the first scenes in which she struggles with a pen while writing a letter. This anime is one of the most beautiful ones I've ever seen, and I'm happy to share a recipe from this wonderful show.

YIELD **2** SERVINGS   PREP **15** MINUTES   COOK **1** HOUR

LEMON GARLIC POTATOES

1 tablespoon olive oil

6 small yellow potatoes, peeled and cut in half lengthwise

2 cloves garlic, grated

Zest and juice of 1 small lemon

½ teaspoon salt

¼ teaspoon black pepper

1 teaspoon dried oregano

1 to 2 cups (240 to 480 ml) chicken or vegetable stock

ROASTED SEA BREAM

2 tablespoons olive oil, divided

½ small lemon, thinly sliced and seeded

½ small onion, thinly sliced

2 whole sea breams
(or any white-fleshed fish, such as tilapia, red snapper, or branzino), gutted and scaled

½ teaspoon salt

¼ teaspoon black pepper

6 sprigs parsley

2 cloves garlic, grated

½ tablespoon unsalted butter

2 handfuls frozen peas

TOMATO RICE

1 cup (185 g)
long-grain white rice

½ tablespoon olive oil

½ small onion, chopped small

1½ tablespoons tomato paste

¼ teaspoon paprika

¼ teaspoon ground cinnamon

¼ teaspoon salt

Pinch black pepper

1½ cups (360 ml)
chicken or vegetable stock

1 tablespoon unsalted butter

FOR SERVING

4 leaves Romaine lettuce

2 wedges lemon

4 wedges tomato

2 pinches salt

1 To make the lemon garlic potatoes: Preheat the oven to 400°F (200°C; gas mark 6).

2 Grease a small baking dish with the 1 tablespoon olive oil, then add the potatoes, garlic, lemon zest and juice, ½ teaspoon salt, ¼ teaspoon pepper, and oregano. Add the stock until it covers the potatoes halfway, then mix everything to combine.

3 Cover with foil and bake for 30 minutes. Remove the foil and continue to bake for 20 to 25 minutes, until the potatoes are fork-tender and the liquid has reduced by half.

4 Meanwhile, make the roasted sea bream: Line a large baking tray with aluminum foil, then brush the aluminum foil with ½ tablespoon of the olive oil. Lay out half of the slices of lemon and onions on the tray where the fish will be placed.

5 On a cutting board, pat the fish dry using paper towels and score 3 lines on both sides of each fish. Place the fish on top of the lemons and onions. Cover both sides of the fish with the remaining 1½ tablespoons olive oil, then season with the ½ teaspoon salt and ¼ teaspoon pepper on both sides and inside the cavities. Open the cavities and stuff with the remaining lemons and onions, parsley sprigs, and garlic.

6 Bake for 20 to 25 minutes, until easily flaked when scraped with a fork. The fish can bake in the oven with the lemon garlic potatoes after the foil is removed from the potatoes in step 3. In the last minutes of baking the fish, place a thin slice of the butter on each fish, along with the frozen peas.

7 To make the tomato rice: Rinse the rice in a fine-mesh strainer with running water until the water runs clear, then set aside.

8 In a medium pot (with a lid), heat the ½ tablespoon olive oil over medium heat, then add the onions and cook until translucent, about 2 minutes. Add the tomato paste and cook for 3 more minutes, or until darkened. Add the rice, paprika, cinnamon, ¼ teaspoon salt, and pinch of pepper and cook for 30 seconds. Add the stock and unsalted butter and stir. Cover with the lid and bring to a boil. Once boiling, reduce the heat to medium-low and cook for another 15 to 18 minutes. Remove from the heat, let rest for a few minutes, and then fluff with a spatula.

9 To serve: Place 2 lettuce leaves on the top half of each plate, then from left to right place the ingredients in this order on the lettuce: a lemon wedge, 2 tomato wedges, 3 lemon garlic potatoes, and a scoop of tomato rice. Remove the stuffing from the roasted sea bream, then place it on the bottom half of each plate. Drizzle the fish with juices and some peas. Serve the extra lemon garlic potatoes on the side and enjoy while steaming hot.

SPINACH CHEESE QUICHE

★ ANIME ★
FULLMETAL ALCHEMIST: BROTHERHOOD
SEASON 1 EPISODE 1
FULLMETAL ALCHEMIST

This series follows two brothers, Edward and Alphonse (Al) Elric, as they try to find a way to restore Alphonse's body. During a human transmutation gone wrong, Edward lost his right arm and leg, and Al lost his entire body. Luckily, even at a young age and while he was in excruciating pain, Edward was able to transfer Al's soul into a large suit of steel armor. As a way for Al to cope, Edward suggests that Al keep a list of foods that he will eat once he gets his body back, which includes Granny's stew and Winry's apple pie, among others. Al also adds Gracia Hughes' delicious quiche to the list, when they meet her in this episode, which is almost as good as their mother's.

YIELD 8-10 SERVINGS   **PREP** 10 MINUTES   **REST** 30 MINUTES   **COOK** 1.5 HOURS

SPECIAL TOOLS

9-inch (23 cm) fluted tart/quiche pan

Pie weights or uncooked rice or beans

BUTTER PIECRUST

1½ cups (180 g) all-purpose flour, plus more for dusting

Pinch of salt

⅔ cup (150 g) unsalted cold butter, cut into ½-inch (12 mm) cubes

1 large egg, beaten

¼ cup (60 ml) ice water, plus more if needed

FILLING

4 strips bacon, cut into ¼-inch (6 mm) pieces

½ small onion, cut into small dice

2 cups (60 g) spinach leaves

4 large eggs

1 tablespoon cornstarch

1½ cups (360 ml) heavy whipping cream

½ cup (72 g) diced Brie

¼ teaspoon grated nutmeg

¼ teaspoon freshly ground black pepper

FOR SERVING

Simple salad

《 CONTINUED 》

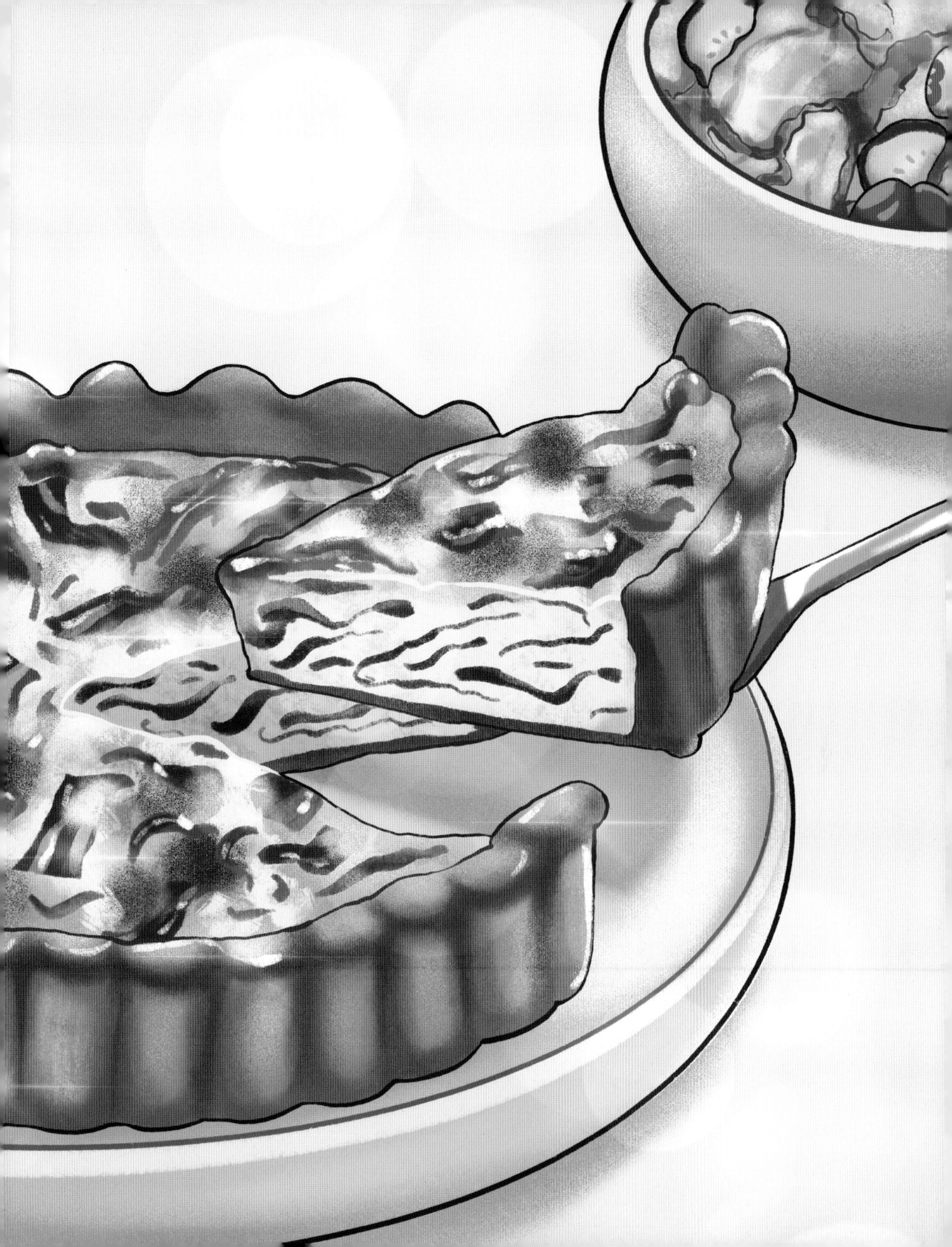

SPINACH CHEESE QUICHE STEPS

1 To make the butter piecrust: In a large bowl, stir together the flour and salt. Add the cold butter and squish the butter into the flour mixture with your fingertips until the entire mixture resembles a mealy or sandy texture. Add the ¼ cup (60 ml) ice water and knead until a clump of dough forms. (Every brand of flour required different hydration; if your dough does not form into a clump, then add small amounts of ice water until it comes together.)

2 Dust the work surface and rolling pin with flour and roll out the dough until it's ⅛ inch (3 mm) thick, then place it on the 9-inch (23 cm) fluted tart/quiche pan. Let the dough overhang the edges and carefully press it into the grooves of the pan using the back of your hand. Cut the overhanging dough 1 inch (2.5 cm) from the top of the pan—the extra overhang will ensure the dough does not shrink during cooking. Place the pie shell in the freezer, uncovered, for 30 minutes.

3 Preheat the oven to 400°F (205°C; gas mark 6). Take the pie shell from the freezer and place some parchment paper on top. Weigh down the center with the pie weights.

4 Bake for 25 minutes, then take out of the oven and remove the parchment paper and pie weights. Bake for another 10 to 15 minutes, until golden. Remove from the oven a second time and let cool to room temperature. Keep the oven on and reduce the heat to 350°F (175°C; gas mark 4).

5 Meanwhile, make the filling: Heat a large skillet over medium heat, then fry the bacon pieces until crispy. Transfer to a paper towel-lined plate and discard the extra grease from the skillet. Let cool.

6 Add the onions to the skillet and cook over medium heat until translucent and soft, about 2 minutes, then add the spinach and cook until wilted, about 1 minute. Remove from the heat and transfer to a cutting board. Roughly chop the mixture until the spinach is halved in length, then thoroughly pat dry with paper towels.

7 In a large bowl, whisk the eggs and cornstarch until the egg white clumps are smoothed out. Add the heavy cream and whisk again, then add the diced Brie, nutmeg, pepper, cooled bacon, and mixture of onions and spinach. Mix everything together, then pour the filling into the cooled piecrust. Cover the edges of the piecrust with aluminum foil.

8 Bake for 40 to 45 minutes, until the top has set and the quiche has a slight jiggle but is not soupy. Remove from the oven and let the quiche cool for 15 to 20 minutes to solidify.

9 Carefully remove the quiche from the pan and take off the foil. Cut the quiche into wedges and serve cold or warm with the simple salad.

LUFFY'S FAVORITE MEAT

★ ANIME ★

ONE PIECE

SEASON 4 EPISODE 37

THE PIRATES' BANQUET AND OPERATION ESCAPE FROM ALABASTA!

The Straw Hat Pirates travel around the globe and eat all kinds of indigenous cuisines. Luffy, the protagonist, is often seen enjoying huge pieces of roasted meat. In this episode, King Cobra throws a banquet feast for the Straw Hats to say thank you for saving his kingdom and his daughter. Luffy, who is known to practically inhale food and steal off others' plates, does exactly that to his crewmate Usopp's dismay. To teach him a lesson, Usopp puts hot sauce on Luffy's rice ball, causing him to literally spit fire. While this recipe has multiple spices, you can rest assured that no fire hazards will occur at the family dinner table.

YIELD **4** SERVINGS   PREP **15** MINUTES   MARINATE **12** HOURS   REST **1** HOUR   COOK **1** HOUR

SPECIAL TOOLS

Kitchen pliers

TURKEY LOLLIPOPS

4 turkey legs

PIRATE SPICE RUB

1½ tablespoons salt

1 tablespoon garlic powder

½ tablespoon sweet paprika

½ tablespoon onion powder

3 teaspoons brown sugar

1 teaspoon cayenne pepper

1 teaspoon ground cumin

1 teaspoon ground cinnamon

⅛ teaspoon grated nutmeg

1 teaspoon black pepper

GOLDEN BASTING LIQUID

¼ cup (55 g) unsalted butter

2 tablespoons honey

3 sprigs thyme

Zest and juice of ½ large lemon

Pinch salt

2 garlic cloves, minced

FOR SERVING

Cooked rice (optional)

Hot sauce (optional)

《 CONTINUED 》

LUFFY'S FAVORITE MEAT STEPS

1. To make the turkey lollipops: Place a cutting board on your work surface and hold a turkey leg by the tip of the bone. Carefully carve around the bone where the meat ends on the leg with a sharp knife. Remove visible tendons and bones using pliers, then push the meat upward to create a meat lollipop. Repeat with the remaining turkey legs.

2. To make the pirate spice rub, in a small bowl, combine all the rub ingredients.

3. Wrap a baking tray with aluminum foil and place an oven-safe wire rack on top. Lay the turkey lollipops on the wire rack and pat them dry with paper towels. Sprinkle the pirate spice rub on and under the turkey skin, then pat to adhere. Refrigerate on the wire rack in the tray, uncovered, for 12 hours.

4. Take the turkey lollipops out of the refrigerator and let them come to room temperature, 1 hour to 1 hour 30 minutes, before baking.

5. Meanwhile, make the golden basting liquid: In a medium saucepan, combine the butter, honey, thyme, lemon zest and juice, and pinch of salt over medium heat and bring to a simmer. Let simmer until thick and the color turns yellow to golden, 9 to 10 minutes. Add the garlic in the last minute of cooking. Remove from the heat and set aside.

6. Preheat the oven to 450°F (230°C; gas mark 8) and move an oven rack to the middle.

7. Add 1 cup (240 ml) of water to the bottom of the baking tray, then wrap the exposed turkey leg bones of the lollipops on the wire rack with aluminum foil. Place the tray on the middle rack of the oven and bake for 20 minutes, then reduce the temperature to 300°F (150°C; gas mark 2) and continue to cook for another 30 minutes. Ten minutes into the 30-minute cooking time, start glazing the turkey lollipops with the golden basting liquid every 10 minutes. When an instant-read thermometer inserted into one of the legs reaches 155°F (69°C), remove the turkey legs from the oven.

8. Let the turkey rest, covered with aluminum foil, for 20 to 30 minutes to let it continue cooking with its residual heat until the internal temperature reaches 165°F (73°C). Remove the aluminum foil and serve alone or with cooked rice. You may want to keep some hot sauce handy in case anyone gets greedy!

"I've never lost to anyone's stomach, so eat to your heart's content!"

—Terracotta, *One Piece*

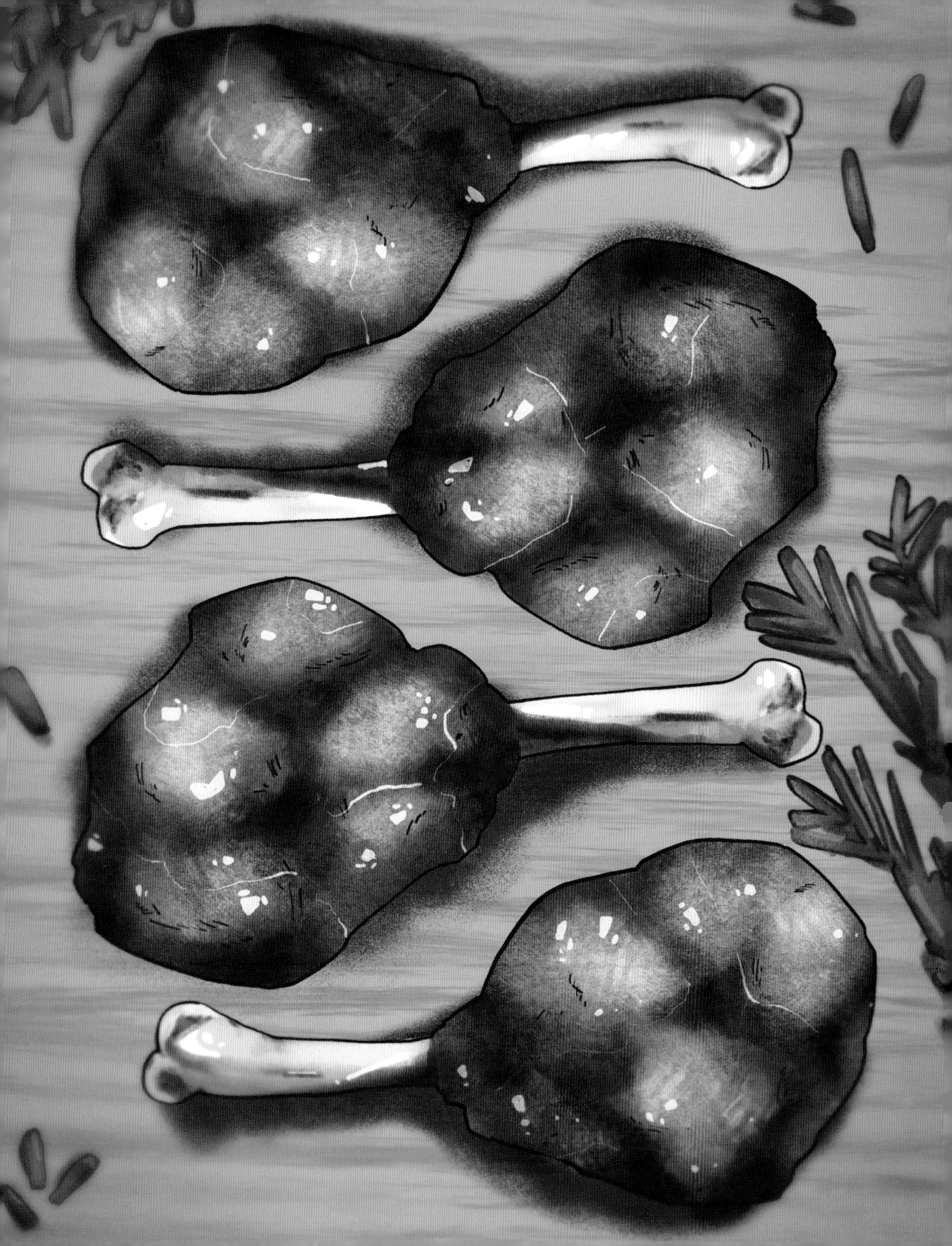

OMURICE

★ANIME★
BLEND-S
SEASON 1 | EPISODE 1
FIRST-TIME
SUPER SADIST

Maika is a normal high school girl who just happens to work as a part-time waitress . . . at a role-playing maid café where her persona is to be "sadistic." Each member of the waitstaff has a different persona, and Maika's menacing smile lands her the role of the sadistic waitress. She proves her capabilities by writing a derogatory term in ketchup on omurice (omelet rice), which the customers very much enjoy. The great thing about omurice is that you can write whatever you want on yours!

YIELD **2** SERVINGS | PREP **10** MINUTES | COOK **15** MINUTES

CHICKEN RICE

1 tablespoon unsalted butter

2 boneless, skinless chicken thighs, sliced into ½-inch (12 mm) cubes

1 teaspoon garlic powder

Pinch each salt and black pepper, plus more to taste if needed

½ small onion, cut into small dice

1 small carrot, peeled and cut into small dice

2 cups (410 g) day-old short-grain white rice

½ tablespoon soy sauce

2 tablespoons ketchup

¼ cup (34 g) frozen peas

OMELETS

3 large eggs

1 tablespoon milk

Pinch each salt and black pepper

1 tablespoon unsalted butter, divided

FOR SERVING

Ketchup

4 cherry tomatoes

2 sprigs curly parsley

1 To make the chicken rice: Heat a medium skillet over medium heat, then melt the 1 tablespoon butter. Add the chicken thigh pieces and season with the garlic powder and pinch each of salt and pepper. Cook until all sides are browned, 2 to 3 minutes per side. Remove the chicken from the pan and set aside.

2 Add the onions to the pan and cook until translucent, about 2 minutes. Add the carrots and cook, stirring occasionally, for 3 more minutes. Add the day-old rice, breaking it up with a spatula. Add the soy sauce and ketchup and continue to cook and stir until fully combined with the rice.

3 Add the chicken and all its juices back into the pan. Add the frozen peas and cook for 1 minute, or until warmed through. Taste and season with more salt and pepper, if needed. Remove from the heat and set aside.

4 To make the omelets: In a medium bowl, crack the eggs and whisk until combined and there are no visible egg-white lumps. Add the milk and season with a pinch each of salt and pepper.

5 Heat a separate medium nonstick skillet over medium heat. Melt ½ tablespoon of the butter, then add half of the egg mixture. Let the egg set for 30 seconds, then quickly swirl the egg with a chopstick to create ridges, about another 30 seconds. Run a spatula along the sides of the pan to detach egg from the pan. Reduce the heat to medium-low.

6 To assemble the omurice: While the egg is still custardy, divide the chicken rice in half. Place one-half on the middle of the egg lengthwise. Fold one side of the egg to the middle, then do the same with the other side, creating a blanket for the rice. Push the omurice to the edge of the pan then carefully flip it over onto a plate with the seam side down. You may refine the omurice into its iconic football-like shape by compressing it with paper towels. Place paper towels on top of the omurice and squeeze and shape as necessary. Repeat this step for the second omurice.

7 To serve: Write or draw a message on the omurice with ketchup. Place 2 tomatoes and 1 sprig of curly parsley on each plate.

"Thank you for coming!
Please never come back again!"

—Maika Sakuranomiya, *Blend-S*

GINGER CHICKEN MEATBALLS

★ANIME★
JUJUTSU KAISEN
SEASON 1 | EPISODE 13
TOMORROW

While Yuji Itadori, the protagonist, and his mentor, Nanami, are engaged in an intense battle against the cursed spirit Mahito, their friends are elsewhere worrying about them. In the JuJu Stroll at the end of the episode, this recipe is featured when Megumi Fushiguro brings the concerned group chicken meatballs. When asked about them, he says that Yuji taught him how to make them (at this point, the group does not know if Yuji is alive or dead). Nobara then comments that the meatballs are Yuji's legacy, which Maki objects to immediately. While Yuji's friends couldn't appreciate these meatballs under those tense circumstances, I hope you can enjoy them with your loved ones!

YIELD **4** SERVINGS · PREP **15** MINUTES · COOK **15** MINUTES

CHICKEN MEATBALLS

1½ pounds (680 g) ground chicken

1 large egg

2 scallions, thinly sliced

2 teaspoons ground ginger

5 cloves garlic, minced

1½ tablespoons soy sauce

¼ teaspoon salt

⅛ teaspoon black pepper

BROTH

6½ cups (1.5 L) water

½ teaspoon dashi powder

2 tablespoons soy sauce

Salt and black pepper, to taste

1½ tablespoons white miso

1 bundle oyster mushrooms

1 large carrot, peeled and sliced ¼ inch (6 mm) thick

1 bundle crown daisies (or bok choy)

1 piece (3 inches, or 7.5 cm, long) large leek, sliced ¼ inch (6 mm) thick

((CONTINUED))

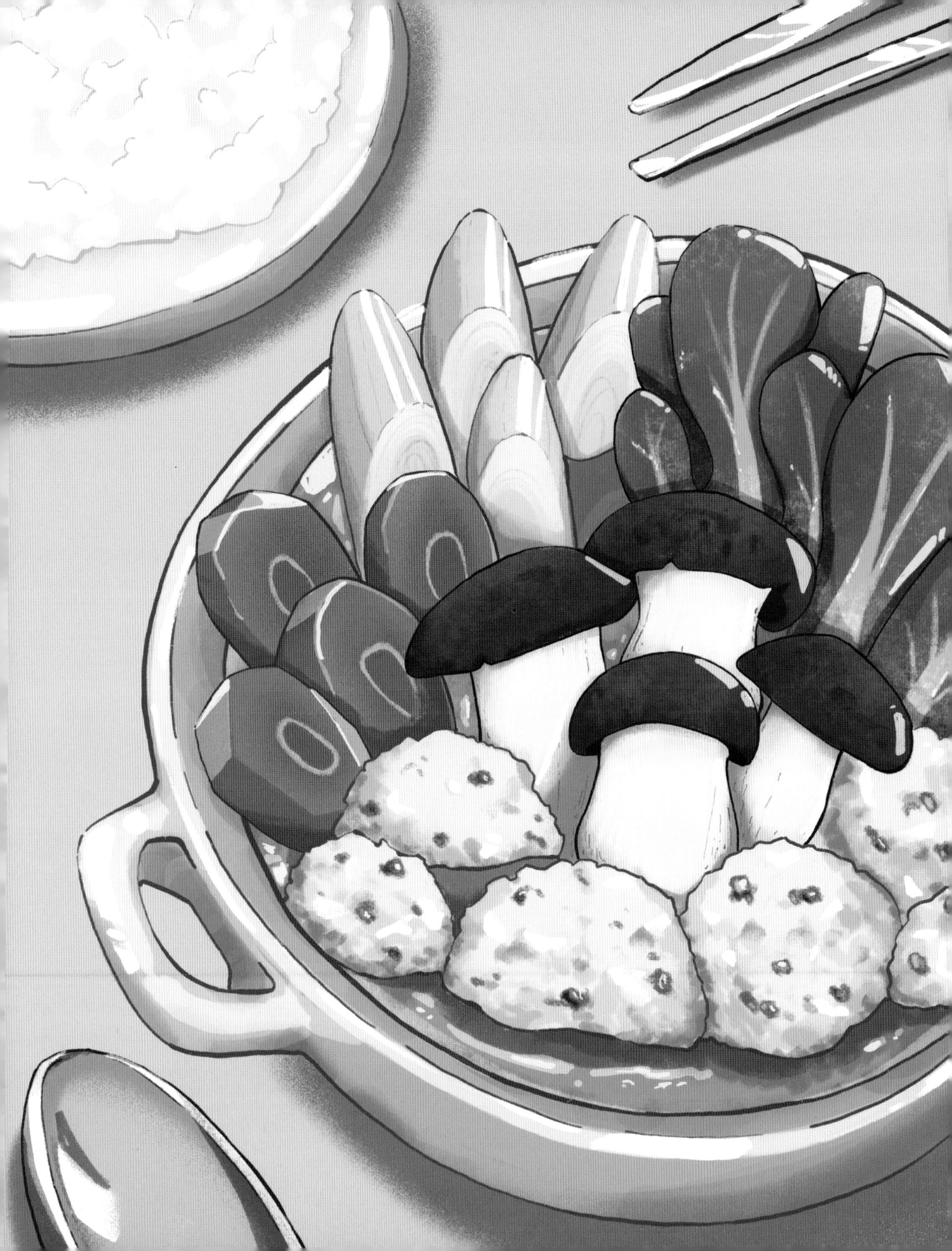

GINGER CHICKEN MEATBALLS STEPS

1 To make the chicken meatballs: In a large bowl, mix the ground chicken and egg in one direction until combined and becomes a paste.

2 Add the scallions, garlic, 1½ tablespoons soy sauce, salt, and pepper to the meat mixture and combine well. (You may test the flavor by frying a small piece of the mixture and adjusting the seasonings as you see fit.)

3 To make the broth: In a large pot, combine the water, dashi powder, and 2 tablespoons soy sauce and stir to combine. Bring to a boil over high heat, then reduce the heat to medium and let simmer while you form the meatballs.

4 To form the meatballs, hold a spoon in each hand and grab a 1½-inch (4 cm) portion of the meat mixture with one spoon, pushing it into the simmering broth with the other spoon. Repeat until all the meat is used; this recipe makes about 35 meatballs.

5 Dissolve the miso with a little hot broth in a ladle or small bowl, then add the miso, mushrooms, carrots, crown daisies, and leeks to the broth and cook for 8 minutes. The meatballs are cooked when they become firm, 8 to 10 minutes. Ladle into individual serving bowls and serve hot.

NOTE

For an even heartier meal, you can add ramen or udon noodles to cook in the broth or serve the dish with rice.

"Oh, those are super easy to make. Even Fushiguro can make them. I taught him how."

—Yuji Itadori, *Jujutsu Kaisen*

SASHA'S STOLEN BREAD AND POTATO RATION SOUP

★ ANIME ★

ATTACK ON TITAN

SEASON 1 | EPISODE 3

A DIM LIGHT AMID DESPAIR, HUMANITY'S COMEBACK, PART 1

The diet in the earlier seasons of *Attack on Titan* consisted of rations—usually bread and potato—because meat was scarce and there was a food shortage in general. Sasha, one of the cadets, often stole food—thanks to the elites in the inner circles hoarding resources—with one of the items being bread. In this episode, Sasha is punished for eating a boiled potato and forced to run around the camp for hours until she drops, along with getting no dinner. This recipe is inspired by the cadets' limited food supply and is a beginner-friendly recipe that is inexpensive to make. Once the corps grants you some more funding, be sure to splurge by adding a tablespoon of cream to the soup when it is ready to serve for a luxurious mouthfeel!

 YIELD 4 SERVINGS **PREP 15 MINUTES** **REST 1.5 HOURS** **COOK 1 HOUR**

SASHA'S STOLEN BREAD

1 cup (240 ml) warm water

1 tablespoon sugar

½ (¼-ounce, or 7-g) packet instant dry yeast

3 cups (360 g) all-purpose flour, plus more for dusting

¼ cup (60 ml) olive oil

1 teaspoon salt

1 large egg

1 tablespoon water

GARLIC CHIPS AND OIL

2 tablespoons olive oil

3 cloves garlic, thinly sliced

Pinch salt

POTATO RATION SOUP

2 tablespoons olive oil

½ medium onion, cut into small dice

1 celery rib, cut into small dice

1 small carrot, peeled and cut into small dice

3 russet potatoes, peeled and cut into small dice

2 cups (480 ml) unsalted vegetable stock

2 teaspoons salt

2 pinches black pepper

《 CONTINUED 》

1 To make Sasha's stolen bread: In a large bowl or the bowl of a stand mixer, stir together the warm water, sugar, and yeast. Cover with plastic wrap and leave somewhere warm for 10 minutes, or until bubbling. Once bubbling, add the all-purpose flour, ¼ cup (60 ml) olive oil, and 1 teaspoon salt.

2 If using a stand mixer, mix on medium-high speed with a dough hook attachment for 10 minutes, until it comes together as a ball of dough. If mixing by hand, knead the dough on a floured work surface for 15 minutes, or until smooth.

3 Once the dough is soft, smooth, and elastic, oil a large bowl with the olive oil and place the dough inside. Cover with a towel and preheat the oven to 200°F (93°C; gas mark ¼). Once the temperature is reached, turn off the oven and place the dough inside for an hour to let it rise. After an hour, or when doubled in size, remove the dough from the oven and degas it by punching it in the center.

4 Place the dough on a flour-dusted surface. Flatten the dough into a circle and divide it into 4 equal-size pieces. Roll each piece into a ball, then flatten each ball with a flour-covered rolling pin to get rid of any visible air bubbles. Tightly roll each flattened ball into a log 5 inches (12.5 cm) long and 2½ inches (6 cm) wide. Gently place the logs onto a parchment-lined baking tray, leaving 2 inches (5 cm) of space in between them. Cover again with a towel and let rest in the oven for another 15 to 20 minutes, until when gently poked, they bounce back 80 percent of the way.

5 Remove the dough from the oven and preheat the oven to 375°F (190°C; gas mark 5).

6 In a small bowl, stir together the egg and 1 tablespoon water. Brush the egg wash onto the surface of the bread. Using a sharp knife or a blade, score 3 straight lines across the bread crosswise. Bake for 20 to 25 minutes, until golden.

7 Meanwhile, make the garlic chips and oil: Heat a small skillet over medium heat, then add the 2 tablespoons olive oil and reduce the heat to medium-low. Add the garlic slices, separate them into a single layer with a spatula, and cook until golden brown and crisp, about 3 minutes. Remove the garlic chips from the pan with a slotted spoon and place on a paper towel-lined plate. Sprinkle with the pinch of salt. Transfer the garlic oil from the pan to a heatproof bowl.

8 To make the potato ration soup: Heat a large pot (with a lid) over a medium heat, then add the reserved garlic oil, onions, celery, and carrots. Cook for 3 to 4 minutes, until glossy and transparent. Add the potatoes, vegetable stock, salt, and pepper. Cover with the lid and cook for 15 to 20 minutes, until the potatoes are soft. Use a potato masher to disintegrate the potatoes into the soup to thicken it, then cook for another 5 minutes, uncovered.

9 Ladle the soup into bowls, crush some garlic chips on top, and serve with fresh-from-the-oven Sasha's stolen bread.

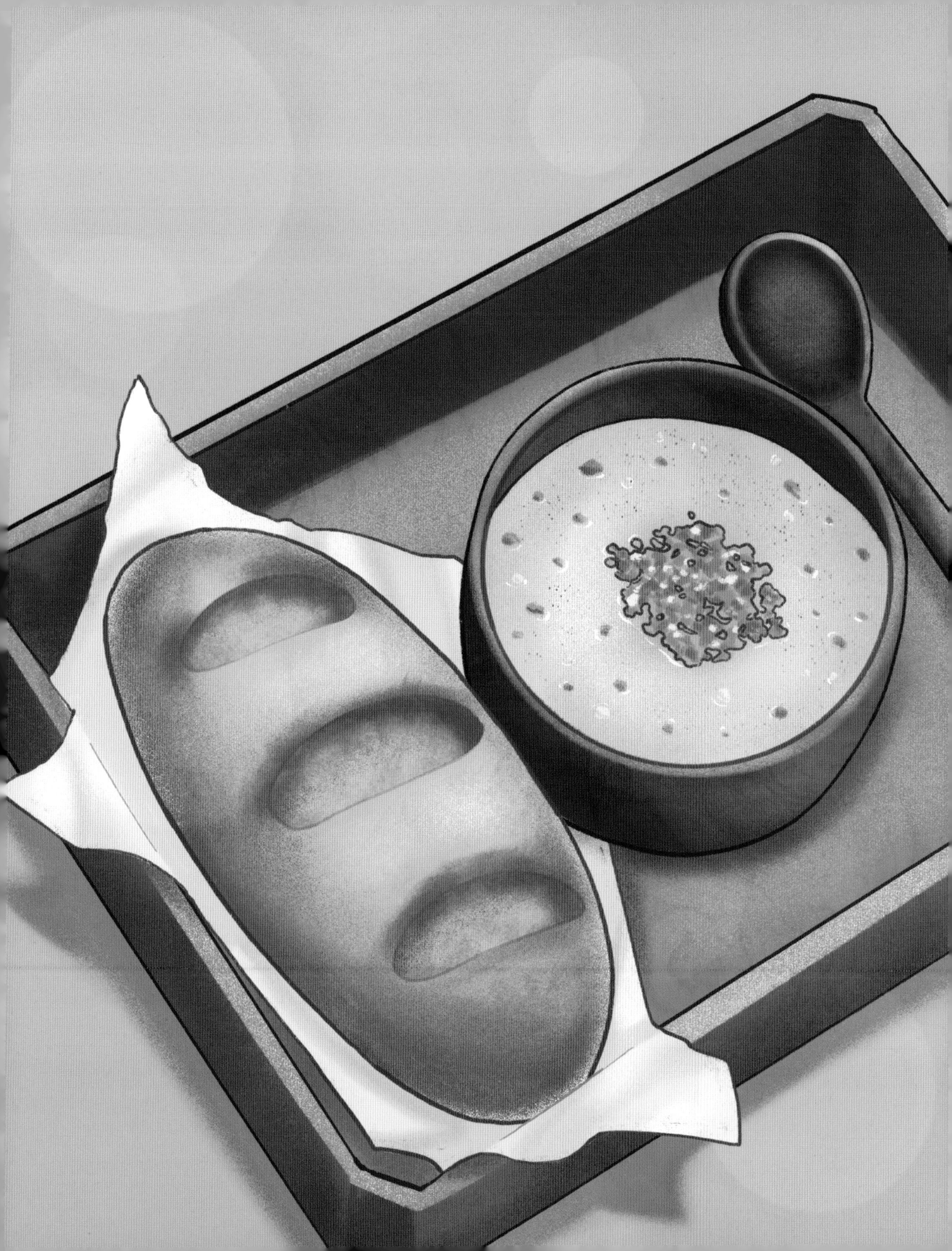

GOLDEN ROASTED CORNISH HEN

★ ANIME ★
SPIRITED
AWAY

Of course I had to include a dish from one of Studio Ghibli's most beloved films! While exploring an abandoned amusement park, Chihiro's parents come across an empty restaurant with enough food for a feast and start indulging in all that it has to offer, with her mom biting into what looks to be a golden roasted bird. Soon, her parents transform into pigs as a representation of greed. Instead of a whole chicken, this recipe uses a Cornish game hen. It's smaller, which allows for a faster cook time, and because the marinade has a high sugar content, the shorter time allows for perfect caramelization in the oven.

YIELD 2 SERVINGS · PREP 10 MINUTES · MARINATE 3 HOURS · COOK 65 MINUTES

SPECIAL TOOLS

Kitchen twine

INGREDIENTS

1 small Cornish game hen
(about 1¾ pounds, or 794 g)

½ teaspoon salt

¼ teaspoon black pepper

4 cloves garlic, 2 whole and 2 minced, divided

2 scallions, trimmed and cut in half lengthwise

1 tablespoon light soy sauce

1 tablespoon dark soy sauce

2 tablespoons oyster sauce

1 teaspoon honey

½ tablespoon dark brown sugar

1 teaspoon Chinese five-spice powder

Oil, for greasing

Cooked rice or steamed buns, for serving

1 Dry the Cornish game hen by patting with paper towels. Rub salt and pepper on the skin and inside the cavity. Stuff the cavity with the 2 whole garlic cloves and the scallions.

2 In a small bowl, combine the minced garlic, light soy sauce, dark soy sauce, oyster sauce, honey, brown sugar, and Chinese five-spice powder. Rub the marinade all over the outside and inside of the hen. Place the hen in a large resealable plastic bag and refrigerate for at least 3 hours, or overnight for full flavor.

3 Preheat the oven to 350°F (175°C; gas mark 4). Remove the Cornish hen from the refrigerator and pat dry with paper towels. Cut the wing tips with kitchen shears and tie the legs together using kitchen twine. Place an oven-safe wire rack on a baking tray. Grease the rack with oil, then lay the hen, breast side up, on the rack.

4 Cook for 30 minutes, then flip the hen back side up. Turn the hen over carefully so as not to tear the skin and continue to cook until a thermometer inserted into the thickest part of the thigh reads 165°F (74°C), about 30 minutes more. Carefully turn the hen over once again so that the breast side is up and cook until the skin is dark brown and glistening, about 5 minutes more. Transfer to a serving platter and let rest for at least 5 minutes.

5 Remove and discard the garlic cloves and scallions and break the Cornish hen into sections with kitchen shears. Serve with cooked rice or steamed buns.

NOTE

If you want to use a whole chicken, bake it for 1 hour 15 minutes, or until the internal temperature reaches 160°F (71°C) on an instant-read thermometer, flipping it halfway through the baking time. When both sides are golden, 50 to 60 minutes into the baking time, cover it with aluminum foil to prevent further coloration, removing the foil for the last 5 minutes of baking. Remove the chicken from the oven and let rest for 15 minutes, covered with foil, allowing the residual heat to continue cooking the chicken until the internal temperature reaches 165°F (74°C).

"You humans always make a mess of things. Like your parents who gobbled up the food of the spirits like pigs. They got what they deserved."

—Yubaba, *Spirited Away*

MYSTERY SIZZLING STEAK

★ ANIME ★
TOKYO GHOUL
SEASON 1 EPISODE 1
TRAGEDY

This episode is aptly named, as Ken Kaneki is attacked by Rize (a ghoul), barely survives, and turns into a half-ghoul as a result of having Rize's organs transplanted into him. Because of his new anatomy, Kaneki is now dependent on . . . well, let's just say that it's a mystery. For my version of mystery sizzling steak, however, I made the classic Japanese hamburg steak that Kaneki enjoys earlier in the episode on his "date" with Rize. It is drizzled with a rich red wine sauce and served on a sizzling plate for extra flair.

YIELD **4** SERVINGS   PREP **15** MINUTES   COOK **45** MINUTES

SPECIAL TOOLS

4 sizzling (or fajita) plates with wooden bases

SIDES

4 small baking potatoes, sliced into wedges

1 head broccoli, cut into 1-inch (2.5 cm) pieces

1 tablespoon oil

2 teaspoons garlic powder

2 teaspoons onion powder

Salt and black pepper, to taste

HAMBURG STEAK

1 tablespoon oil, divided, for cooking

½ medium onion, finely chopped

4 cloves garlic, minced

¾ teaspoon plus pinch salt, divided

1 pound (454 g) ground beef

3 teaspoons garlic powder

2 teaspoons onion powder

½ teaspoon smoked paprika

Pepper, to taste

RED WINE SAUCE

1 tablespoon butter

½ tablespoon oil

1½ tablespoons flour

⅓ cup (80 ml) red wine

⅓ cup (80 ml) unsalted beef stock

⅛ teaspoon Dijon mustard

Salt and black pepper, to taste

《 CONTINUED 》

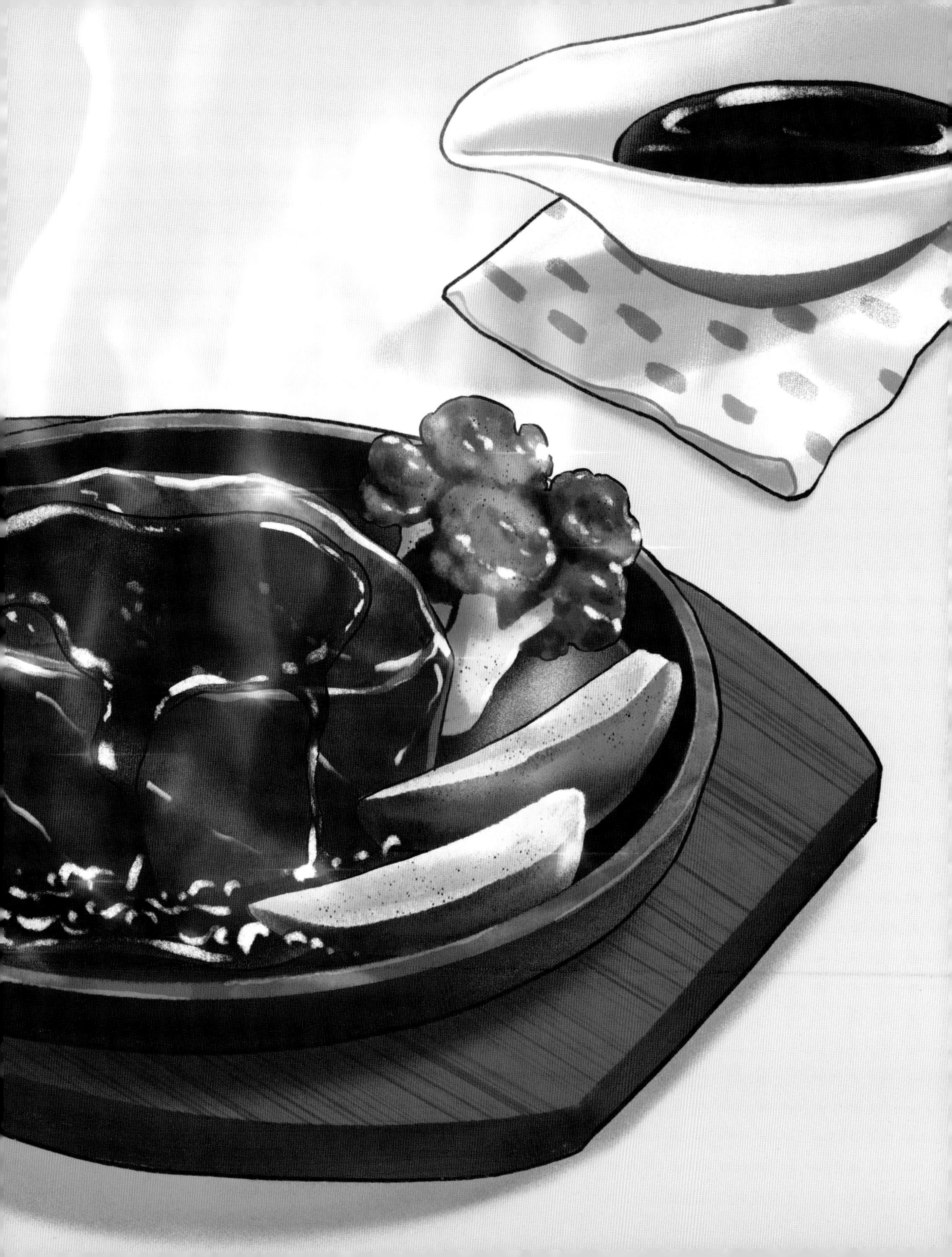

MYSTERY SIZZLING STEAK STEPS

1 To make the sides: Preheat the oven to 450°F (230°C; gas mark 8). Line a sheet pan with parchment paper and set aside.

2 In a medium bowl, toss the potato wedges and broccoli with the 1 tablespoon oil, 2 teaspoons each garlic and onion powders, and salt and pepper. Spread the potatoes and broccoli in a single layer on the prepared sheet pan. Bake for 7 minutes, then remove the pan from the oven and transfer the broccoli from the pan to a plate. Return the potatoes to the oven to cook for 23 minutes more, flipping them halfway through the baking time.

3 Meanwhile, make the hamburg steak: Heat a medium skillet (with a lid) over medium heat, then add ½ tablespoon of the oil. Once hot, add the onions and reduce the heat to medium-low. Cook, stirring occasionally, for 12 to 15 minutes, or until caramelized in color. Add the garlic to the onions and cook for 2 minutes. Stir in the pinch of the salt, then remove from the heat and let cool to room temperature.

4 In a large bowl, combine the ground beef, 3 teaspoons garlic powder, 2 teaspoons onion powder, smoked paprika, remaining ¾ teaspoon salt, and pepper to taste, and cooled onion-garlic mixture. Mix until well combined and sticky. (You may test the flavor by frying a small piece of the mixture and adjusting the seasonings as you see fit.) Form the mixture into 4 patties.

5 Add the remaining ½ tablespoon oil to the same skillet that the onions and garlic were cooked in and heat over medium heat. Add the hamburg patties and cook for 3 minutes per side, or until browned, then cover with the lid and cook for another 7 minutes, or until desired doneness (for medium, cook to an internal temperature of 155°F, or 69°C). Remove the patties from the pan and place on a paper towel-lined plate. Preheat the sizzling plates.

6 To make the red wine sauce: Add the butter and ½ tablespoon oil to the same pan that the hamburg patties were cooked in. Once the butter is melted, add the flour and stir until it forms a paste. Add the red wine and whisk until there are no lumps and the liquid makes a soft sizzle sound to indicate that the alcohol has evaporated. Add the beef stock, Dijon mustard, and salt and pepper, then cook for 2 minutes while stirring to combine. Transfer to a gravy boat.

7 To serve: Place the heated sizzling plates on their bases, then place a hamburg steak in the center of each plate with some roasted broccoli and potatoes at the right of it. Drizzle the meat with the red wine sauce.

SPICY HARLOT SPAGHETTI

★ ANIME ★

JOJO'S BIZARRE ADVENTURE: DIAMOND IS UNBREAKABLE

SEASON 3 EPISODE 10

LET'S GO EAT SOME ITALIAN FOOD

★

Chef Tonio Trussardi makes harlot spaghetti, a dish inspired by pasta puttanesca, with his own twist, omitting capers and adding sweet cherry tomatoes to contrast the saltiness of the anchovies and olives. Okuyasu eats it despite not liking spicy food and cleans the entire plate. A small, inconsequential side effect is that Okuyasu's teeth fall out while eating, but he grows new ones, so all's well that ends well, I guess? My version, luckily, has none of the side effects and all the flavor!

YIELD 4 SERVINGS   **PREP** 10 MINUTES   **COOK** 35 MINUTES

SPECIAL TOOLS

Garlic press (optional)

INGREDIENTS

14 ounces (397 g) cherry tomatoes (about 25)

¼ cup (60 ml) plus 1 tablespoon olive oil, divided

Pinch black pepper, plus more to taste

14 ounces (397 g) spaghetti

6 anchovy fillets in oil, drained

Pinch crushed red pepper flakes

1 cup (128 g) sliced black olives

6 cloves garlic

Salt, to taste (optional)

¼ cup (13 g) chopped fresh parsley, or to taste

½ cup (50 g) grated Parmesan

《 CONTINUED 》

SPICY HARLOT SPAGHETTI STEPS

1 Preheat the oven to 450°F (230°C; gas mark 8). Place the cherry tomatoes on a baking tray and drizzle with 1 tablespoon of the olive oil and the pinch of black pepper. Bake the tomatoes for 25 minutes, or until blistered and soft. Remove from the oven and mash them in a medium bowl. While the cherry tomatoes bake, make the other recipe components.

2 Cook the spaghetti according to the package instructions.

3 Heat a medium skillet over medium heat. Add the remaining ¼ cup (60 ml) olive oil and the anchovies. Cook until the anchovies have melted or are reduced in size, about 5 minutes.

4 Add the red pepper flakes, olives, and garlic, crushing the garlic with a garlic press right into the pan. (If you don't have a garlic press, mince the garlic before you start cooking.) Cook for 2 minutes. Add the mashed roasted cherry tomatoes and season with black pepper.

5 Drain the spaghetti, keeping the cooking water. Toss the drained spaghetti in the tomato sauce, along with 2 to 4 tablespoons of the cooking water (add more water for a thinner sauce). Season with salt, if needed, and sprinkle with a little chopped parsley.

6 Serve the spaghetti on plates with the grated Parmesan and more parsley sprinkled over the top.

"We don't have a menu here. . . . It means that I will determine the dishes by looking at the customers."

—Tonio Trussardi, *Jojo's Bizarre Adventure: Diamond Is Unbreakable*

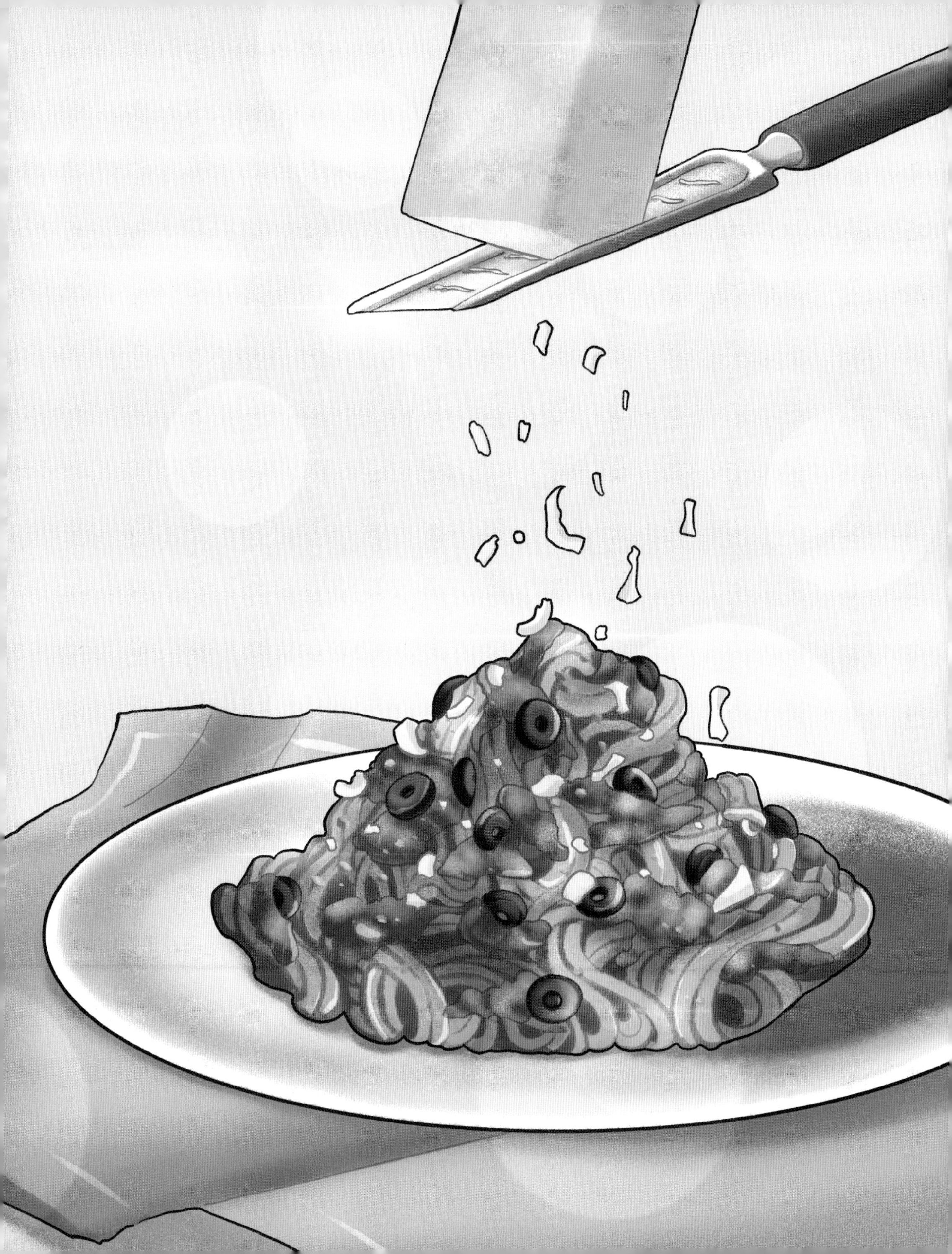

SUPER SPICY MABO TOFU

★ ANIME ★
ANGEL BEATS!
SEASON 1 EPISODE 6
FAMILY AFFAIR

Otonashi and Angel enjoy some "infamous mabo tofu that's too spicy for anyone to eat" while eating alone in the cafeteria and breaking a school rule while doing so. Here, Otonashi learns that Angel has a high tolerance for spicy food. Though the circumstances are a little bit dire, it could almost be considered a date! Hopefully, when you make this dish for your crush, you aren't dead in what could be the equivalent of purgatory in a high school, fighting the Shadows and trying to move on, instead of enjoying this lovely meal for two with some candles and flowers. You may be more familiar with this dish by its Chinese name, mapo tofu.

YIELD 2 SERVINGS PREP 10 MINUTES COOK 20 MINUTES

SPECIAL TOOLS

Mortar and pestle or spice grinder

TOFU PREPARATION

1 package (500 g) soft tofu, cut in half crosswise and then slice into 1-inch (2.5 cm) cubes

½ teaspoon salt

SICHUAN PEPPERCORN POWDER AND OIL

1 teaspoon Sichuan peppercorns

1½ tablespoons canola oil (or any neutral oil)

SUPER SPICY MABO TOFU

½ tablespoon canola oil (or any neutral oil)

4 cloves garlic, minced

1 piece (1 inch, or 2.5 cm, long) ginger root, minced

2 green scallions, white and green parts separated, thinly sliced, divided

2 tablespoons Chinese fermented soybeans (doubanjiang), minced

1½ tablespoons Chinese fermented black beans (douchi), minced

1½ teaspoons sugar

¼ pound (113 g) ground beef (substitute with pork, mushrooms, or lentils)

1½ cups (360 ml) unsalted chicken stock (substitute vegetable stock or water)

½ tablespoon cornstarch

½ teaspoon sesame oil

1 To prepare the tofu: Bring a medium pot of water to a boil. Add the salt, then carefully slide in the tofu. Boil for 2 minutes, or until some pieces are floating. Boiling makes the tofu firmer, helping it keep its shape in the sauce. Carefully remove the tofu from the water using a slotted spoon and set aside.

2 To make the Sichuan peppercorn powder and oil: Heat a large pot (or wok) over low heat, then add the Sichuan peppercorns and toast them without oil until fragrant, 2 to 3 minutes. Remove from the heat.

3 In a well-ventilated area, grind the toasted Sichuan peppercorns into a fine powder using the mortar and pestle or spice grinder. Be careful not to inhale the peppercorn fumes. Heat the same large pot over medium heat, then add 1½ tablespoons of canola oil. Add half of the toasted Sichuan peppercorn powder and let bubble for 2 minutes to create Sichuan peppercorn oil. Transfer to a heatproof bowl and set aside.

4 To make the super spicy mabo tofu: Heat the ½ tablespoon of canola oil in the same pot over medium heat. Add the garlic, ginger, and white parts of the scallions and cook until fragrant and slightly browned. Add the fermented soybeans and constantly stir until the red oils release, about 2 minutes. Add the fermented black beans and sugar and mix until combined. Add the ground beef. Cook, breaking up the ground beef into fine crumbles with a wooden spoon, until browned, crisp, and oils release, 5 to 6 minutes.

5 Add the chicken stock. Mix until everything is incorporated and the pastes are dissolved in the stock. Increase the heat to medium-high and bring to a boil.

6 In a small bowl, combine the cornstarch and 1 tablespoon of the liquid from the pot to make a slurry. Add the slurry to the pot and stir to mix well. Cook for another 2 minutes, or until the sauce thickens and becomes glossy.

7 Reduce the heat to low, then add the tofu to the pot. Let simmer until warmed through, 1 to 2 minutes. Pour the sauce over the tofu, or carefully push the tofu forward with a spatula, to mix with the sauce. Do not attempt to flip the tofu, as it will break.

8 Finish by adding 1 tablespoon of the Sichuan peppercorn oil, ¼ teaspoon of the Sichuan peppercorn powder (or to taste), and the sesame oil, gently mixing in the same manner as in step 7.

9 Tilt the pot to slide all its contents into a shallow serving bowl. Sprinkle with the green parts of the scallions and more Sichuan peppercorn powder.

BURI DAIKON

★ ANIME ★

RASCAL DOES NOT DREAM OF BUNNY GIRL SENPAI

SEASON 1 EPISODE 11

THE KAEDE QUEST

Mai makes this simmered yellowtail and daikon (Japanese radish) dish for her boyfriend, Sakuto, and his little sister, Kaede, prompting the younger girl to say she wished she could cook as well as her. Mai tells her it's all about practice, and later in the episode, she helps Kaede regain some confidence after she was cyberbullied.

YIELD 4 SERVINGS · PREP 10 MINUTES · COOK 35 MINUTES

INGREDIENTS

1 pound (454 g) yellowtail, sliced into 1-inch-thick (2.5 cm) fillets

½ pound (227 g) Japanese radish (daikon)

3 tablespoons sake

2 tablespoons mirin

4 tablespoons soy sauce

2 tablespoons brown sugar

1 piece (1 inch, or 2.5 cm, long) ginger root, sliced into matchsticks

1 scallion, green part only, finely chopped

《 STEPS 》

1 In a large pot, bring enough water to a boil to submerge the yellowtail fillets. Once boiling, submerge the yellowtail fillets in the water and blanch for less than 1 minute, or until all sides turn white. Remove with a slotted spoon and set aside.

2 Peel the radish and slice it into 1-inch-thick (2.5 cm) rounds. Trim around the top and bottom edges of each round with a small knife or peeler to prevent the edges from breaking when cooking. Slice each round in half.

3 Clean the pot used for blanching the yellowtail and bring enough water to a boil over high heat to submerge the radish. Once boiling, submerge the radish and boil for 10 minutes to remove sliminess and bitterness. Strain the water from the daikon and rinse in clean water.

4 In a large saucepan, combine the sake, mirin, soy sauce, brown sugar, and ginger and bring to a boil. Turn the heat to medium and add the prepared daikon. Let simmer for 15 minutes. Reduce the heat to medium-low and add the prepared yellowtail. Place a round piece of parchment paper to fit on top of the simmering broth to allow full contact with it. Simmer for 8 to 10 minutes.

5 Remove from the heat and ladle into a large bowl to serve from. Top with the chopped scallions.

NOTE
This dish is even better the next day once the flavors and color of the broth infuse the ingredients. It can also be enjoyed hot or cold.

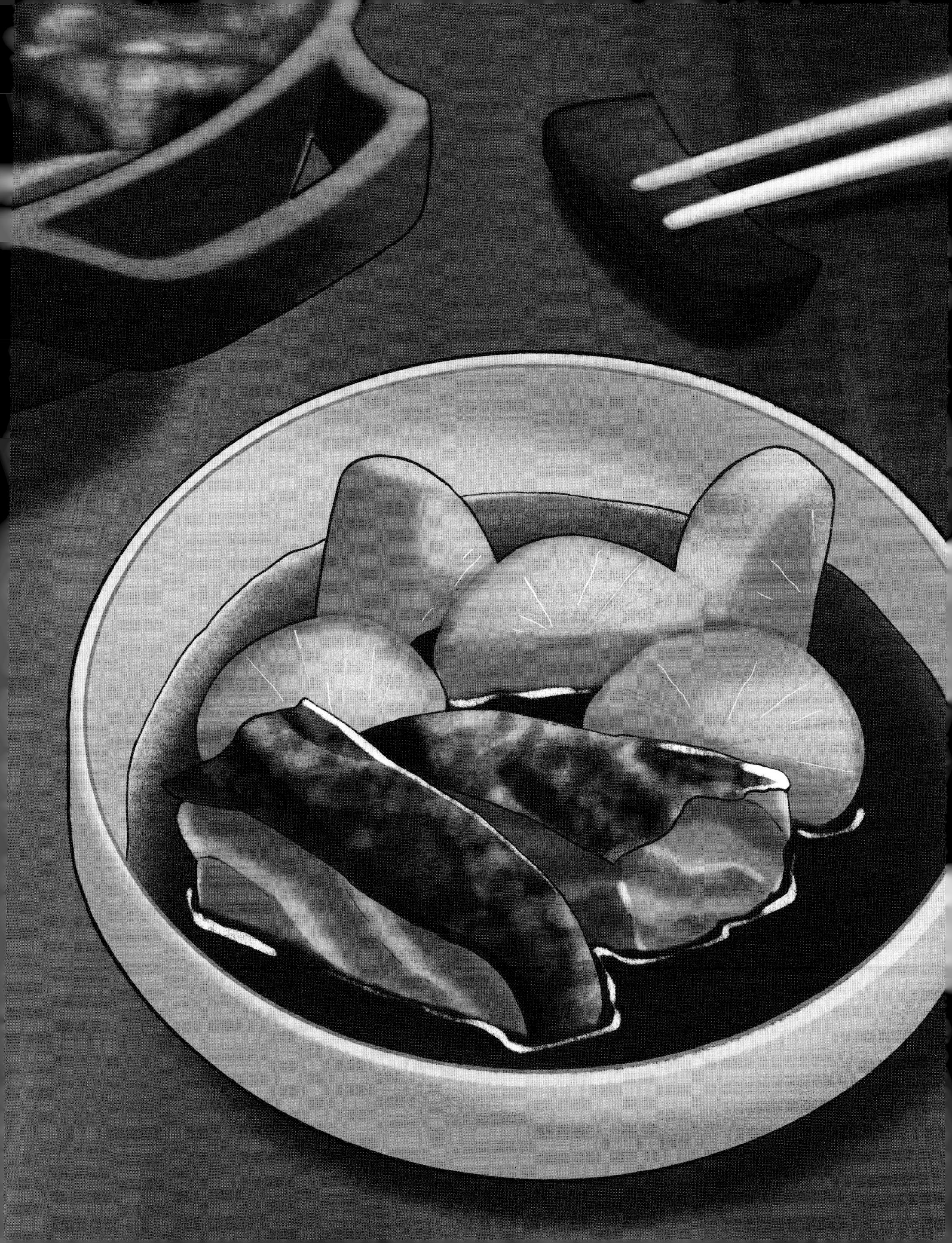

LAND AND SEA MIX OKONOMIYAKI

★ ANIME ★

HIMOUTO! UMARU-CHAN R

SEASON 2 EPISODE 12

EVERYONE AND UMARU

Okonomiyaki translates to, basically, "whatever you like," and is a savory batter filled with cabbage, along with any fillings of your choosing, and topped with mayonnaise and a sweet-and-savory sauce. If that sounds familiar, it's because it sounds like a pizza, which is what okonomiyaki is often called! In this episode, Umaru wants pizza, but her brother chooses to hold an okonomiyaki party instead, against her wishes, though she ends up enjoying it. There are two main styles of okonomiyaki: Osaka and Hiroshima. The key difference between the two is that Osaka style has all the fillings mixed in the batter, and Hiroshima style has layers of ingredients. I recommend you serve this dish with cola, Umaru's favorite drink.

YIELD 4 SERVINGS   PREP 15 MINUTES   COOK 15 MINUTES

OKONOMIYAKI BASE AND FILLINGS

⅔ cup (80 g) all-purpose flour

1 teaspoon baking powder

Pinch salt

½ teaspoon dashi powder (or a bouillon cube)

¾ cup (180 ml) water

½ cup (80 g) peeled and grated Japanese mountain yam (nagaimo or yamaimo)

3 large eggs, beaten

Oil, for greasing

3 cups (210 g) finely chopped cabbage

2 scallions, finely chopped

12 small-size shrimp, peeled and deveined

1 boiled octopus leg (4 inches, or 10 cm, long), cut into ¼-inch-thick (6 mm) slices

2 squid heads, lightly scored and cut into ½-inch (12 mm) squares

2 slices mozzarella, cut into ½-inch (12 mm) squares

8 thin slices (6 inches, or 15 cm, long) pork belly

FOR SERVING

Okonomiyaki sauce, to taste

Kewpie mayo (Japanese mayo), to taste

Dried bonito flakes (katsuobushi), to taste

Dried seaweed flakes (aonori), to taste

1 To make the okonomiyaki base: In a large bowl, combine the flour, baking powder, and salt. Whisk to break up any lumps.

2 In a small bowl, dissolve the dashi powder in the water, then add it to the bowl of flour. Whisk until there are no lumps and it resembles a pancake batter. Add the grated mountain yam and eggs. Incorporate them but do not overmix.

3 Meanwhile, heat a medium nonstick skillet (with a lid) over medium heat and grease lightly with oil.

4 Finish the batter by adding the cabbage, scallions, shrimp, octopus, squid, and mozzarella as fillings, making sure to coat everything in the batter.

5 Add one-quarter of the batter to the hot pan and shape it into an 8-inch (20 cm) circle, ½ inch (12 mm) thick. Once shaped, place the pork belly slices in a single layer on top, covering the batter. Cover with the lid and cook for 4 minutes, or until the bottom is golden. Remove the lid and, using two spatulas on both sides of the okonomiyaki, confidently flip it over.

Gently shape the edges with a spatula by gently pushing the sides of the okonomiyaki toward the center. Continue cooking, uncovered, until the pork belly is crispy, about 4 minutes. Flip again, using the two spatulas, with the bacon side up.

6 To serve: Brush a layer of okonomiyaki sauce over the okonomiyaki. Create Umaru's design by drawing a large circle for a hamster face with Kewpie mayo on top of the okonomiyaki, close to the edges. Then, draw 2 smaller circles at the top of the circle for ears. Continue to draw the hamster with the Kewpie mayo by making two ¾-inch (2 cm) lines for the eyes that tilt up toward the center and 2 longer lines above the eyes, also tilting up, for eyebrows. Lastly, draw an infinity symbol (horizontal 8) for the nose on the center of the okonomiyaki, then sprinkle bonito flakes on each side of the face for cheeks and around the perimeter of the outline of the hamster face. Sprinkle seaweed flakes on top of the entire okonomiyaki.

7 Slide the okonomiyaki onto a serving plate or leave it in the skillet. Chop into it using a spatula to create triangular slices and serve hot.

"Well, for okonomiyaki . . .
a MIX is the only way to go!"

—Umaru Doma, *Himouto! Umaru-chan R*

PIKACHU CURRY

ANIME
POKÉMON CAFÉ MIX

Curry has been a staple in the Pokémon franchise and is consistently shown in the anime and video games. This recipe comes from the free video game *Pokémon Café Mix*, now known as *Pokémon Café ReMix*, and is available to play on the Nintendo Switch and smart phones. It's a puzzle-based video game in which you complete puzzles to make delectable drinks and dishes to serve at your Pokémon Café! The more you play, you can also collect additional Pokémon, though you get to start with Eevee, who is one of my favorites. This dish is a recreation of the Piquant Pikachu Curry from the game.

YIELD 4 SERVINGS | PREP 15 MINUTES | COOK 1.5 HOURS | DECORATE 20 MINUTES

SPECIAL TOOLS

Star-shaped cookie cutters

PIKACHU TURMERIC RICE

½ tablespoon unsalted butter

½ small onion, finely chopped

2 cloves garlic, minced

1½ cups (300 g) short-grain white rice

2 cups (480 ml) vegetable stock

1½ teaspoon turmeric powder

¼ teaspoon salt

Pinch black pepper

PIKACHU DECORATIONS

1 sheet dried seaweed (nori)

1 slice mozzarella cheese

1 piece (1 inch, or 2.5 cm, long) carrot, peeled

APPLE VEGETABLE CURRY

1 tablespoon olive oil

8 slices carrot, shaped into stars

8 slices potato, shaped into stars

1 teaspoon each salt and black pepper, plus more to season

½ tablespoon unsalted butter

1 medium onion, minced

3 cloves garlic, grated

1 piece (¼ inch, or 6 mm, long) ginger root, grated

1 small Fuji apple, peeled and grated

3 cups (720 ml) unsalted vegetable stock

2 Japanese curry cubes (such as Vermont Curry or Golden Curry)

8 slices green bell pepper, shaped into stars

Honey, to taste

CONTINUED

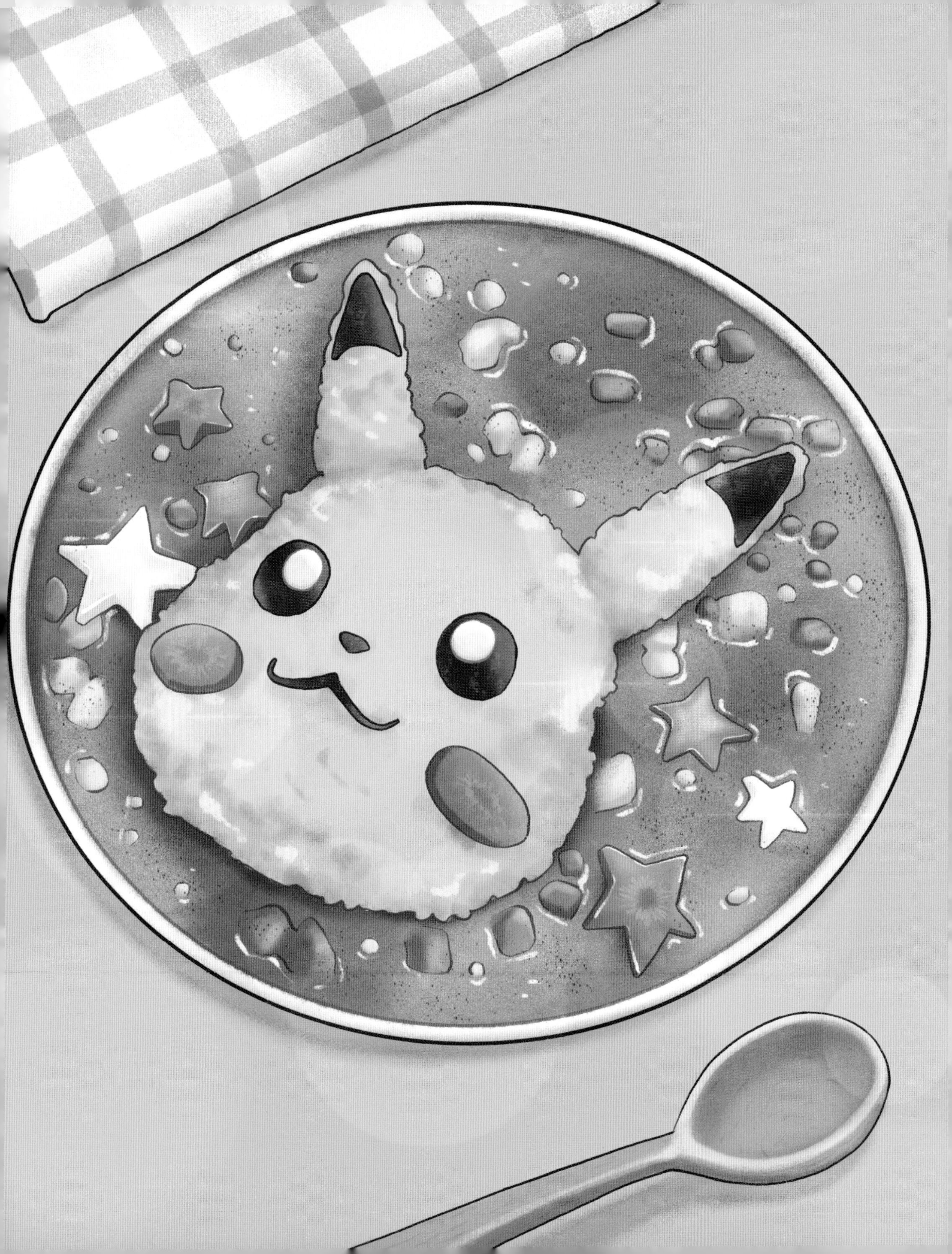

1 To make the Pikachu turmeric rice: Heat a medium pot (with a lid) over medium heat, then melt the ½ tablespoon butter. Add the chopped onions and minced garlic and cook until fragrant, about 2 minutes.

2 Meanwhile, rinse the rice in a fine-mesh strainer with running water until the water runs clear, then add the rinsed rice to the pot, along with the vegetable stock, turmeric powder, ¼ teaspoon salt, and pinch of pepper. Stir, cover with the lid, and let come to a boil over medium heat, about 15 minutes. Once boiling, reduce the heat to medium-low and cook for 15 to 18 minutes, until the rice is tender, opaque, and fully cooked through. Remove from the heat and gently fluff the rice with a spatula.

3 To decorate: Lay a piece of plastic wrap on your work surface. For Pikachu's face, place about ¾ cup (125 g) of the turmeric rice in the middle of the plastic wrap and bring together all edges of the plastic wrap. Compress the rice into a flat circle. (The plastic wrap helps prevent staining your fingers yellow from the turmeric.) Squeeze a small indent on both sides of the circle to make Pikachu's cheeks prominent. Place the Pikachu face onto a large dinner plate and remove the plastic wrap.

4 To make Pikachu's ears, place about ¼ cup (42 g) of turmeric rice in the middle of the same piece of plastic wrap and roll into a 2½-inch-long (6 cm) log. Shape one end of the log into a point; this point indicates the top of the ear. Arrange the base of Pikachu's ear onto its head. Remove the plastic wrap and repeat this step for the second ear. Once both ears are placed, use the plastic wrap to gently bind the head and ears together by compressing the connecting edges. Repeat step 3 and this step for the remaining Pikachu rice plates.

5 Using kitchen shears, cut the nori sheet into 8 small ovals for the eyes, 4 small triangles for the noses, 4 large but narrow number-three (3) shapes for the mouths, and 8 triangles for the tops of Pikachu's ears. Place these face details on the Pikachu rice. For Pikachu's pupils, cut 8 tiny circles from the mozzarella slices and place them on top of Pikachu's nori eyes. For the blush, slice the carrot into two ⅛-inch-thick (3 mm) coins. Carefully shape them into ovals with a paring knife, then place on Pikachu's cheeks. Cover the Pikachu rice while waiting for the curry to cook to prevent hardening.

6 To make the apple vegetable curry: In a medium nonstick skillet, heat the olive oil over medium heat. Add the star-shaped carrots and potatoes and pinch each of salt and pepper and cook for 6 to 8 minutes, until all sides of the veggies are golden brown. Transfer the cooked vegetables to a heatproof bowl and set aside. (Precooking vegetables helps to keep their shape in the sauce.)

7 Heat a medium pot (with a lid) over medium heat, then melt the butter. Add the minced onion, reduce the heat to medium-low, and cook for 15 to 20 minutes, stirring occasionally, until caramelized.

8 Increase the heat to medium and add the grated garlic and ginger. Stir together and cook until fragrant, about 2 minutes. Add the vegetable stock, apple, and 1 teaspoon each of salt and pepper. Cover with the lid and bring to a boil. Once boiling, add the curry cubes, cooked carrot and potato stars, bell pepper stars, and honey. Cook for 8 to 10 minutes, or until the curry has thickened and the root vegetables are fork-tender but not falling apart, stirring occasionally.

9 To serve: Carefully spoon the curry around the Pikachu turmeric rice on each plate and serve hot.

"A vegetable-loaded curry with a kick to it. Enjoy a big plate and fuel your energy with Pikachu's smile."

—Piquant Pikachu Curry description, *Pokémon Café Mix*

SOUP DUMPLINGS

Before Chihiro's parents turn into pigs (see Golden Roasted Cornish Hen on page 98), they enjoy a plentiful feast that includes what I thought were ginormous dumplings, but according to an animator on the film, they are the stomachs of coelacanth, a deep-sea fish. I decided to stick with my dumpling theory here, for your sake, and replicate how they look in the Studio Ghibli film, translucent and juicy. I also kept the size to something a little more manageable to eat!

YIELD **4** DUMPLINGS · PREP **40** MINUTES · REST **70** MINUTES · COOK **3.25** HOURS

SPECIAL TOOLS

Bamboo steamer or large pot with a steamer insert

CHICKEN JELLY SOUP (ASPIC)

2 pounds (907 g) chicken wings

½ small onion, peeled and cut in half

2 scallions, trimmed and cut in half lengthwise

1 piece (1 inch, or 2.5 cm, long) ginger root, thinly sliced

4 cloves garlic, cut in half lengthwise

½ tablespoon Shaoxing cooking wine

1 teaspoon salt

JUICY PORK FILLING

½ pound (227 g) ground pork

½ tablespoon soy sauce

1 teaspoon Shaoxing cooking wine

½ teaspoon sesame oil

¼ teaspoon sugar

¼ teaspoon salt

⅛ teaspoon pepper

1 piece (½ inch, or 12 mm, long) ginger root, grated

2 scallions, white and green parts separated, finely chopped, divided

DUMPLING WRAPPERS

1½ cups (180 g) all-purpose flour, plus more for dusting

½ cup (120 ml) plus 1 tablespoon boiling water

1 teaspoon canola oil

DIPPING SAUCE

3 tablespoons black vinegar

1 tablespoon garlic chili oil

1 tablespoon soy sauce

1 piece (1 inch, or 2.5 cm, long) ginger root, thinly sliced

((CONTINUED))

HOW-TO
DUMPLING FOLDING

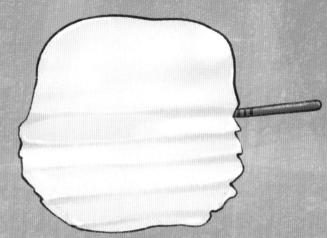

1. roll out dough + make striations

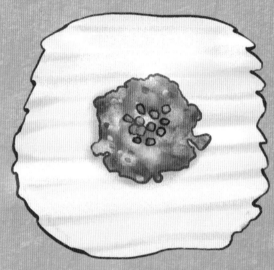

2. add pork filling + scallions

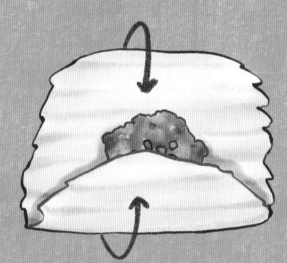

3. fold + match seams

4. cut extra + tuck and seal sides

5. add wing decorations

1 To make the chicken jelly soup (aspic): In a large pot (with a lid), combine all the aspic ingredients and add enough water to submerge everything. Bring to a boil over medium-high heat, then cover with the lid, reduce the heat to medium, and let cook for 2 hours, stirring occasionally. Uncover and skim off any scum and oil that is floating on the surface. Add enough water to cover once more and cook for another hour, skimming any scum and oil off the surface. Add enough water to cover for the third time and cook until the liquid has reduced in half, about an hour, skimming any scum and oil off the surface. Strain the liquid into a heatproof container and discard the ingredients (at this point they will have no flavor left). Cover the strained liquid and refrigerate until gelatinous, about an hour. Roughly slice the aspic into ¼-inch (6 mm) cubes.

2 To make the juicy pork filling: In a medium bowl, combine the ground pork, soy sauce, Shaoxing wine, sesame oil, sugar, salt, and pepper and mix until it becomes a paste. Add the ginger and the white part of the scallions and mix until combined. Add the cubed aspic and gently mix to ensure that the aspic keeps its shape.

3 To make the dumpling wrappers: Add the flour to a large bowl and pour over the boiling water while mixing with a spatula until the flour and water are fully absorbed. Continue to mix and, once warm and a dough forms, turn the dough out onto a sparingly flour-covered surface. Knead the dough with your hands until soft, about 10 minutes. Once soft, flatten the dough into a rectangle and spread it with the canola oil. Fold the dough like a letter for an envelope, with the top side folded to the middle and the bottom side folded over the top. Continue kneading until the oil is absorbed, about 5 minutes. Let the dough rest under plastic wrap for 10 minutes.

4 Divide the dough into 4 equal-size pieces. Using a rolling pin, roll out each piece into a 9-inch (23 cm) circle, ⅛ inch (3 mm) thick. Make striations in the dough circles by lifting them and placing a chopstick underneath. Pull the chopstick upward to make a ridge, then solidify the ridge by pinching the dough. Continue to make striations in one direction throughout the dough circles, spacing them 1 inch (2.5 cm) apart.

5 Add one-quarter of the juicy pork filling to the center of one of the dumpling wrappers, along with some of the chopped green parts of the scallions. Seal the dumpling together by folding the opposite edges in the middle, making sure the seams match. Cut off excess dough on the sides and compress and tuck the side seals.

6 With the extra dough, make the "wing" decorations by flattening the dough into a thin layer and cutting out sixteen ½-inch-tall (12 mm) triangles. Working with one triangle at a time, press the right and left sides of the triangle together to make a cone. Add water to the base of the wing and adhere it to the middle of a dumpling, pressing them together and rubbing the edges of the base of the wing to remove any seams. Form 3 more wings and adhere them around the middle of the dumpling, evenly spacing them apart. Place the completed dumpling on its own piece of parchment paper, then set it aside under a cloth or plastic wrap to prevent it from drying out. Repeat step 6 and this step for the remaining wings and dumplings.

7 Steam the dumplings on their pieces of parchment paper in the bamboo steamer or large pot with a steamer insert for 15 to 20 minutes, until firm to the touch. If using a pot with a steamer insert, leave the lid open and slightly tilted to allow the water to run off the sides and not onto the dumplings, which may cause a bumpy effect on the surface of the dumplings.

8 Meanwhile, make the dipping sauce: In a small bowl, combine all the sauce ingredients and stir to mix well.

9 Spoon some dipping sauce onto each plate, then place a dumpling on top. Serve hot.

> ## "Come on! Quit eating! Let's get out of here!"
>
> —Chihiro Ogino, *Spirited Away*

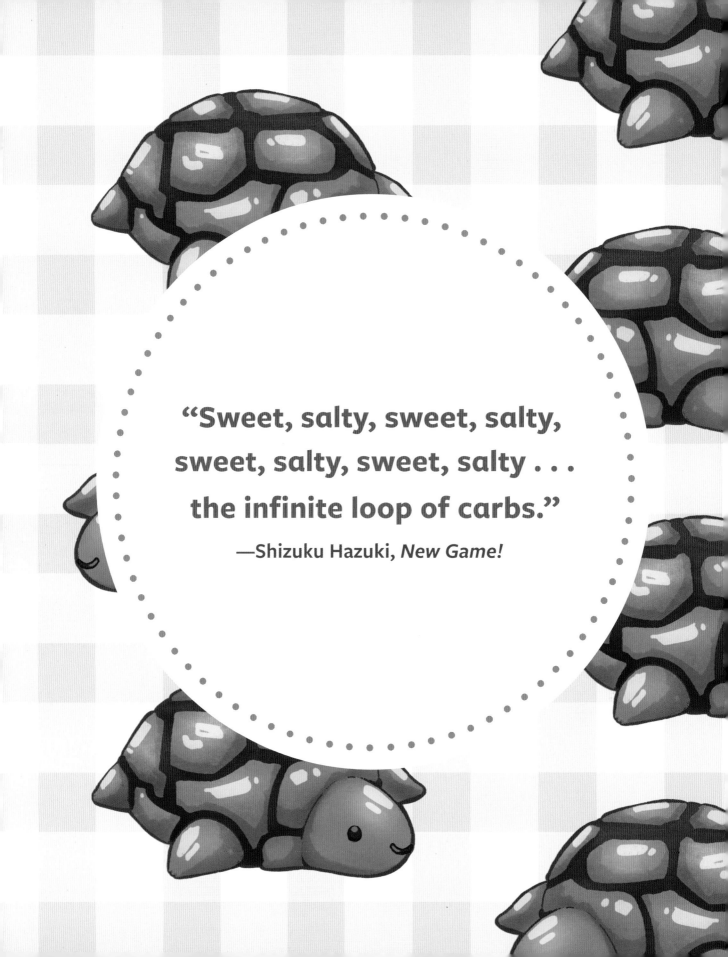

"Sweet, salty, sweet, salty, sweet, salty, sweet, salty . . . the infinite loop of carbs."

—Shizuku Hazuki, *New Game!*

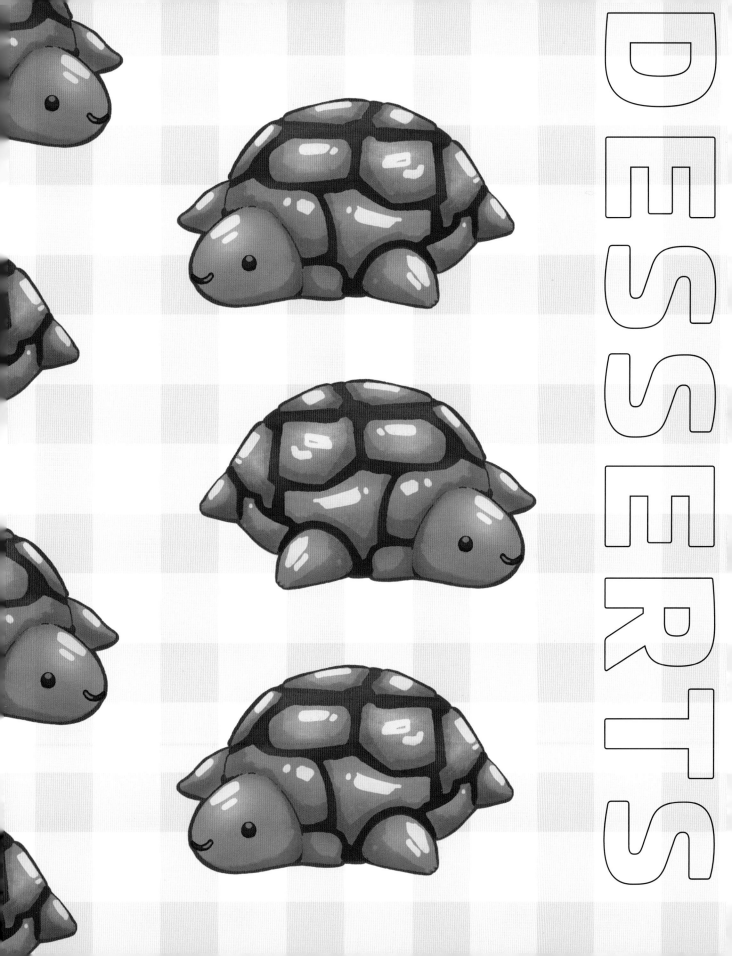

DESSERTS

STRAWBERRY PANCAKES WITH MACARONS

ANIME
YOUR NAME

Mitsuha and Taki (female and male protagonists respectively) are high school students from different places—Mitsuha, a rural Japanese village, and Take, Tokyo—who discover a phenomenon in which they switch bodies at random. At one point, Mitsuha spends Taki's hard-earned money on sweets, which prompts the two to set boundaries for what they can and can't do while inhabiting each other's bodies. I've created this recipe with all the fixings, so you can make all of them or pick and choose what you want!

YIELD 2 SERVINGS **PREP** 45 MINUTES **REST** 30 MINUTES **COOK** 40 MINUTES

SPECIAL TOOLS

Sifter

MINI PINK MACARONS

⅔ cup (75 g) almond flour

1 cup (120 g) confectioners' sugar

Pinch salt

2 large egg whites, at room temperature

¼ teaspoon cream of tartar

2 tablespoons granulated sugar

2 drops pink gel food coloring

WHITE CHOCOLATE STRAWBERRY BUTTERCREAM

⅓ cup (60 g) chopped white chocolate

2 tablespoons heavy whipping cream

⅓ cup (75 g) unsalted butter, at room temperature

Pinch salt

2 large egg whites

¼ cup (50 g) granulated sugar

2 tablespoons strawberry jam, strained

MINI PANCAKES

¾ cup (90 g) all-purpose flour

1½ teaspoons baking powder

1 tablespoon granulated sugar

Pinch salt

⅔ cup (160 g) warm milk

2 tablespoons unsalted butter, melted

1 large egg

1 teaspoon vanilla extract

½ to 1 teaspoon canola oil, for cooking

WHIPPED CREAM

1 cup (240 ml) heavy whipping cream

½ tablespoon granulated sugar

1 teaspoon vanilla extract

《 CONTINUED 》》

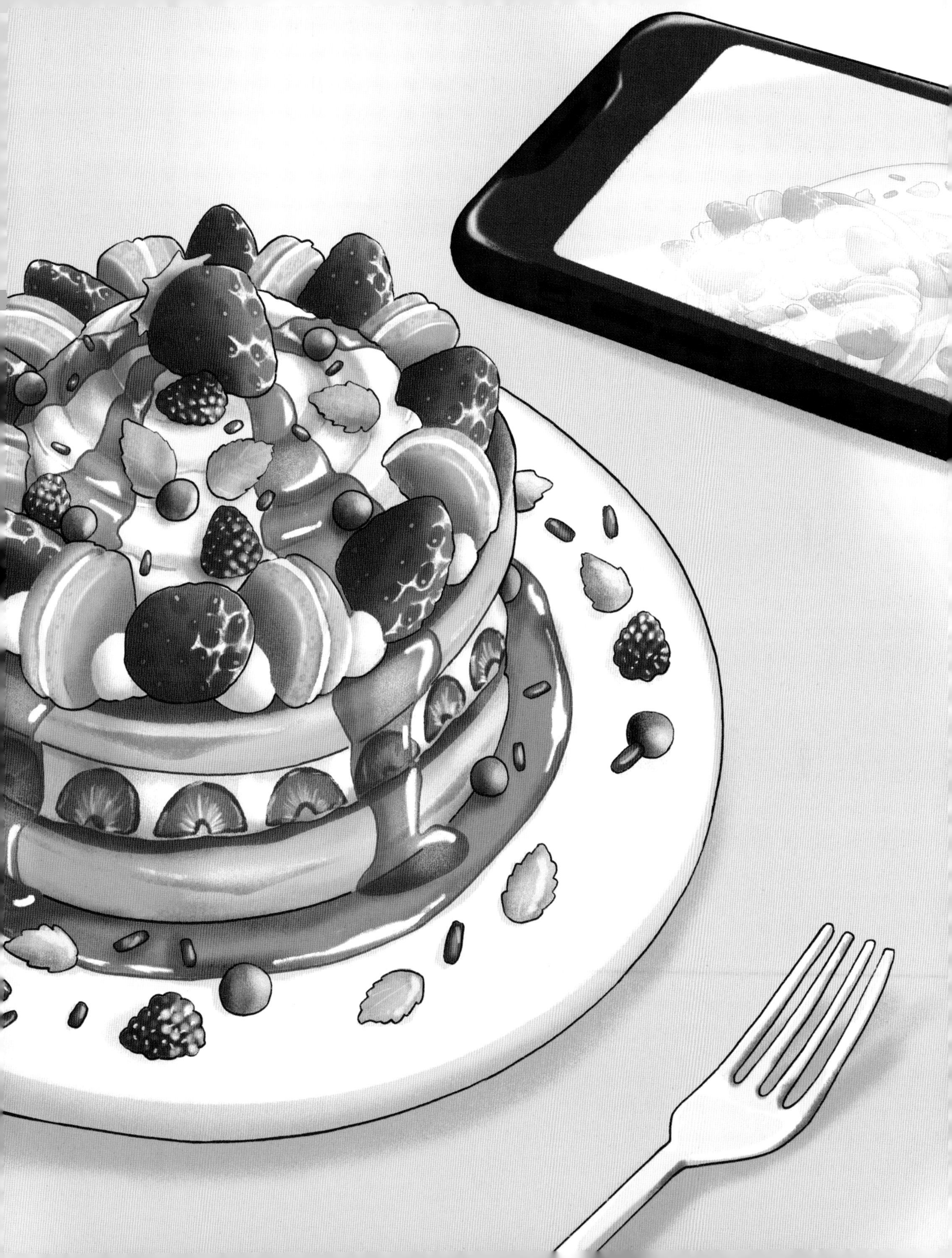

FOR ASSEMBLY

36 small strawberries, 18 trimmed and sliced in half, 16 trimmed and left whole, and 2 left whole with stems

¼ cup (35 g) pomegranate seeds

¼ cup (35) blueberries

¼ cup (30 g) raspberries

Strawberry Glaze (see Honey's Strawberry Shortcake on page 136, step 10, but only make the glaze; do not follow the instruction to drizzle over strawberries)

Fresh mint leaves, to taste, for decorating

·················《 **STRAWBERRY PANCAKES WITH MACARONS STEPS** 》··················

1 To make the mini pink macarons: Sift together the almond flour, confectioners' sugar, and pinch of salt into a medium bowl, then mix until fully combined.

2 In a large bowl, using a hand mixer with a whisk attachment, whip the 2 egg whites and cream of tartar on medium-high speed until soft peaks form. Gradually add the 2 tablespoons granulated sugar into the egg whites, whipping until stiff peaks form.

3 Fold the stiffened egg whites into the almond flour and confectioners' sugar mixture one-third at a time, aiming to fold less than thirty times total and adding the pink food coloring right before finished combining. Place the batter in a piping bag fitted with a ⁵⁄₁₆-inch (8 mm) piping tip.

4 Line a baking tray with parchment paper or a silicone mat. Pipe the macarons into 1-inch (2.5 cm) rounds, leaving 2 inches (5 cm) of space between each one. Pipe a total of 32 macaron shells. Let the macarons dry at room temperature for 15 to 20 minutes. Check the dryness by gently touching the exterior; it must not stick to your fingers.

5 Preheat the oven to 320°F (160°C; gas mark 3). Bake the macarons for 15 to 20 minutes, until they are solid when touched. Let cool on the tray before adding the filling.

6 To make the white chocolate strawberry buttercream: In a small microwave-safe bowl, combine the white chocolate and heavy whipping cream. Microwave until the cream is hot, about 30 seconds. Mix the melted white chocolate and hot cream for 2 minutes, or until well combined.

7 In a medium bowl, using a hand mixer with a whisk attachment, whip the ⅓ cup (75 g) butter with the pinch of salt on medium speed until pale and fluffy, about 5 minutes. Add the cooled white chocolate mixture to the butter and combine with a spatula until smooth.

8 Prepare a double boiler by bringing at least 1½ inches (4 cm) of water to a boil in a small saucepan. Find a heatproof bowl that will fit on top of the saucepan without touching the water and set it aside. Once the water is boiling, add the 2 egg whites and ¼ cup (50 g) granulated sugar to the heatproof bowl, constantly whisking the mixture until it reaches 160°F (70°C), measuring with a candy thermometer. Remove the bowl from the heat, then, using a hand mixer with a clean whisk attachment, whip the egg whites on high speed until stiff peaks form. Add the egg whites to the white chocolate–butter mixture, one-third at a time, until well combined and fluffy. Gently fold in the strawberry jam.

9 Finish the macarons by placing the white chocolate strawberry buttercream in a piping bag. Cut a small hole at the tip and pipe the buttercream onto a cooled macaron shell. Top with another macaron shell. Repeat with the remaining macaron shells for a total of 16 cookies.

10 To make the mini pancakes: In a medium bowl, stir together the flour, baking powder, 1 tablespoon granulated sugar, and pinch of salt.

11 In a small heatproof bowl, stir together the warm milk and melted butter. Add the egg and vanilla to the bowl and fully combine. Gradually add the wet ingredients to the bowl with the dry ingredients, mixing until combined.

12 Heat a large nonstick skillet over medium heat. Add ½ teaspoon canola oil and swirl in the pan to coat, wiping off excess oil with a paper towel. Ladle the batter into the pan and create 4-inch (10 cm) pancakes. Reduce the heat to medium-low and wait for the pancakes to bubble before flipping, 2 to 3 minutes. Cook for another 2 to 3 minutes, until golden brown. Repeat this step if working in batches. (There should be enough batter for 4 pancakes).

13 To make the whipped cream: In a medium bowl, combine the heavy cream, ½ tablespoon granulated sugar, and 1 teaspoon vanilla. Using a hand mixer with a whisk attachment, whip on medium speed, gradually increasing to high speed, until stiff peaks form, about 3 minutes.

14 To assemble: Place a pancake on a plate, top it with whipped cream, and decorate the pancake's perimeter with half of the cut strawberries, cut sides down and top ends facing out. Stack another pancake on top, then add a mountain of whipped cream in the center and place a strawberry with a stem on top. Decorate the perimeter of the top pancake with eight mini pink macarons, equally spaced apart, placing a stemmed strawberry in between each one. Use whipped cream to adhere them to the pancake, if needed. Place the pomegranate seeds, blueberries, and raspberries on top of the pancake and around the plate. Lastly, drizzle the top of the pancake with the strawberry glaze and decorate with the mint leaves. Repeat this step for the second plate. Serve immediately.

NOTE

The white chocolate strawberry buttercream can be made ahead of time and stored in an airtight container in the refrigerator for up to 1 week and in the freezer for up to 1 month. To revive, simply let it come to room temperature and whisk until it becomes smooth again.

MANGO PARFAIT

★ ANIME ★
MAID-SAMA
SEASON 1 EPISODE 4
NET IDOL AOI

Misaki is a high school girl who is class president and has a reputation for being strict. She also has a secret part-time job working at a maid café, which her classmate Usui finds out about but promises not to tell anyone. Usui comes to the café often and is a fan of this mango parfait. Let's get layering!

YIELD **2** SERVINGS   PREP **15** MINUTES

LAYERS

2 mangoes, peeled and seeds removed

½ tablespoon plus 1 teaspoon (optional) sugar, divided

2 pinches salt, divided

½ block (4 ounces, or 113 g) cream cheese, at room temperature

1½ cups (360 ml) heavy whipping cream, divided

2 teaspoons vanilla extract, divided

FOR ASSEMBLY

½ cup (15 g) cornflakes

2 generous scoops vanilla ice cream

2 cherries

1 large mango, peeled, seed removed, and sliced ¼ inch (6 mm) thick

1 small apple, cut into wedges lightly soaked in lemon juice

《 STEPS 》

1 To make the layers: Slice the flesh of the 2 mangoes into a blender and blend until smooth. Strain the purée in a fine-mesh strainer into a bowl, then mix in 1 teaspoon of the sugar (if using) and pinch of the salt.

2 Add the cream cheese to a small bowl and, using a hand mixer with a whisk attachment, whip on high speed until softened, about 1 minute. Add ½ cup (120 ml) of the heavy cream, 1 teaspoon of the vanilla, and remaining pinch of salt to the bowl and whip on high speed until creamy, about 2 minutes. In a medium bowl, combine the remaining 1 cup (240 ml) heavy cream, remaining ½ tablespoon

sugar, and remaining 1 teaspoon vanilla. Using the hand mixer with a clean, dry whisk attachment, whip on medium speed, gradually increasing to high speed, until medium-stiff peaks form, about 2 minutes. Place in a piping bag with a ½-inch (12 mm) star-shaped tip.

3 To assemble: In each parfait glass, place a layer of mango purée, followed by a whipped cream cheese layer, then a layer of cornflakes. Top with a scoop of vanilla ice cream, a generous swirl of whipped cream, and a cherry. Add mango slices, apple wedges, and more mango purée. Serve immediately.

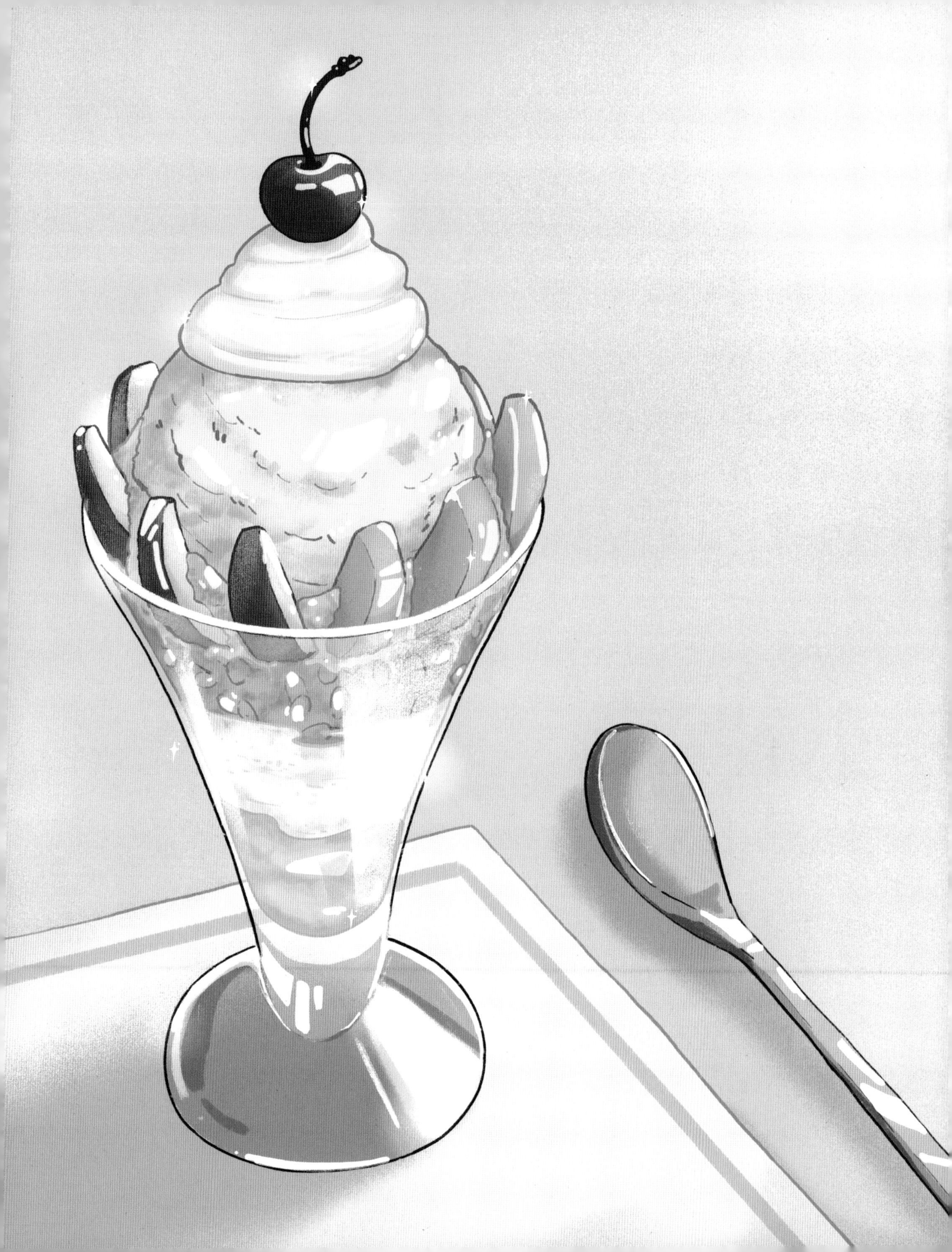

APRICOT CANELÉS

★ ANIME ★
THE WAY OF THE HOUSEHUSBAND
SEASON 1 EPISODE 4

Tatsu, a mob boss turned househusband, is married to Miku. In this episode, Miku's parents are making a last-minute visit, prompting Tatsu to quickly whip up homemade canelés (French custard pastries with a soft center and crispy exterior) with homemade jam. It's not mentioned what kind of jam he uses, but it looks like apricot from the color and appearance. I made the recipe a little easier by using store-bought jam!

YIELD 6 CANELÉS · **PREP** 15 MINUTES · **REST** 30 MINUTES · **COOK** 1 HOUR

SPECIAL TOOLS

Canelé mold pan or mini muffin tin

INGREDIENTS

3 egg yolks

½ cup (100 g) sugar

2 tablespoons dark rum

1 teaspoon vanilla extract

Pinch salt

½ cup (60 g) flour

1 cup (240 ml) milk

2 tablespoons apricot jam, strained, plus 2 tablespoons for topping

2 tablespoons unsalted butter, divided

Prepared hot Darjeeling tea, for serving

《 STEPS 》

1 In a medium bowl, stir together the egg yolks, sugar, rum, vanilla, and salt. Whisk in the flour until fully combined and there are no lumps.

2 In a small pot, heat the milk, strained apricot jam, and 1½ tablespoons of the butter to a slow simmer over medium heat.

Remove from the heat and add one-third of the milk mixture to the egg yolk mixture. Whisk until fully combined and smooth, then repeat with the remaining two-thirds of the milk mixture. Strain the mixture with a fine-mesh strainer into a clean container, cover with a lid, and refrigerate for at least 30 minutes and up to 48 hours.

3 In a small skillet, melt the remaining ½ tablespoon butter. Grease 6 canelé molds with the melted butter using a brush. Flip the pan upside down onto a parchment-lined baking tray to remove excess butter, then place the canelé pan in the refrigerator until the butter has hardened and is set.

4 Preheat the oven to 450°F (230°C; gas mark 8). Remove the canelé batter from the refrigerator and stir to reconstitute. Pour the batter into the pan, leaving a ¼-inch (6 mm) allowance to rise.

5 Bake for 15 minutes, then reduce the temperature to 375°F (190°C; gas mark 5) and bake for another 40 minutes, or until desired exterior color (see Notes right).

6 Let the canelés cool to room temperature, then place a small dollop of apricot jam on top of each one. Serve with the Darjeeling tea.

NOTES

- It's recommended to refrigerate the canelé batter in step 2 for 48 hours before baking to produce a richer result—the flour becomes more hydrated the longer it rests—but Tatsu was in a hurry! No matter how long you refrigerate the batter, the canelés will be delicious.
- You may bake the canelés for less time for a more golden color, or longer for a darker color that produces a more bitter caramel taste. Subtract or add 5 minutes to the second baking time, depending on your oven.

"I want you to give me some homemaking tips, Tatsu!"

—Miku's mom, *The Way of the Househusband*

SHEEP'S MILK PORRIDGE
WITH APPLES AND GOAT CHEESE

ANIME
SPICE AND WOLF II
SEASON 1 | EPISODE 0
WOLF AND AMBER MELANCHOLY

Holo, a wolf deity and protagonist Kraft Lawrence's traveling partner, falls ill at Nora's house, where they stopped for dinner. She is fed this flavorful porridge to adjust "the balance between the four humors." This dish is rich in nutrients, good for rehydration, and has a nice thermal balance with the hot porridge and cold toppings. Plus, it's a perfect marriage of sweet and savory!

YIELD 4 SERVINGS | PREP 5 MINUTES | COOK 25 MINUTES

INGREDIENTS

4 cups (1 L) sheep's milk (or dairy or nondairy milk of choice)

1 tablespoon unsalted butter

2 tablespoons honey

1 cinnamon stick

¼ teaspoon grated nutmeg

½ teaspoon salt

1 cup (160 g) wheat porridge (also known as cream of wheat, hot cereal, or farina)

¼ teaspoon vanilla extract

1 Fuji apple, thinly sliced, for topping

¼ cup (68 g) goat cheese, for topping

STEPS

1 In a medium saucepan (with a lid), combine the sheep's milk, butter, honey, cinnamon stick, nutmeg, and salt. Turn the heat to medium-low, cover with the lid, and cook for 20 minutes, stirring occasionally.

2 Remove the cinnamon stick, then slowly add the wheat porridge while stirring. Increase the heat to medium and bring to a boil, then reduce the heat to medium-low and cook for 5 minutes, stirring occasionally. Cook longer if you desire a thicker consistency. (The porridge thickens as it cools.)

3 Stir in the vanilla and remove from the heat.

4 Serve in bowls topping each with one-quarter of the apple slices, then spread a tablespoon of goat cheese across the top of the porridge and apples.

RASPBERRY JAM THUMBPRINT COOKIES

ANIME
THE SECRET WORLD OF ARRIETTY

In this Studio Ghibli film, Arrietty and her family are tiny people who live in the nooks and crannies of a suburban home. Oftentimes, they "borrow" ingredients from their hosts. Arrietty likes to grind up cookies to use as baking flour, so I "borrowed" Arrietty's idea and used ground-up cookies in this recipe! Arrietty served these cookies to Spiller, when he helped bring her injured father home.

YIELD 10 COOKIES · **PREP** 10 MINUTES · **COOK** 10 MINUTES

SPECIAL TOOLS

12-cup muffin tin

10 cupcake liners

INGREDIENTS

1 cup (120 g) crushed digestive cookies

½ cup (48 g) rolled oats

2 tablespoons sugar

½ teaspoon ground cinnamon

2 pinches salt

¼ cup (60 g) unsweetened smooth applesauce

2 tablespoons unsalted butter, melted

5 tablespoons (100 g) raspberry jam

Prepared hot matcha tea, for serving

« STEPS »

1 Preheat the oven to 350°F (175°C; gas mark 4). In a food processor or high-powered blender, blend the crushed cookies and oats until the cookies are turned into crumbs and most of the oats are halved in size. Add the sugar, cinnamon, and salt and pulse until combined. Add the applesauce and butter and pulse until the dough comes together.

2 Line 10 muffin cups with the cupcake liners, then scoop 1½ tablespoons of dough into each cup. Push the dough tightly into the base of each cup. Make a 1½-inch (4 cm) circular indent in the center of the dough by slightly pressing with your thumb. Add 1½ teaspoons of raspberry jam in each indentation.

3 Bake for 10 minutes, or until the cookies are slightly browned and hardened and the jam has thickened. (Bake for 15 minutes for extra-crisp cookies.) Remove the cookies from the tin, still in the liners, and set on a rack. Let cool for at least 15 minutes to allow the cookies to harden more. Serve with the matcha tea.

CHOCOLATE CORNETS

★ ANIME ★
LUCKY STAR
SEASON 1 EPISODE 1

In the first episode of *Lucky Star*, Konata Izumi, the protagonist, asks her friend Tsukasa which end of a chocolate cornet (a cone-shaped Japanese pastry filled with chocolate custard) she eats first, sparking a conversation about which end is "the head." In a later scene, another friend, Miyuki, suggests to "tear off the thin end and dip it in the chocolate cream on the fat end." This recipe is enough for a batch of six, so hopefully you and your friends can try eating them in all the different ways possible!

YIELD **6** CORNETS PREP **10** MINUTES REST **1.5** HOURS COOK **30** MINUTES

SPECIAL TOOLS

6 cornet molds

MILK BREAD

⅓ cup (80 ml) warm milk

2½ tablespoons sugar

2 large eggs, divided

½ (¼-ounce, or 7-g) packet active dry yeast

1½ cups (180 g) all-purpose flour, plus more for dusting

1 tablespoon milk powder

Pinch salt

2 tablespoons unsalted butter, at room temperature, divided, plus more for greasing

CHOCOLATE CUSTARD

2 egg yolks

2 tablespoons sugar

Pinch salt

2 tablespoons cornstarch (or potato starch)

1½ cups (360 ml) milk

½ cup (85 g) semisweet or dark chocolate chips

1 teaspoon vanilla extract

⟪ STEPS ⟫

1 To make the milk bread: In a bowl of a stand mixer, combine the warm milk, 2 tablespoons sugar, 1 egg, and yeast. Mix with a dough hook attachment on medium speed until incorporated, about 5 seconds.

2 In a medium bowl, whisk together the flour, milk powder, and pinch of salt. Add the dry ingredients to the bowl with the wet ingredients. Mix on medium-high speed for 2 minutes, or until a dough forms, scraping the flour from the sides of the bowl if needed. Turn the stand mixer off and add 1 tablespoon of the butter. Turn the mixer back on medium-high speed until the butter is incorporated, 3 to 4 minutes.

⟪ CONTINUED ⟫

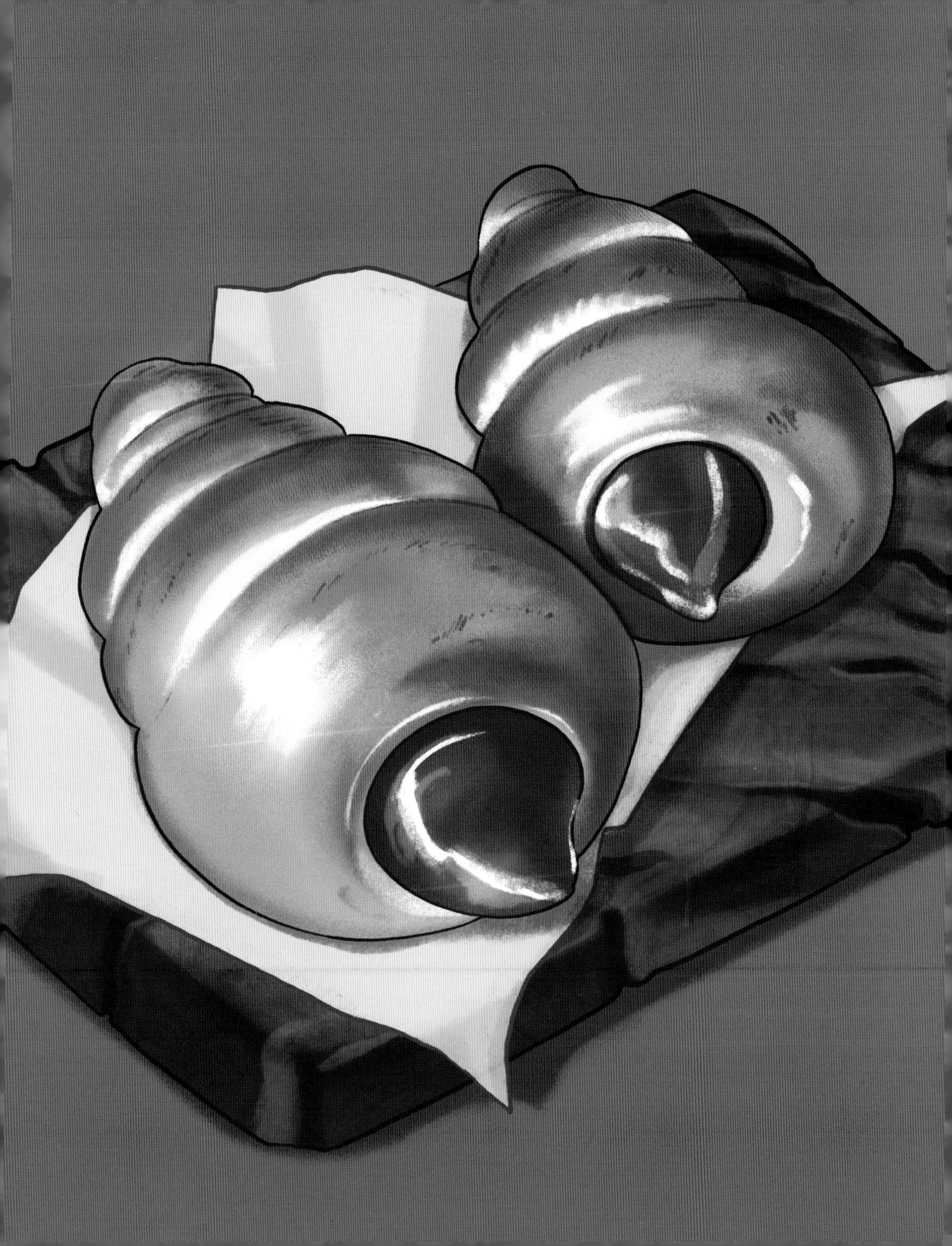

Repeat with the remaining 1 tablespoon butter. Once all the butter is incorporated, continue to knead the dough on medium speed until it is soft and smooth, about 4 minutes.

3 Remove the dough from the bowl, grease the bowl (you can use nonstick cooking spray, oil, or butter), return the dough to the bowl, and cover with plastic wrap. Place in a warm spot and leave to rise until doubled in size, 45 to 50 minutes. The dough is ready when you poke it in the center and the hole does not collapse. Degas the risen dough by punching it in the center. Turn out the dough on a flour-covered work surface. Aggressively pat the dough to remove more gas. Roll the dough into a log and divide it into 6 equal-size pieces.

4 Roll each piece into a ball, then flatten each ball with a flour-covered rolling pin to get rid of any visible air bubbles. Tightly roll each flattened ball into a log, then stretch the dough to 12 inches (30 cm) by placing both hands on the dough and rolling it in a back-and-forth motion from the center of the dough to the edges. Taper one end, making it thinner than the other.

5 Grease the cornet molds with butter. Wrap the dough on the mold by holding the tapered end ¼ inch (6 mm) below the tip of the mold with one hand, then wrapping the dough around to the base. Seal the dough by firmly pinching both ends. Repeat this step for the remaining dough and molds. Place the molds onto a baking tray lined with parchment paper, cover with a towel, and place in a warm spot. Let the dough rise again until doubled in size, about 15 minutes. Preheat the oven to 350°F (175°C; gas mark 4).

6 Prepare an egg wash by beating the remaining egg in a small bowl. Dip a brush into the beaten egg and brush the egg wash onto the surface of the dough. Bake for 12 to 15 minutes, until golden in color. Let cool before removing the molds.

7 Meanwhile, make the chocolate custard: In a medium heatproof bowl, whisk together the egg yolks and 2 tablespoons sugar until pale white. Add the pinch of salt and cornstarch to the bowl and whisk until there are no clumps.

8 In a medium saucepan, bring the milk to a rapid simmer over medium heat, then remove from the heat. Temper the egg yolks by slowly pouring one-third of the heated milk into the bowl with the egg yolk mixture. Whisk until fully combined, then add the remaining two-thirds of the milk and whisk until fully combined. Add the milk and egg yolk contents back into the medium saucepan and turn the heat to medium. Continuously stir until thickened, about 5 minutes. Remove from the heat and pour into a clean medium bowl.

9 Add the chocolate chips and vanilla to the bowl and gently whisk until it is melted and incorporated. Cover the surface of the bowl with plastic wrap so that the plastic wrap is touching the custard and refrigerate until set, about 30 minutes.

10 To assemble: Remove the chocolate custard from the refrigerator and whisk for a minute to reconstitute. Place the custard in a piping bag and cut a ½-inch (12 mm) hole at the tip. Pipe custard into the crevice of a cornet until full. Repeat with the remaining custard and cornets.

OHAGI

★ ANIME ★

RUROUNI KENSHIN

SEASON 1 EPISODE 9

THE STRONGEST
GROUP OF NINJAS:
THE HORRIBLE
ONIWABAN GROUP

Megumi makes Yahiko ohagi to celebrate his recovery from being poisoned. Kaoru then asks Megumi to teach her how to make ohagi so that she can make it for Yahiko next time. Yahiko jokes that he'd rather eat "cakes of dirt" than Kaoru's cooking, and Kaoru retaliates by smacking Yahiko's face into the plate of ohagi, making everyone laugh because he looks like an ohagi! Ohagi is a wagashi (Japanese tea confection) that's made with sticky rice and red bean paste and pairs perfectly with a cup of your favorite tea.

YIELD 10 OHAGI

PREP 20 MINUTES

COOK 2 HOURS

INGREDIENTS

1 recipe Red Bean Paste from the Siberia Sponge Cake recipe (page 177; follow step 1 on page 178, then follow the steps below)

½ cup (90 g) sticky rice (also called sweet rice and glutinous rice)

❮❮ STEPS ❯❯

1 While the red beans are hot, mash 80 percent of them using the back of a wooden spoon or a hand blender, then let cool a bit until safe to handle.

2 Place the sticky rice in a fine-mesh strainer and rinse it with running water until the water runs clear. Add the rice to a small saucepan with the amount of water recommended in the package instructions for cooking ½ cup (90 g). Cook according to the package instructions. Remove the rice from the heat, mash half of the cooked rice in the pot, and mix to combine the different textures found in ohagi.

3 To assemble: Cover your work surface with plastic wrap, at least an 8-inch-long

(20 cm) piece. Grab half a handful (about 1½ tablespoons) of red bean paste and place it on the plastic wrap. Squish it down into a circle that is ⅛ inch (3 mm) thick. With wet, clean hands, to prevent the rice from sticking, grab another half of handful (about 1½ tablespoons) of warm or room-temperature sticky rice and form it into a ball. Place the ball on top of the squished red bean paste. Gather the plastic wrap to enclose the sticky rice with the red bean paste. Tightly twist the plastic wrap to achieve a smooth, circular ohagi; the rice should be completely concealed inside the red bean paste. Open the plastic wrap and place the ohagi onto a plate. Repeat until all the red bean paste and sticky rice are used. Enjoy at room temperature.

HONEY'S STRAWBERRY SHORTCAKE

★ ANIME ★

OURAN HIGH SCHOOL HOST CLUB

SEASON 1 EPISODE 13

HARUHI IN WONDERLAND!

While Haruhi is reminiscing about her first visit to Ouran Academy, the memory turns into a dream sequence inspired by Lewis Carroll's *Alice in Wonderland*. In the dining hall, she comes across the Mad Hatter's tea party in which Honey is dressed as his stuffed rabbit, Usa-chan, and continually eating this cake, because the time is always three o'clock in the afternoon, snack time. I included a recipe for Usa-chan meringue cookies to decorate the cake!

YIELD **5** SERVINGS PREP **45** MINUTES REST **1** HOUR COOK **3** HOURS

SPECIAL TOOLS

6 x 3-inch (15 x 7.5 cm) round cake pan

Sifter

Toothpick

USA-CHAN MERINGUE COOKIES

2 large egg whites

⅔ cup (135 g) sugar

Pink gel food coloring

1 teaspoon vanilla extract

1 scant teaspoon black gel food coloring

GENOISE (SPONGE CAKE)

4 large eggs

⅔ cup (135 g) sugar

1 cup (130 g) cake flour

Pinch salt

2 tablespoons milk, at room temperature

2 tablespoons unsalted butter, melted

1 teaspoon vanilla extract

WHIPPED CREAM

3 cups (720 ml) heavy whipping cream

1 tablespoon sugar (optional)

SIMPLE SYRUP

¼ cup (60 ml) water

¼ cup (50 g) sugar

STRAWBERRY GLAZE

½ cup (100 g) sugar

½ cup (120 ml) water

2 tablespoons strawberry jam

1 tablespoon cornstarch

5 small strawberries, trimmed and left whole

FOR ASSEMBLY

¼ cup (80 g) strawberry jam

8 large strawberries, trimmed and sliced in half

《 CONTINUED 》

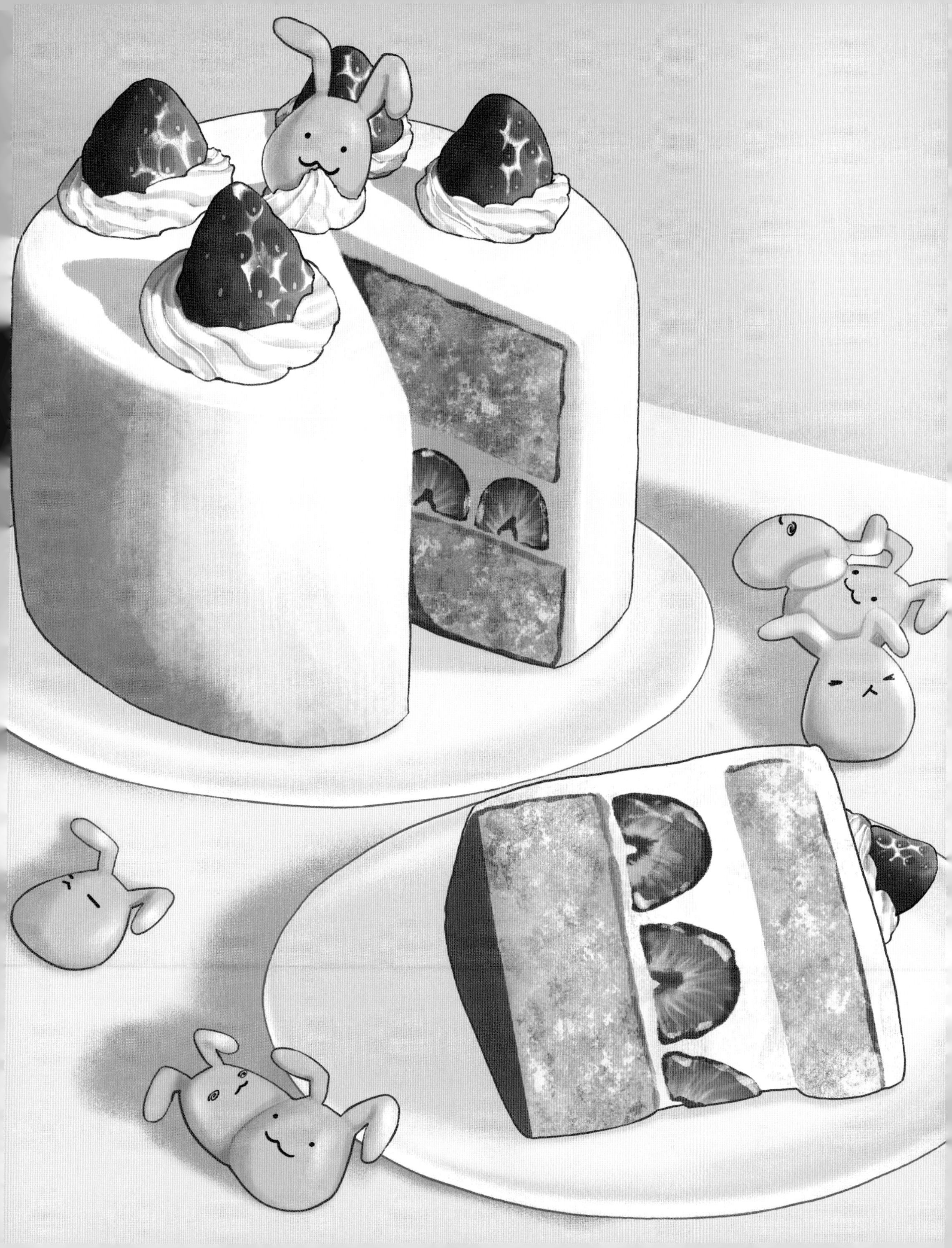

HONEY'S STRAWBERRY SHORTCAKE STEPS

1 To make the Usa-Chan meringue cookies: Prepare a double boiler by bringing at least 1½ inches (4 cm) of water to a boil in a small saucepan. Find a heatproof bowl that will fit on top of the saucepan without touching the water and set it aside. Once the water is boiling, add the egg whites and ⅔ cup (135 g) sugar to the heatproof bowl and whisk together. Place the heatproof bowl on top of the saucepan and constantly whisk the mixture to 122°F (50°C), measuring with a candy thermometer. (If you do not have a thermometer, place a small amount of egg whites on your fingers and feel if the sugar has dissolved.) Remove from the heat.

2 Using a hand mixer with a whisk attachment, whip the egg whites on high speed until stiff peaks form, about 3 minutes. Fold in 3 drops of the pink gel food coloring and the 1 teaspoon vanilla with a spatula. Place the pink meringue batter into a piping bag with a ¼-inch (6 mm) tip, or cut a hole of that size at the tip. Line a baking tray with parchment paper. Pipe the shape of Usa-Chan onto the prepared tray by drawing a 1¼-inch (3 cm) circle for the head with chubby cheeks and 1-inch-long (2.5 cm) thin ears pointing in different directions. Pipe 15 cookies, then place the leftover meringue in a small bowl and add 1 drop of the black food coloring. Dip a toothpick into the black meringue to draw on two dots for the eyes and a horizontal number-three (3) shape for the mouth.

3 Preheat the oven to 175°F (80°C) and place the tray of meringue cookies inside. Leave the oven door slightly ajar and bake for 2 hours, or until the tops are set and the cookies cleanly peel off the parchment paper and the bottoms are dried. Let cool on the baking tray.

4 After the cookies are done baking, make the genoise: Preheat the oven to 355°F (180°C; gas mark 4). Line the sides and bottom of the 6 x 3-inch (15 x 7.5 cm) round cake pan with parchment paper.

5 Place the eggs and ⅔ cup (135 g) sugar in a heatproof mixing bowl and whisk together. Heat the eggs and sugar over a double boiler, like in step 1, whisking constantly until the mixture reaches 100°F (38°C). Remove from the heat, then, using a hand mixer with a whisk attachment, mix on high speed until the volume has tripled, turned lighter, and ribbons are left in the batter while mixing, about 10 minutes. Whisk on low speed for another minute to get rid of large air bubbles.

6 Sift together the cake flour and salt into a small bowl, then fold the dry mixture into the batter using a spatula. In a small bowl combine the milk, butter, and 1 teaspoon vanilla. Add to the batter in three stages and fold with the spatula until just combined, making sure to scrape the bottom of the bowl for any loose liquids. Transfer the batter to the prepared cake pan and immediately place in the oven.

7 Bake for 25 to 30 minutes, or when touched you hear sounds of bubbles popping and the cake springs back to its original height. Immediately after baking, place a piece of parchment paper on top of the cake and flip over to remove from the pan onto a rack for 10 minutes to achieve a smooth top. Flip back to its original position and let cool to room temperature.

8 To make the whipped cream: In a medium bowl, using a hand mixer with a whisk attachment, whip the heavy cream and 1 tablespoon sugar (if using) on medium-high

speed until soft peaks form, 2 to 3 minutes. Remove one-third of the cream to another bowl and continue to whip the rest of the cream on medium-high speed into stiff peaks, about 2 more minutes. Set both whipped cream batches aside.

9 To make the simple syrup: In a small saucepan, bring the ¼ cup (60 ml) water and ¼ cup (50 g) sugar to a boil over medium heat, then reduce the heat to a simmer until the sugar is dissolved, stirring occasionally, 4 to 5 minutes. Set aside and let cool.

10 To make the strawberry glaze: In a separate small saucepan, stir together the ½ cup (100 g) sugar, ½ cup (120 ml) water, strawberry jam, and cornstarch. Heat over medium heat until thickened and glossy, stirring occasionally, about 8 minutes. Place the 5 small strawberries on a wire rack, then drizzle them with the glaze to cover.

11 To assemble: Slice the cooled genoise in half lengthwise into 2 layers. Lightly brush and dab simple syrup onto the sides of both cake halves that were exposed by the cut. Apply a thin layer of strawberry jam on the bottom cake layer on top of the simple syrup, then apply a thin layer of the stiff whipped cream using an offset spatula. Place the halved strawberries in a single layer, cut sides down, to cover the entire cake surface, then add more of the stiff whipped cream to fully cover them. Level the top layer of whipped cream, then place the top cake layer, with the simple-syrup side facing up. Apply a thin, even layer of the stiff whipped cream all over the entire cake to crumb-coat it. Place the cake in the refrigerator for 30 minutes, until chilled and the outer layer of whipped cream has hardened.

12 Remove the cake from the refrigerator and add an even layer of the soft whipped cream all over the cake using an offset spatula. Place the leftover soft whipped cream in a piping bag fitted with a star-shaped tip and pipe five 1½- to 2-inch (4 to 5 cm) circles equally spaced around the perimeter of the cake, along with a dollop in the middle. Place a prepared shiny strawberry in the middle of each piped circle. When ready to serve, place a Usa-Chan cookie on the middle dollop of whipped cream and scatter more cookies around the cake.

"I love anything chocolate, Usa-chan, and all of you ladies!"

—Mitsukuni "Honey" Haninozuka, *Ouran High School Host Club*

MINI MATCHA MOCHI PANCAKES

★ ANIME ★
TOKYO REVENGERS
SEASON 1 | EPISODE 23
END OF WAR

Mikey and Emma are hanging out on her birthday, being affectionate and close. Their friends, thinking Emma is cheating on her boyfriend, Draken, follow them around to find out for sure. However, it's revealed that Mikey and Emma are half siblings, and Draken already knew this! These mini matcha mochi pancakes are inspired by the ones Emma orders while she and Mikey are out celebrating her birthday.

YIELD **4** SERVINGS | PREP **10** MINUTES | COOK **15** MINUTES

WHITE CHOCOLATE MATCHA CREAM

¼ cup (60 ml) boiling water

1 tablespoon matcha powder

1 cup (240 ml) heavy whipping cream

3½ ounces (100 g) white chocolate, finely chopped

Pinch salt

MINI MATCHA MOCHI PANCAKES

¾ cup (120 g) sweet rice flour

¾ cup (90 g) all-purpose flour

⅓ cup (65 g) sugar

2 tablespoons matcha powder

1½ teaspoons baking powder

Pinch salt

2 eggs, at room temperature

1¼ cups (300 ml) milk, at room temperature

1 teaspoon vanilla extract

2 tablespoons unsalted butter, melted

1½ teaspoons canola oil, divided, for cooking

WHIPPED CREAM

1 cup (240 ml) heavy whipping cream

½ tablespoon sugar

1 teaspoon vanilla extract

FOR ASSEMBLY

3½ ounces (100 g) semisweet chocolate, roughly chopped

1 To make the white chocolate matcha cream: Add the boiling hot water and 1 tablespoon matcha powder to a heatproof mixing cup and whisk to combine.

2 Place the matcha mixture in a medium saucepan and add the 1 cup (240 ml) heavy cream, white chocolate, and pinch of salt. Heat over a medium heat, stirring occasionally until thick, 8 to 10 minutes. Remove from the heat and let cool to room temperature.

3 To make the mini matcha pancakes: In a medium bowl, whisk together the sweet rice flour, all-purpose flour, ⅓ cup (65 g) sugar, 2 tablespoons matcha powder, baking powder, and pinch of salt.

4 In a separate medium bowl, crack the eggs and mix them until there are no visible egg white lumps. Whisk in the milk, 1 teaspoon vanilla, and melted butter. Add the dry ingredients to the bowl with the wet ingredients and whisk just until combined.

5 Heat a large nonstick skillet over medium heat. Add ½ teaspoon of the oil and swirl in the pan to coat, wiping off excess oil with a paper towel. Ladle the batter into the pan and create 4-inch (10 cm) pancakes. Reduce the heat to medium-low and wait for the pancakes to bubble before flipping, 2 to 3 minutes. Cook for another 2 to 3 minutes, until the color turns a darker green and the batter is set. Transfer to a baking tray. Repeat this step with the remaining batter. (There should be enough batter for 12 pancakes.)

6 To make the whipped cream: In a medium bowl, combine the 1 cup (240 ml) heavy cream, ½ tablespoon sugar, and 1 teaspoon vanilla. Using a hand mixer with a whisk attachment, whip on medium speed, gradually increasing to high speed, until stiff peaks form, about 3 minutes.

7 To assemble: Place 3 pancakes on each serving plate, drizzle with the white chocolate matcha cream, and top with the semisweet chocolate chunks. Pipe a mountain of whipped cream at the side of the pancakes.

"You're hanging out with your little sister on her birthday, Mikey?"

—Draken, *Tokyo Revengers*

CAT DONUTS

★ ANIME ★
NEW GAME!
SEASON 1 EPISODE 10
FULL-TIME EMPLOYMENT
IS A LOOPHOLE IN THE LAW
TO MAKE WAGES LOWER

The team at Eagle Jump, a video game company, are working overtime through the weekend. Coincidentally, everyone buys boxes of cat donuts as a treat because the donut shop by the office is having a half-price sale. I'm happy that I get to share my delicious recipe for honey milk donuts with you, which received a lot of praise when I posted it on Reddit.

YIELD **12** DONUTS · PREP **15** MINUTES · REST **1.5** HOURS · COOK **10** MINUTES · DECORATE **20** MINUTES

SPECIAL TOOLS

Sifter

HONEY MILK DONUTS

½ cup (120 ml) warm milk

1 teaspoon active dry yeast

2 large eggs

1½ tablespoons honey

2¼ cups (270 g) all-purpose flour, plus more for dusting

⅛ teaspoon grated nutmeg

3 tablespoons salted butter, at room temperature, divided, plus more for greasing

Canola oil, for frying

FOR DECORATING

24 roasted almonds

1 cup (120 g) confectioners' sugar, plus 2 teaspoons for thickening

2 tablespoons milk

Yellow, teal, and pink gel food coloring

½ teaspoon instant coffee powder

《 CONTINUED 》

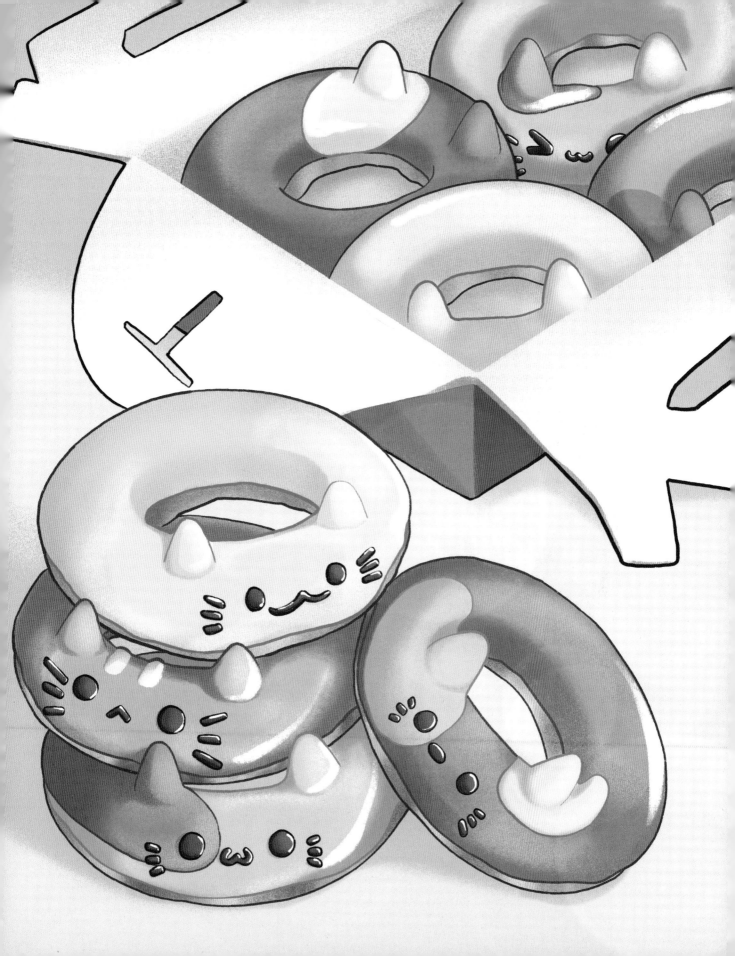

1 To make the honey milk donuts: In the bowl of a stand mixer, combine the warm milk, yeast, eggs, and honey.

2 Sift the flour into the bowl and add the nutmeg. Combine on medium speed with a dough hook attachment for 8 minutes, or until incorporated and soft. Add 1½ tablespoons of the butter and combine for 2 minutes. Add the remaining 1½ tablespoons butter and combine for another 2 minutes, or until the dough is super soft, smooth, and elastic.

3 Grease a clean bowl with butter and add the dough to it. Cover with plastic wrap and let the dough sit somewhere warm for an hour, or until doubled in size.

4 Turn out the dough on a work surface lined with parchment paper and degas it. Smack the big pockets of air gently out of the dough by turning it over and patting it repeatedly. Divide the dough into 12 equal-size pieces. Form each piece into a ball by kneading. Working with one ball at a time, create a smooth dough by holding the piece of dough with both hands and pushing in your thumbs underneath while curling/folding the edges to the underside. Pinch the bottom seam together where the edges meet. Now, hold the piece of dough again with both hands and, using your thumbs, pierce a hole in the center, stretching the hole to 1½ inches (4 cm) wide while working the dough into a donut shape, about 3½ inches (9 cm) wide. You won't be removing any dough from the hole but working it into the rest of the dough to shape the donut. Repeat with the remaining dough balls.

5 Line a baking tray with parchment paper. Place the donuts on the baking tray, cover the tray with a towel, and let the donuts rise again, somewhere warm, for 30 minutes. The donuts are done rising when you gently poke the surface and the dough springs back 75 to 80 percent of the way. If it does not spring back, then the donut is ruined and will absorb too much oil; if it springs all the way back, then it is not done proofing.

6 Fill a large heavy-bottomed pot with at least 3 inches (7.5 cm) of the canola oil and heat the oil between 350°F (175°C), measuring with a thermometer or a small piece of dough sizzling when it hits the hot oil. Working in batches, place 3 donuts in the oil at a time and cook for 2 minutes per side. Remove from the oil and place onto a rack to cool completely.

7 To decorate the donuts: For the cat ears, use a small knife to poke 2 small holes on each end of the top of each donut, then snugly fit an almond in each hole.

8 In a small bowl, mix the 1 cup (120 g) confectioners' sugar and milk together for royal icing. Divide the royal icing among four bowls. Add the yellow, teal, and pink food colorings to three of the bowls and the instant coffee powder for brown to the remaining bowl. Stir to incorporate the colors.

9 To ice the donuts, lay a donut, top side down, in the icing color of choice to fully coat the top, almond ears and all. Use a chopstick to pick up the donut by the hole, letting most of the excess icing drip off. Place onto a rack to let the icing set, about 5 minutes. Repeat for the remaining donuts. To create cat spots, use a chopstick to hold the donut through the hole. (Holding the donut with your hands can melt and crack the base icing coat.)

Lightly dip the donut diagonally onto another icing color or two to add the spots. Lift with the chopstick, let the excess icing drip off, and place back onto the rack to set for another 5 minutes. Repeat for the remaining donuts.

10 Moving on to the face details, add a teaspoon each of confectioners' sugar to the brown and pink icings and mix until they turn into a thick paste. Place the icings into separate small piping bags and cut a small hole at the tip of each bag. Using either color, pipe the mouth by drawing a horizontal number-three (3) or an upside-down V shape on a donut. With the same color, draw small dots for the eyes or a horizontal

V shape for a wink and 3 whiskers per cheek. If you want, add a nose with the same color by drawing a small circle that connects to the middle peak of the mouth. Let the facial features set, about 5 minutes. Repeat for the remaining donuts.

11 Pack your donuts in a box and get ready to brighten your coworkers' day!

NOTES
- **If you are allergic to nuts, you can use small chocolate candies or dried fruit for the ears.**
- **Try to keep the cats' facial features small. This will result in a cuter anime-style character.**

"It's like a donut party."

—Rin Toyama, *New Game!*

CHARMY'S AFTER-BATTLE DESSERT

★ ANIME ★
BLACK CLOVER
SEASON 1   EPISODE 78
PEASANT TRAP

Throughout this anime, Charmy is seen making, eating, or thinking about food constantly. Her "after-battle dessert" is named so because she offers it to the winner of the duels as a reward, and in this episode, she gives it to Yuno, who makes her swoon with his kind comments. To replicate this dessert, I created giant vanilla-milk cupcakes topped with homemade strawberry buttercream frosting.

YIELD **6** CUPCAKES   PREP **20** MINUTES   COOK **15** MINUTES

SPECIAL TOOLS

6-cup jumbo muffin tin

6 jumbo cupcake liners

Sifter

SOFT VANILLA-MILK CUPCAKES

1½ cups (180 g) all-purpose flour

2 tablespoons milk powder

1 teaspoon baking powder

Pinch salt

½ cup (115 g) unsalted butter

1 cup (200 g) granulated sugar

2 large eggs, at room temperature

1 teaspoon vanilla extract

½ cup (120 ml) whole milk

STRAWBERRY BUTTERCREAM FROSTING

½ cup (115 g) unsalted butter, at room temperature

¼ cup (25 g) freeze-dried strawberries, ground into powder

Pinch salt

1 teaspoon vanilla extract

1¼ cups (150 g) confectioners' sugar

3 tablespoons heavy whipping cream

Zest of 1 organic lemon

½ tablespoon fresh lemon juice

ICING GLAZE

2 tablespoons milk

¼ cup (30 g) confectioners' sugar

Pinch salt

FOR ASSEMBLY

4 strawberries, trimmed and left whole

4 sprigs (1 inch, or 2.5 cm, long) rosemary

4 vanilla wafer cookies

1 To make the soft vanilla-milk cupcakes: Preheat the oven to 350°F (175°C; gas mark 4). Line the cups of the muffin tin with the cupcake liners and set aside.

2 In a medium bowl, sift together the flour, milk powder, baking powder, and pinch of salt.

3 In a separate medium bowl, cream the ½ cup (115 g) butter and granulated sugar with a whisk until pale yellow. Add the eggs, 1 teaspoon vanilla, and ½ cup (120 ml) milk and stir to incorporate.

4 Add the dry ingredients to the bowl with the wet ingredients and fully incorporate until there are no clumps, scraping down the sides of the bowl if needed. Distribute the batter evenly among the cups of the prepared muffin tin.

5 Bake for 22 to 25 minutes, until slightly browned, the tops have puffed, and a toothpick inserted into the center of a cupcake comes out clean. Once warm to the touch, remove the cupcakes, still in the cupcake liners, from the tin and transfer to a rack to cool completely.

6 To make the strawberry buttercream frosting: Add the ½ cup (115 g) butter to a medium bowl and mix with a spatula until softened. Add the freeze-dried strawberry powder, salt, 1 teaspoon vanilla, and 1¼ cups (150 g) confectioners' sugar and, using a hand mixer with the whisk attachment, whip on medium speed until combined, about 2 minutes. Add the heavy cream and whip on medium speed until fluffy and stiff peaks form, 4 to 5 minutes. Add the lemon zest and juice and mix for another minute. Place the buttercream in a piping bag with a ½-inch (12 mm) round tip, or cut a hole of that size at the tip.

7 To make the icing glaze: In a small bowl, mix the 2 tablespoons milk, ¼ cup (30 g) confectioners' sugar, and pinch of salt until syrupy.

8 To assemble: Working with one cooled cupcake at a time, still in the liner, pipe the strawberry buttercream around the perimeter of the top of the cupcake, then drizzle the icing glaze on the peak (center) of the cupcake, letting it drip down the top (the buttercream perimeter will prevent it from dripping farther down the sides). Top with a strawberry and a sprig of rosemary. Push a vanilla wafer into the cupcake behind the strawberry so that it stands upright.

> **"I could watch you fight like that all day long. Here, I brought your usual post-battle dessert!"**
>
> —Charmy Pappitson, *Black Clover*

KIKI'S CHOCOLATE CAKE

ANIME
KIKI'S DELIVERY SERVICE

A Studio Ghibli classic, *Kiki's Delivery Service* is about the young witch-in-training, Kiki, who uses her flying powers to run errands for people. Madame, whom Kiki helped with a herring pie to deliver to her granddaughter, gifts Kiki this chocolate cake as a thanks for all her help, but Kiki isn't able to eat it because she has to save her friend who is in danger. I made this cake as a two-tiered chocolate cake, filled with a whipped ganache and topped with a silky ganache glaze. I prefer bitter chocolate, but feel free to use whatever chocolate you like!

 YIELD 8 SERVINGS **PREP 1 HOUR** **REST 1 HOUR** **COOK 45 MINUTES** **DECORATE 20 MINUTES**

SPECIAL TOOLS

2 (9-inch, or 23-cm) round cake pans

Sifter

Rotating cake stand (optional)

CHOCOLATE CAKE

Nonstick cooking spray, for greasing

1 cup (240 ml) milk

½ cup (115 g) unsalted butter, melted

1 teaspoon vanilla extract

1 cup (240 ml) boiling water

1¼ cup (120 g) unsweetened cocoa powder

2 cups (240 g) all-purpose flour

1¾ cup (350 g) sugar

1½ teaspoons baking powder

1½ teaspoons baking soda

¼ teaspoon salt

WHIPPED GANACHE

1⅔ cups (405 ml) heavy whipping cream

1¼ cups (400 g) chopped 70% cacao dark chocolate or dark chocolate chips

CHOCOLATE GANACHE GLAZE

1 cup (240 ml) heavy whipping cream

1 cup (175 g) chopped semisweet chocolate or semisweet chocolate chips

2 tablespoons unsalted butter

FOR DECORATING

¼ cup (40 g) white chocolate melts

Red and green gel food coloring

《 CONTINUED 》

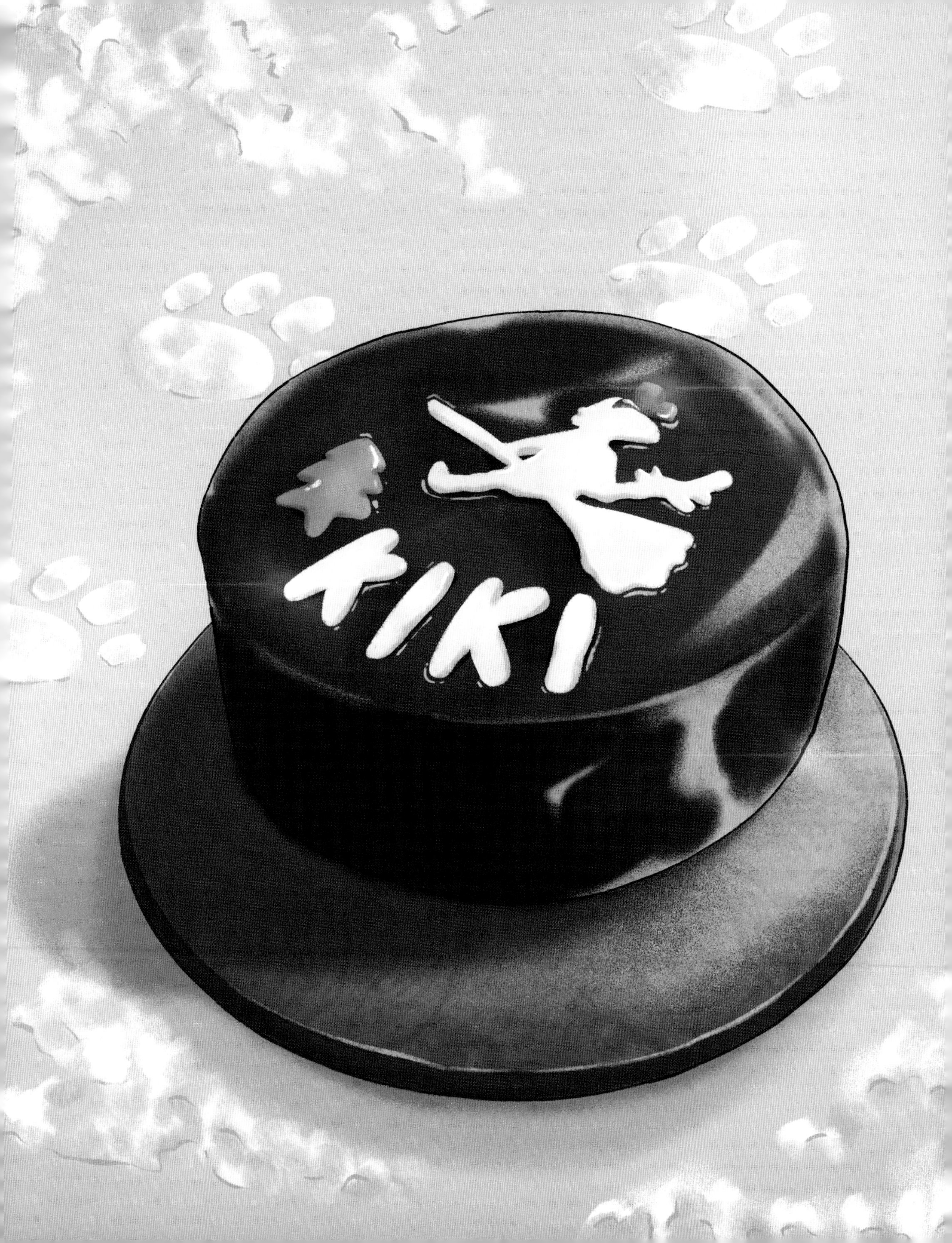
KIKI

KIKI'S CHOCOLATE CAKE STEPS

1 To make the chocolate cake: Preheat the oven to 325°F (165°C; gas mark 3). Line the sides and bottoms of the two 9-inch (23 cm) round cake pans with parchment paper. Grease the parchment paper with nonstick cooking spray and set aside.

2 In a large bowl, stir together the milk, melted butter, and vanilla extract. In a small heatproof bowl, mix the boiling water with the cocoa powder. Add the cocoa mixture to the bowl with the rest of the wet ingredients and combine well. In a separate medium bowl, sift together the flour, sugar, baking powder, baking soda, and salt together. Add the dry ingredients to the bowl with the wet ingredients and mix until combined. Do not overmix.

3 Divide the cake batter between the two prepared pans, tap the pans twice on a surface to get rid of large air bubbles, and bake for 45 minutes, or until the tops are flat and a toothpick inserted into the center comes out clean. Immediately after baking, place a piece of parchment paper on top of each cake and flip over to remove from the pan onto a rack for 10 minutes to achieve a smooth top. Flip the cakes back to their original positions and let cool to room temperature.

4 To make the whipped ganache: In a microwave-safe container, microwave the 1⅔ cups (405 ml) heavy cream until hot, 1 to 2 minutes. Put the 1¼ cups (400 g) dark chocolate into a medium heatproof bowl, then pour over the hot heavy cream and stir until all the chocolate is melted. Refrigerate until the melted chocolate is cool to the touch, about 15 minutes. Remove from the refrigerator and, using a hand mixer with a whisk attachment, whip until fluffy or stiff peaks form.

5 To assemble: Once the cakes have rested and cooled, level them if needed. Place one cake on the rotating cake stand (if using) or a plate and spread and smooth half of the whipped ganache on top. Place the second cake on top and add the rest of the whipped ganache over the top and the sides. Fill in any gaps between the cake layers. Smooth the exterior using an offset spatula for a polished look. Place the layered cake in the refrigerator until the chocolate ganache has set and is solid to the touch, about 15 minutes.

6 Meanwhile, make the chocolate ganache glaze: In a microwave-safe container, microwave the 1 cup (240 ml) heavy cream until hot, 1 to 2 minutes. Put the 1 cup (175 g) semisweet chocolate and butter into a medium heatproof bowl, then pour in the hot heavy cream. Stir until all the chocolate and butter is melted.

7 Set up a drizzling station consisting of a wire rack on top of a baking tray. Remove the cake from the refrigerator and place it on the rack. Carefully pour the chocolate ganache glaze over the top of the cake to cover it entirely. Once glazed, transfer the cake to a cake stand or a serving plate to set.

8 To decorate: Make a stencil on a piece of parchment paper by first tracing the cake pan's circumference with a pencil. Within the cake pan outline, draw Kiki at the top half of the cake, riding her broomstick with Jiji (her cat) hanging onto the back of her dress; KIKI in large capitalized letters beneath Kiki on her broomstick; and a small and simple pine tree in the remaining space on the left side of the scene. Use the illustration on page 149 for reference.

9 Melt the white chocolate melts according to the package instructions. Once melted, divide among three small bowls, adding red food coloring to one, green to another, and leaving the third white. Stir to incorporate the colors, then transfer to three piping bags, cutting a ⅛-inch (3 mm) hole at their tips. Wait until the melted chocolate turns from hot to warm to allow the chocolate to thicken and make it easier to pipe and fill in the stencil shapes. Run over the designs with a small spatula or toothpick while warm to get a smooth surface. Wait for the chocolate decorations to harden, then transfer carefully onto the cake using an offset spatula for support and serve.

NOTE

White chocolate–melt decorations are extremely fragile, so I recommend making multiple decorations in case one breaks. Melted white chocolate melts that haven't had food coloring added are extremely forgiving, so if you make a mistake, simply microwave the chocolate until melted and use it again.

"It's dusty with flour. . . . I think, by tomorrow, I'll be a white cat."

—Jiji, *Kiki's Delivery Service*

CAT COOKIES

★ ANIME ★
KAKEGURUI XX
SEASON 2 · EPISODE 4
THE CONNECTED GIRLS

The students of Hyakkaou Private Academy participate in a school-wide gambling ring in which the winnings are used to determine their social statuses. In the episode before this one, two mean girls harass a girl, whom they call "Mittens Girl" because she is a "housepet" with a low status in the school, trying to force her to gamble with them and purposely lose. Rei Batsubami saves the girl from the situation, and as a thank you, "Mittens Girl" gifts him these cute cat cookies the next day.

YIELD 8 COOKIES · **PREP** 30 MINUTES · **FREEZE** 30 MINUTES · **COOK** 8 MINUTES · **DECORATE** 20 MINUTES

COOKIES

¼ cup (55 g) unsalted butter, soft and at room temperature

¼ cup (50 g) granulated sugar

1 large egg

1 teaspoon vanilla extract

Pinch salt

1 cup (120 g) all-purpose flour

½ teaspoon baking powder

ICING

¼ cup (30 g) confectioners' sugar

2½ teaspoons milk (or water), divided

Red and brown gel food coloring

½ teaspoon unsweetened cocoa powder

((STEPS))

1 To make the cookies: In a large bowl, using a hand mixer with a beater attachment, cream the butter and granulated sugar until combined and pale yellow. Add the egg, vanilla, and salt and mix on medium-high speed until fluffed, doubled in volume, and ribbons are left in the batter while mixing, 5 to 6 minutes.

2 In a medium bowl, whisk the flour and baking powder until fully combined. Add the dry ingredients to the bowl with the wet ingredients and mix on medium speed until

the dough comes together as a ball, about 3 minutes.

3 Place the dough in between two pieces of parchment paper and roll to ¼-inch (6 mm) thickness with a rolling pin. Place in the freezer for about 30 minutes, or until the dough is rock hard.

4 Make a cat stencil with parchment paper and a pencil. Start by tracing around the bottom of a drinking cup (with a diameter of around 2½ inches, or 6 cm). Draw cat ears on top of the circle by drawing 2 triangles with rounded points. Cut out the parchment-paper cat and erase any pencil markings.

5 Take out the frozen dough from the freezer and place it on a cutting board. Remove the top piece of parchment paper and place the cat stencil on the dough as a guide to cut around. Cut out the cookies with a small knife and place them onto a baking tray lined with parchment paper.

6 Place the cookies in the freezer again and preheat the oven to 350°F (175°C; gas mark 4).

7 Bake the cookies for 8 to 9 minutes, or until slightly browned on the edges. Let cool completely on a rack before decorating.

8 Meanwhile, make the icing: In a small bowl, mix the confectioners' sugar and 2 teaspoons of the milk until incorporated and thick. Divide the icing among three small bowls.

Add 2 drops of red food coloring to one bowl, a scant drop of brown food coloring to another bowl for light brown, and the cocoa powder and remaining ½ teaspoon of milk to the third bowl for dark brown. Stir to incorporate the colors into the icing. Place each icing color in a small piping bag. Place the smallest tip on each piping bag or cut a tiny hole at the tip of each piping bag and draw the facial details on the cooled cookies. With the red icing, draw circles for the eyes and fill them in. With the light brown icing, draw a wide oval for the nose and a horizontal D shape for the smile and fill them in. With the dark brown icing, add 3 thick lines for whiskers at the side edges of each cookie.

9 Let the icing set at room temperature before gifting to your friends.

NOTE
Freezing the cookie dough makes it easier to cut out precise shapes. It also helps the cookies keep their shapes during baking.

"You were a knight in shining armor. . . . Anyway, thank you! These are for you, if you'd like."
— "Mittens Girl," *Kakegurui XX*

DEADLY DELICIOUS BLUEBERRY MERINGUE PIE

★ANIME★
THAT TIME I GOT REINCARNATED AS A SLIME

SEASON 1 EPISODE 11
GABIRU IS HERE!

Shion cooks dinner for the gang and everyone except Rimuru declines the offer to eat it. Rimuru, confused, doesn't think much of it until Shion brings out the dish: an amorphous blob of blue and purple so foul that waves of evil waft up from it, and he even thinks it's possessed. I wanted to make my own version of this deadly dish, but deadly *delicious*!

YIELD **6** SERVINGS PREP **25** MINUTES REST **3.5** HOURS COOK **40** MINUTES

SPECIAL TOOLS

6 x 3-inch (15 x 7.5 cm) round cake pan

Pie weights or uncooked rice or beans

Kitchen torch (optional)

SHORT-CRUST PASTRY

1 cup (120 g) all-purpose flour

1 tablespoon sugar

6 tablespoons cold unsalted butter, cut into ¼-inch (6 mm) cubes

Pinch salt

2 large eggs, 1 cold and 1 beaten, divided

BLUEBERRY LEMON FILLING

3 cups (435 g) blueberries

¼ cup (50 g) sugar

1 tablespoon fresh lemon juice

2 teaspoons lemon zest

¼ teaspoon salt

2 tablespoons tapioca starch or cornstarch

1 tablespoon unsalted butter

SWISS MERINGUE

3 large egg whites

1 cup (200 g) sugar

¼ teaspoon cream of tartar

1 teaspoon vanilla extract

Navy blue gel food coloring

FOR DECORATING

Silver luster dust (optional)

《 CONTINUED 》》

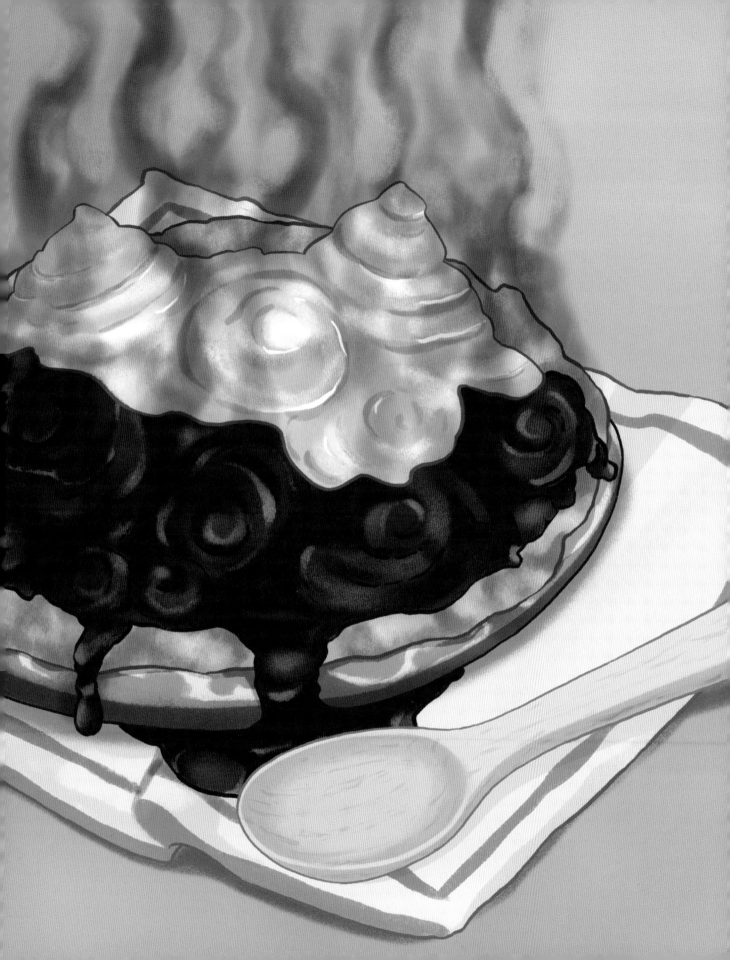

DEADLY DELICIOUS BLUEBERRY MERINGUE PIE STEPS

1 To make the short-crust pastry: In a medium bowl, combine the flour, 1 tablespoon sugar, pinch of salt, and cubed butter. Squish the butter and flour together with your fingertips until the mixture resembles grainy sand. Crack in the cold egg and use your hands to mix it into a dough. Knead a few times to make it come together. Place the dough on a piece of plastic wrap and roughly shape it into a circle ½ inch (12 mm) thick. Refrigerate until hardened, about 20 minutes.

2 Preheat the oven to 400°F (205°C; gas mark 6). Remove the short-crust pastry from the plastic wrap and place between two pieces of parchment paper. Roll out the dough with a rolling pin into a 9-inch (23 cm) circle. Place the dough circle on the cake pan, then press it into the pan with 2-inch-tall (5 cm) sides. Dock the dough all over with a fork, then place a piece of parchment paper on top and add the pie weights.

3 Bake for 15 minutes. Carefully remove the pie weights and parchment paper. Dock areas with a fork where the pastry has puffed, if any. Brush all surfaces of the pie shell with the beaten egg and place back in the oven until golden brown, 5 to 8 minutes. Let cool.

4 Meanwhile, make the blueberry lemon filling: In a medium saucepan, mix the blueberries, ¼ cup (50 g) sugar, lemon zest, lemon juice, and ¼ teaspoon salt together. Turn the heat to medium and cook, stirring occasionally, until the blueberries are soft, about 8 minutes. Transfer 2 tablespoons of released blueberry juice from the pan to a small bowl. Add the tapioca starch to the bowl and mix to make a slurry. Add the slurry to the saucepan, stir to combine, and let simmer until thickened, about 3 minutes. Remove from the heat and mix in the butter. Let the mixture come to room temperature before pouring it into the cooked pie shell. Once added to the pie shell, refrigerate until set, 3 to 4 hours.

5 Right before serving the pie, make the Swiss meringue: In a large bowl, using a hand mixer with a whisk attachment, mix the egg whites, 1 cup (200 g) sugar, and cream of tartar on medium speed until just combined, about 1 minute.

6 Prepare a double boiler by filling a saucepan slightly larger than the bowl with the egg whites with at least 1½ inches (4 cm) of water and bringing it to a boil. Once the water is boiling, reduce the heat to medium and place the bowl on top. Whisk constantly until the mixture reaches 160°F (71°C), measuring with a candy thermometer. Remove the bowl from the heat and, using the hand mixer with a clean, dry whisk attachment, whip on medium-high speed, until stiff peaks form, 5 to 7 minutes. Add the vanilla and 3 drops of the food coloring and gently fold in using a spatula. Transfer the meringue to a piping bag, cut a ¾-inch (2 cm) hole at the tip, and use immediately.

7 To decorate: Pipe 3 large mountains of swirls on one-half of the pie, and make it messy! You may torch the tops of the meringue with a kitchen torch for color, or leave the meringue as is. (The egg whites in the meringue have been cooked by the hot sugar, so it is safe to consume without torching or browning). Sprinkle the meringue with luster dust (if using) and serve immediately.

MONSTER CELL TRUFFLES

★ ANIME ★
ONE-PUNCH MAN

SEASON 2 EPISODE 7
THE CLASS S HEROES

Monster cells are mutated virus cells that transform humans into monsters upon ingestion. Multiple characters take them over the course of the anime/manga, but they first appear in this episode. I replicated their look and portability, but for a more palatable taste, I adapted them into rich, soft chocolate truffles with a crunchy chocolate-coated exterior.

YIELD **12** TRUFFLES · PREP **10** MINUTES · FREEZE **10** MINUTES · COOK **15** MINUTES

TRUFFLES

1 cup (170 g) finely chopped white chocolate

¼ cup (60 ml) heavy whipping cream

3 tablespoons unsalted butter, at room temperature

Pinch salt

Navy blue gel food coloring

Confectioners' sugar, for dusting

CRISPY RICE

1 cup (165 g) white candy melts

Purple and red gel food coloring

½ cup (13 g) crispy rice cereal, with the rice crisps crushed in half

·····《《 STEPS 》》 ·····

1 To make the truffles: Place the chopped white chocolate in a medium microwave-safe bowl. In a small microwave-safe bowl, microwave the heavy cream until it is hot, 40 to 60 seconds (or heat in small saucepan over low heat until hot). Pour the hot heavy cream into the bowl with the white chocolate. Let the chocolate melt into the cream for 1 minute, then whisk until smooth and fully combined.

2 Add the butter and salt and stir to combine. Add 2 drops of the navy blue food coloring and use the whisk to incorporate. (If you want to give the monster cells stripes, make swirls in the batter instead of fully combining the food coloring.) Cover the mixture with plastic wrap, ensuring that it touches its surface. Freeze until solid, about 10 minutes.

····· 《《 CONTINUED 》》 ·····

MONSTER CELL TRUFFLES STEPS (CONTINUED)

3 Line a baking tray with parchment paper and lightly dust it with confectioners' sugar. Using a small scoop or a spoon, scoop white chocolate truffles onto the tray. Once all the truffles are portioned, lightly dust your hands with confectioners' sugar and form each into a ball. Place the truffles back in the refrigerator until needed.

4 To make the crispy rice: If using white candy melts, melt according to the package instructions. Add 2 drops of purple gel food coloring and 1 drop of red to the melted chocolate. Mix with a spatula or whisk until the desired color is reached.

5 Add the crushed crispy rice cereal to the melted chocolate and mix until fully coated. Roll a white chocolate truffle in the mixture to coat the exterior. Remove the truffle with a spoon and place onto a piece of clean parchment paper. Repeat for all the truffles. Let cool until hardened, 3 to 5 minutes.

"The thought of getting stronger tempts you? A monster cell. All you need to do is ingest this into your body."

—Gale Wind, *One-Punch Man*

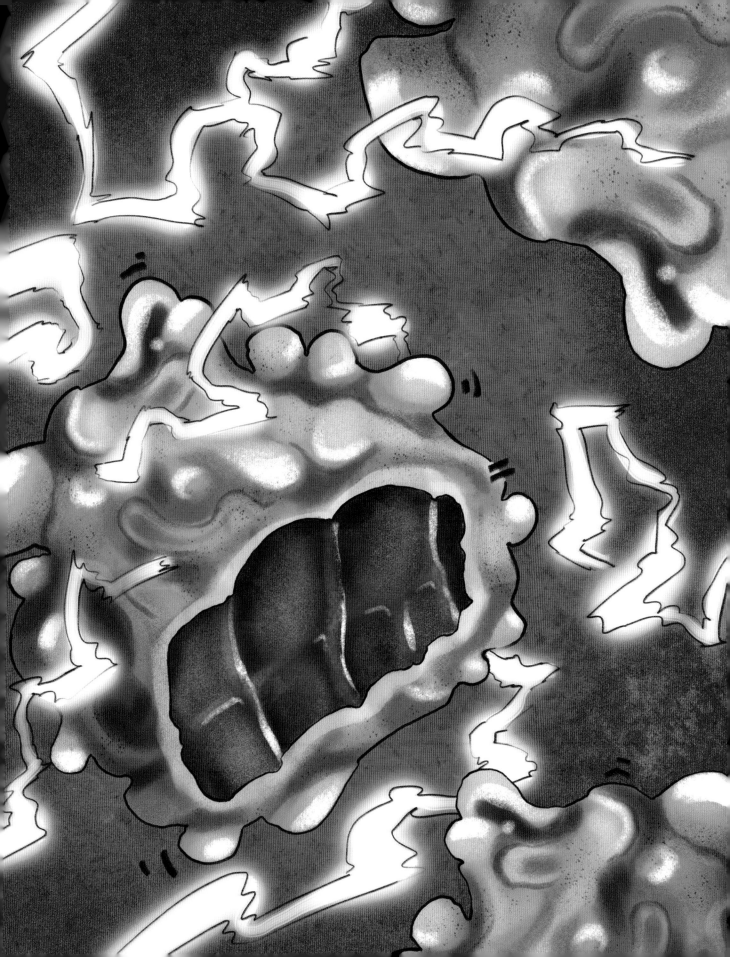

WHIPPED CHOCOLATE CAKE

★ ANIME ★

KOMI CAN'T COMMUNICATE

VOLUME 9 | CHAPTER 116

PREPARING FOR VALENTINES

Komi, a beautiful girl who appears to be aloof, suffers from extreme social anxiety and struggles to make friends as a result. In this chapter of the manga, Komi is invited by her friends to make a chocolate cake for Valentine's Day after school. I made some adjustments to the manga recipe to make it extra creamy and chocolaty.

YIELD 6 SERVINGS · **PREP** 25 MINUTES · **COOK** 40 MINUTES

EQUIPMENT

7 x 3-inch (18 x 7.5 cm) or 8 x 2-inch (20 x 5 cm) round cake pan

WHIPPED CHOCOLATE CAKE

½ cup (85 g) semisweet chocolate chips

¼ cup (55 g) unsalted butter

½ cup (50 g) unsweetened cocoa powder

2 tablespoons hazelnut milk (or any dairy or nondairy milk)

4 large egg whites

½ cup (100 g) sugar, divided

4 large egg yolks

1½ tablespoons brandy (or 1 teaspoon vanilla extract)

2½ tablespoons all-purpose flour

2 pinches salt

SOFT WHIP

1½ cups (360 ml) heavy whipping cream

½ tablespoon sugar

1 teaspoon vanilla extract

《 CONTINUED 》

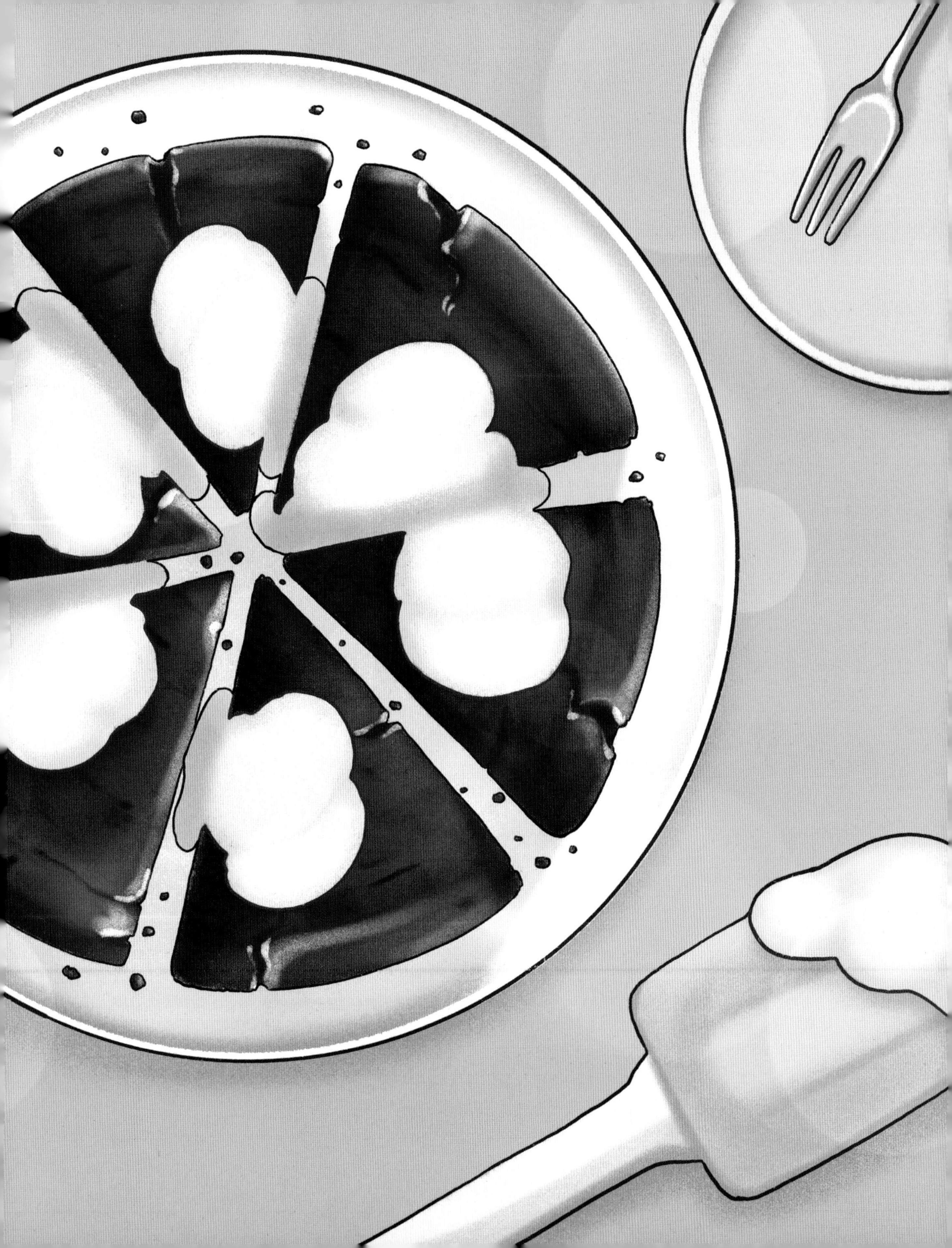

WHIPPED CHOCOLATE CAKE STEPS

1 To make the whipped chocolate cake: Preheat the oven to 350°F (175°C; gas mark 4). Line the sides and bottom of the 7 x 3-inch (18 x 7.5 cm) or 8 x 2-inch (20 x 5 cm) round cake pan with parchment paper and set aside.

2 In a small microwave-safe bowl, microwave the chocolate chips and butter in 15- to 30-second increments, until melted, stirring in between. Add the cocoa powder and hazelnut milk and stir until fully combined.

3 In a medium bowl, using a hand mixer with a whisk attachment, whip the egg whites and ¼ cup (50 g) of the sugar. Start at low speed, and once frothy, increase to medium-high until stiff peaks form, about 6 minutes.

4 In a large bowl, whip the egg yolks and the remaining ¼ cup (50 g) sugar with the same whisk attachment and whip until pale in color and tripled in volume. Add the brandy and mix on low speed until combined. Using a spatula, slowly fold in the melted chocolate in thirds.

5 Whisk one-third of the stiff egg whites into the chocolate-yolk mixture to loosen. Continue to fold in the stiff egg white mixture in one-third increments. Add the flour and salt and fold until combined, aiming to fold less than ten times.

6 Place the chocolate cake batter into the prepared cake pan, lightly tap the pan on a surface to get rid of larger air bubbles, and bake for 18 to 20 minutes, until a toothpick inserted in the center comes out clean. Let the cake rest for a few minutes. (Deflating is normal for soufflé-like cakes and is accurate to the anime.)

7 To make the soft whip: Add all the soft whip ingredients to a medium bowl and, using a hand mixer with a clean whisk attachment, whip on slow speed, gradually increasing to medium-high speed, until soft peaks form, around 3 minutes.

8 Slice the cake into wedges and serve each slice with a dollop of soft whip.

"Food tastes better if you eat it with someone else."

—Osana Najimi, *Komi Can't Communicate*

MOCHA POKÉ PUFFS

★ ANIME ★
POKÉMON XY
SEASON 17 EPISODE 25
A BATTLE BY ANY
OTHER NAME!

Serena has baked two flavors of fresh, human-friendly Poké Puffs for her Pokémon and friends to try—one pink and fruity and the other brown and chocolaty—but Slurpuff comes along and steals one, prompting Slurpuff's trainer, Miette, to insult Serena's Poké Puffs. Later in the episode, Serena and Miette compete in the Poké Puffs Contest, both making it to the final round with a third competitor, but I don't want to spoil who wins! I chose to make the chocolate ones with a mocha twist.

YIELD 8 PUFFS · **PREP** 30 MINUTES · **REST** 30 MINUTES · **COOK** 1 HOUR

SPECIAL TOOLS

Sifter

COFFEE PASTRY CREAM

2 large eggs

1 large egg yolk

¼ cup (30 g) cornstarch

2 cups (480 ml) whole milk

¼ cup (50 g) granulated sugar

1½ tablespoons instant coffee powder

¼ teaspoon salt

1 teaspoon vanilla extract

½ (3.5-ounce, or 100-g) semisweet chocolate bar, finely chopped

CHOCOLATE CREAM PUFFS

⅔ cup (80 g) all-purpose flour

1½ tablespoons unsweetened cocoa powder

¼ cup (55g) unsalted butter

¼ cup (60 ml) water

¼ cup (60 ml) whole milk, plus more if needed

1 teaspoon sugar

¼ teaspoon salt

2 large eggs, beaten

COFFEE DIPLOMAT CREAM

1½ cups (360 ml) heavy whipping cream

CHOCOLATE DIP

1 (3.5-ounce, or 100-g) white chocolate bar

⅓ (3.5-ounce, or 100-g) semisweet chocolate bar

((CONTINUED))

1 To make the coffee pastry cream: In a medium heatproof bowl, whisk together the 2 eggs, egg yolk, and cornstarch thoroughly.

2 In a medium saucepan, stir together the 2 cups (480 ml) milk, ¼ cup (50 g) sugar, instant coffee powder, and ¼ teaspoon salt. Bring to a rapid simmer over medium heat, then remove from the heat. Add one-third of the milk mixture to the egg mixture and whisk immediately until incorporated.

3 Pour the entire egg-milk mixture into the saucepan the milk was heated in and stir to combine. Place over medium heat and continuously whisk until bubbling and thickened into a paste, 2 to 3 minutes. Remove from the heat, add the vanilla and ½ semisweet chocolate bar, and mix until combined. Transfer to a heatproof container and cover the coffee pastry cream with plastic wrap, making sure that the mixture and plastic wrap are touching to prevent a film from forming on the top. Refrigerate until cooled and set into a hard jellylike substance.

4 Meanwhile, make the chocolate cream puffs: Preheat the oven to 450°F (230°C; gas mark 8).

5 In a medium bowl, sift together the flour and cocoa powder and mix to combine. In a medium saucepan, stir together the butter, water, ¼ cup (60 ml) milk, 1 teaspoon sugar, and ¼ teaspoon salt. Bring to a boil over medium heat, then remove from the heat. Add the sifted flour and cocoa powder and vigorously whisk with a spatula until the mixture becomes homogeneous. Place the saucepan over medium-high heat. After 2 to 3 minutes, when stirring, there should be a thin film of the mixture sticking to the bottom of the pan.

Continue cooking for another 2 to 3 minutes until this film disappears and a ball of dough forms. Remove from the heat and transfer to a bowl of a stand mixer.

6 Mix on low speed with a paddle attachment for 2 minutes to cool it down. Add half of the beaten eggs and mix until incorporated. Add the rest of the beaten eggs and mix again until incorporated. Continue to mix until the batter resembles soft peaks, or when the batter is scooped with a spatula or the paddle attachment and raised in the air, it hangs off the tool in a V shape. If the mixture is too dry, add 1 teaspoon of milk at a time and mix until the right consistency is reached.

7 Add the batter to a piping bag and cut a ½-inch (12 mm) hole at the tip. Line a baking tray with parchment paper or a silicone mat. To form the puffs, pipe the batter into 2-inch (5 cm) circles, 1 inch (2.5 cm) tall, for a total of 8 puffs, leaving 2 inches (5 cm) in between each one. Dampen your fingers with water and gently press down any peaks or bumps on the puffs.

8 Bake for 10 minutes, then, without opening the oven, reduce the oven temperature to 350°F (175°C; gas mark 4) and bake for another 30 minutes. Check the puffs by opening the oven and seeing if they are firm and browned; if not, quickly shut the oven door and bake for another 5 minutes. Once baked, turn the oven off with the puffs inside and leave the oven door ajar for 10 minutes. Remove from the oven and, using a toothpick or a small knife, pierce a ¼-inch-wide (6 mm) hole in the bottom of each puff.

9 To make the coffee diplomat cream: Remove the set coffee pastry cream from the refrigerator and whisk until softened.

10 Add the heavy whipping cream to a medium bowl and, using a hand mixer with a whisk attachment, whip on high speed until soft peaks form, about 2 minutes. Add half of the coffee pastry cream to the soft whipped cream and mix until homogenous. Transfer the coffee diplomat cream to a piping bag.

11 To make the chocolate dip: In a small microwave-safe bowl, combine the white chocolate bar and ⅓ semisweet chocolate bar. Microwave until melted, about 40 seconds, then stir to combine.

12 To assemble: Cut a ¼-inch (6 mm) hole at the tip of the piping bag. Pipe the coffee diplomat cream into the hole in the base of each cream puff until full. Clean the bottom of the puffs by swiping away exposed cream with a knife. Dip the tops of the cream puffs into the chocolate dip, letting the excess drip off, then place onto a parchment-lined baking tray and refrigerate until the chocolate sets, about 10 minutes.

13 Place the remaining coffee pastry cream in a piping bag fitted with a basket-weave tip. Pipe vertical lines around the puff that are slightly diagonal and that slightly overlap from the bottom edge of the chocolate dip up to the center of the puff until the top is covered, creating a swirl effect. Repeat until the top is covered. Repeat for the remaining cream puffs and serve.

"They're great! That's the yummiest thing I've ever eaten in my life!"

—Ash Ketchum, *Pokémon XY*

PANDA SHAVED ICE PARFAIT

★ ANIME ★

POLAR BEAR CAFÉ

SEASON 1   EPISODE 5

PANDA GETS
ENTHUSIASTIC/
EVERYONE'S PARFAIT

The owners of Polar Bear Café are having a hard time updating their menu, so Sasako, a human waitress who works there, creates cute parfaits that resemble two of the patrons—Penguin and Panda—as well as the head chef, Polar Bear. Penguin, Panda, and Polar Bear are loving the idea until they witness customers eating their heads! I chose to replicate the adorable Panda parfait.

YIELD 2 SERVINGS · **PREP** 10 MINUTES · **FREEZE** 1 HOUR · **COOK** 10 MINUTES · **DECORATE** 20 MINUTES

CHOCOLATE SHAVED ICE

3 cups (720 ml) whole milk

3 tablespoons unsweetened cocoa powder

¼ cup (60 ml) condensed milk

Pinch salt

VANILLA MILK SHAVED ICE

1½ cups (360 ml) whole milk

¼ cup (60 ml) condensed milk

½ teaspoon vanilla extract

Pinch salt

TOPPINGS

1 pint (16 ounces, or 773 ml) vanilla ice cream

½ cup (60 ml) heavy whipping cream

1 teaspoon sugar

1½ tablespoons matcha powder, divided

1 ounce (28 g) white chocolate, finely chopped

4 sticks Chocolate Pocky (or any chocolate sticklike biscuit)

1 semisweet or dark chocolate bar (3½ ounces, or 100 g), chopped small

« STEPS »

1 To make the chocolate shaved ice: In a small saucepan, stir together all the chocolate shaved ice ingredients. Bring to a simmer over medium heat, stirring occasionally, to fully incorporate, then remove from the heat and let cool. Transfer the mixture to a gallon-size resealable plastic bag, lay the bag on its side in the freezer so that it hardens into a thin layer, and freeze until just about frozen and mostly ice.

« CONTINUED »

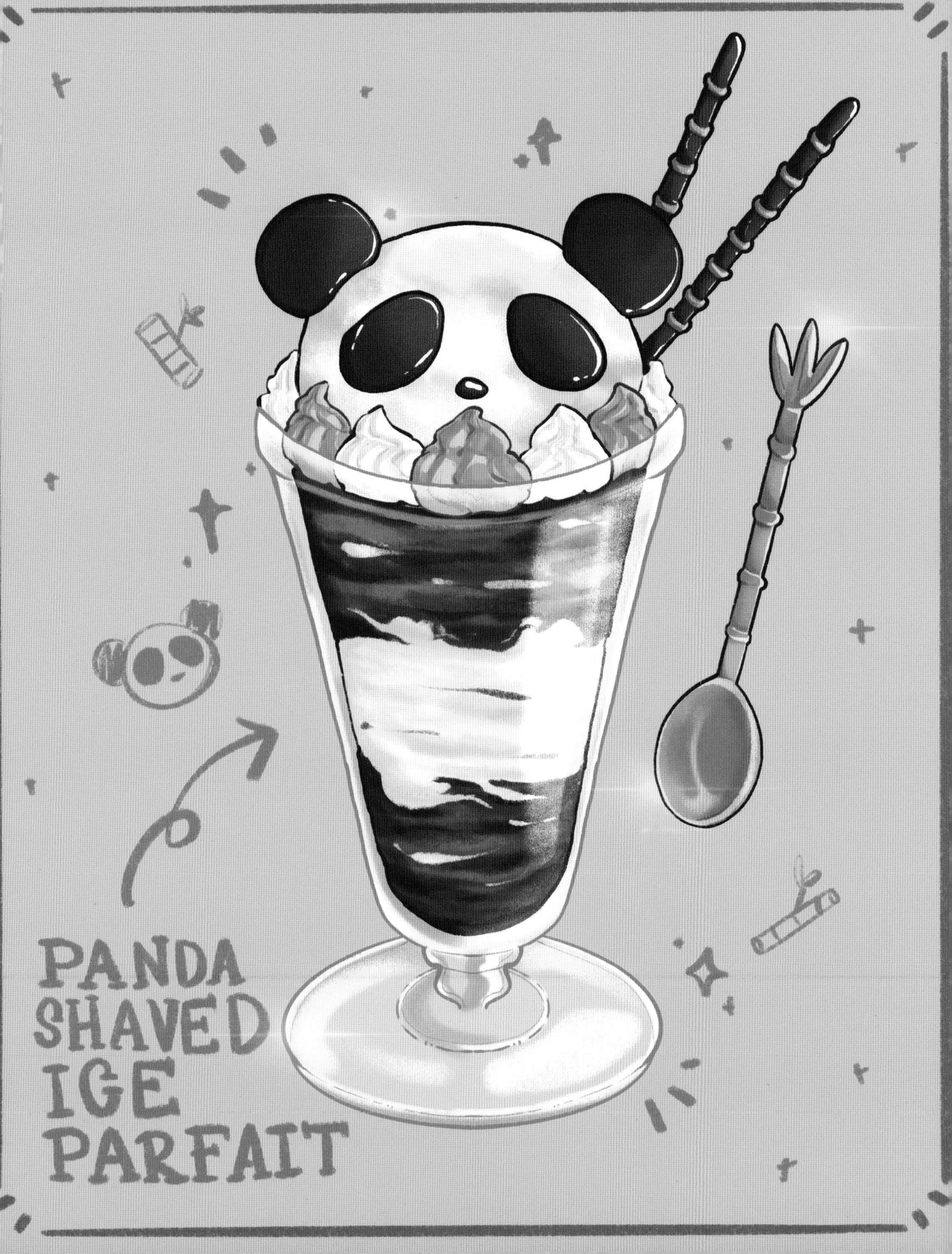
PANDA
SHAVED
ICE
PARFAIT

2 To make the vanilla milk shaved ice: Clean the small saucepan used for the chocolate shaved ice, then add all the vanilla milk shaved ice ingredients and stir to combine. Bring to a simmer over medium heat, stirring occasionally, to fully incorporate, then remove from the heat and let cool. Transfer the mixture to a gallon-size resealable plastic bag, lay the bag on its side in the freezer so that it hardens into a thin layer, and freeze until just about frozen and mostly ice.

3 To prepare and make the toppings: Make panda heads by scooping 2 perfect vanilla ice-cream scoops into a container or tray lined with parchment paper, then place in the freezer. (This helps the ice cream maintain its shape and melt slower when added to the parfait.)

4 In a medium bowl, make whipped cream by combining the heavy cream and sugar. Using a hand mixer with a whisk attachment, whip on high speed for 2 minutes, or until medium-stiff peaks form. Transfer one-half of the whipped cream to a small bowl and fold in 1 tablespoon of the matcha powder. Place the regular whipped cream and the matcha whipped cream in separate small piping bags and refrigerate.

5 Make bamboo biscuits by placing the white chocolate in a microwave-safe bowl and microwaving until melted, about 30 seconds. Add the remaining ½ tablespoon matcha powder to the melted chocolate and mix to combine. Stripe each Pocky with the white chocolate matcha by holding a Pocky over the chocolate bowl and using a spoon to drip a steady, thin stream of chocolate in a horizontal back-and-forth motion along the biscuit. Lay on a plate or tray lined with parchment paper and refrigerate until set, about 2 minutes, or until ready to use.

6 Lastly, make the panda face decorations. In a small bowl, microwave the semisweet or dark chocolate until melted, about 40 seconds. Place the melted chocolate in a piping bag and wait 4 to 5 minutes until slightly cooled and the chocolate becomes thicker and easier to pipe. Meanwhile, line a baking tray with parchment paper. Once the chocolate is slightly cooled, cut a ⅛-inch (3 mm) hole at the tip of the piping bag. Pipe onto the prepared baking tray four ¾-inch (2 cm) semicircles for the ears, four ¾-inch (2 cm) abstract circles, kind of like an ink blot, for the eye spots, and two ⅛-inch (3 mm) ovals for the noses. Refrigerate until set, about 2 minutes, or ready to use.

7 To assemble: Crush the chocolate and vanilla milk ice in the plastic bags with a rolling pin, using a rolling motion, until it has the texture of shaved ice. (You can also pulse the ice in a blender until the texture becomes like grated ice or fresh snow.) In a parfait glass, fill it one-third with chocolate shaved ice, then layer with another third of vanilla milk shaved ice, and then add another layer of chocolate shaved ice ½ inch (12 mm) from the top of the glass. Peel off a perfect scoop of vanilla ice cream from the parchment paper and place on top of the shaved ice, then carefully peel off the panda face decorations from the parchment paper and arrange them onto the scoop of ice cream. Cut ½-inch (12 mm) holes at the tips of the piping bags with whipped cream and pipe small dollops in alternating colors of white and matcha green around the base of the panda head. Lastly, poke 2 bamboo biscuits into the shaved ice behind the panda's head on the right side. Repeat for the remaining parfait. Serve immediately.

KERO'S PURIN

ANIME

CARDCAPTOR SAKURA

SEASON 1 EPISODE 1

SAKURA AND THE STRANGE MAGICAL BOOK

Kero is Sakura's companion in her journey to becoming the master of the cards. One of Kero's personality traits is his affinity for sweets, as he's constantly seen eating desserts—specifically purin (Japanese custard pudding), as witnessed in the first episode of the series. Along with the classic caramel topping, I created Kero's wings out of caramel to decorate each pudding!

YIELD 6 SERVINGS **PREP** 20 MINUTES **COOK** 1 HOUR

SPECIAL TOOLS

6 (8-ounce, or 240-ml) ramekins

CARAMEL

½ cup (100 g) sugar

2 tablespoons water

CLASSIC PURIN

3 large egg yolks

3 large eggs

⅓ cup (65 g) sugar

1 cup (240 ml) heavy whipping cream

2 cups (480 ml) milk

Pinch salt

1 teaspoon vanilla extract

FOR ASSEMBLY

½ cup (120 ml) heavy whipping cream, whipped to stiff peaks

‹‹ STEPS ››

1 To make the caramel: Have the ramekins at the ready and line a baking tray with parchment paper.

2 In a medium saucepan, heat the ½ cup (100 g) sugar and water over medium heat. Gently swirl the pan to cover the sugar with water. (At no point should you mix the caramel with any utensils; swirling is the most efficient way to prevent crystallization.) Watch the caramel closely as it turns an amber color, 9 to 10 minutes, swirling the pan if needed. Once it turns amber, let it cook for another minute, or until it becomes a caramel color. Remove from the heat and quickly pour a ⅛-inch (3 mm) layer into each ramekin.

3 While the caramel is hot, scoop some caramel onto a spoon and with a thin stream of caramel, draw Kero's wing design on the prepared baking tray. Start by drawing 3 horizontal curves, 2 to 2½ inches (5 to 6 cm) tall total, then connect them with a straight vertical line. Draw an identical pair of wings. Repeat for 5 more pairs of wings. Use the illustration on page 171 for reference. Let cool.

‹‹ CONTINUED ››

4 To make the classic purin: In a large heatproof bowl, vigorously mix the egg yolks, eggs, and ⅓ cup (65 g) sugar with a balloon whisk until fully combined, the mixture is pale yellow, and there are no visible egg white lumps when the whisk is lifted from the batter.

5 Add the heavy cream, milk, and salt to the saucepan with the caramel and bring to a simmer over medium heat, stirring occasionally, then remove from the heat. Pour one-quarter of the milk mixture into the bowl with the eggs and quickly whisk until fully combined. Pour in the rest of the milk mixture while stirring the egg mixture. Stir in the vanilla extract.

6 Strain the pudding mixture with a fine-mesh strainer into a pouring mug, then carefully pour it into the ramekins with the caramel layer, filling each ramekin three-quarters full.

7 Preheat the oven to 350°F (175°C; gas mark 2). Lay a small cloth towel in a deep baking dish to prevent the ramekins from moving around. Place the ramekins on top of the towel and cover each one with aluminum foil. Once the oven is at temperature, add boiling water to the baking dish to about halfway up the sides of the ramekins.

8 Carefully place the baking dish into the oven and bake for 50 to 55 minutes, until the tops are set with just a slight jiggle. Let cool.

9 To assemble: Run a knife along the edges of each ramekin, then, working one at a time, center a serving plate over the top, flip upside down, and remove the ramekin. Place the whipped cream in a piping bag with a star-shaped tip and pipe whipped cream on top of each purin. Gently push a pair of wings into the sides of each purin, about ¼ inch (6 mm) deep, and serve

NOTE
- If you prefer a creamier purin, use 2 cups (480 ml) of heavy whipping cream and 1 cup (240 ml) of milk.
- Purin is even better the next day and can be refrigerated for up to 3 days.

"Pudding! Pudding! My dear pudding!"

—Cerberus "Kero", *Cardcaptor Sakura*

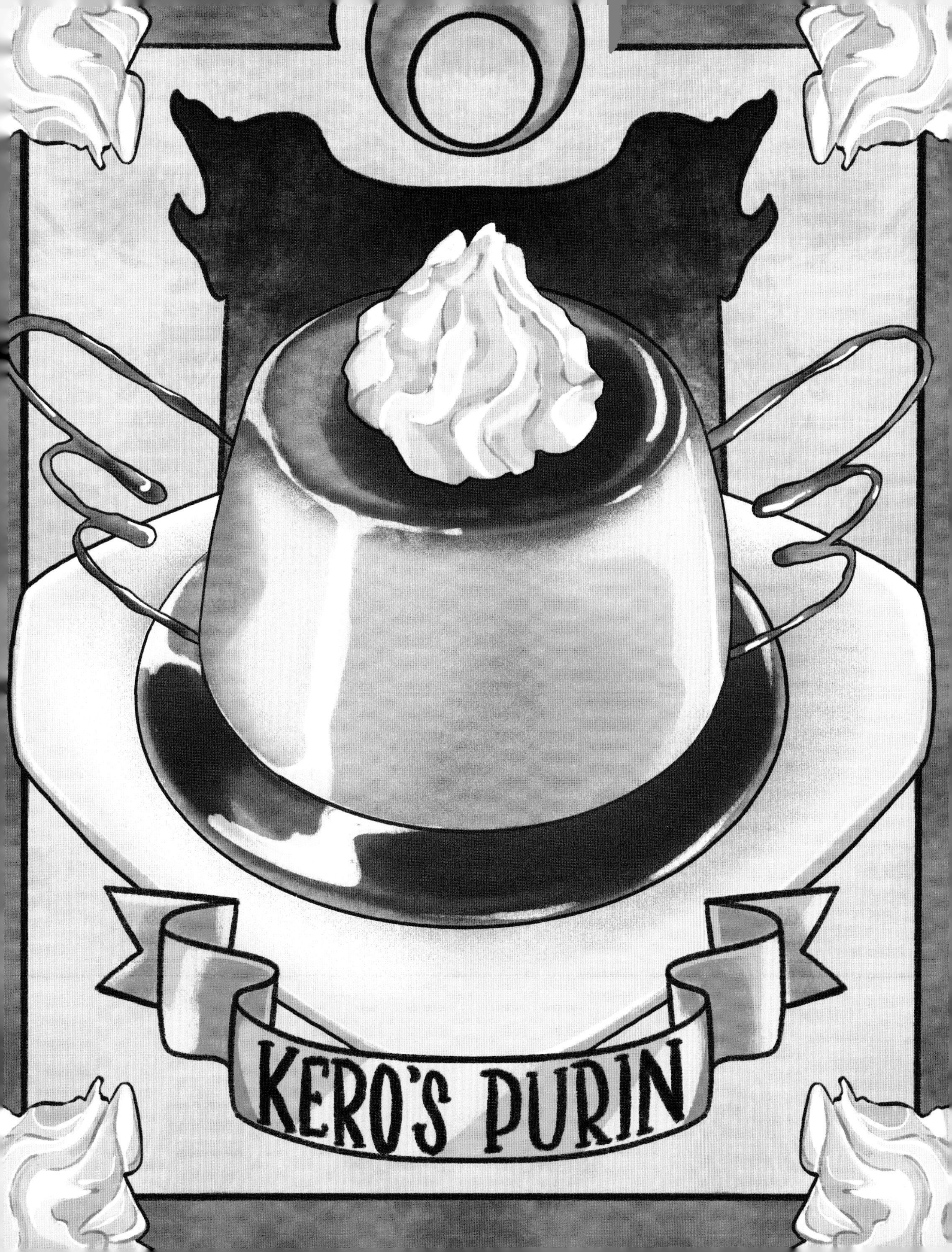
KERO'S PURIN

FRUIT TARTS

★ ANIME ★

THE ANCIENT MAGUS' BRIDE

SEASON 1   EPISODE 12

BETTER TO ASK THE WAY THAN GO ASTRAY

Silky, the housekeeper, serves these tarts as part of a hearty breakfast for the members of the household: Elias, the magus; Chise, whom Elias bought at an auction and is teaching magic; and Ruth, Chise's familiar. This anime has a lot of interesting, delicious-looking foods, mostly British-style meals, because it takes place in Great Britain.

YIELD 12 TARTS · **PREP 15 MINUTES** · **COOK 20 MINUTES**

SPECIAL TOOLS

3½-inch (9 cm) round cookie cutter

3-inch (7.5 cm) round cookie cutter

LEMON CREAM

1 block (8 ounces, or 227 g) cream cheese, at room temperature

2 tablespoons confectioners' sugar

¼ cup (60 ml) heavy whipping cream

Zest of 1 lemon

1 teaspoon vanilla extract

Pinch salt

PASTRIES

2 sheets puff pastry, defrosted

All-purpose flour, for dusting

1 large egg, beaten

2 tablespoons turbinado or sanding sugar

FOR ASSEMBLY

¼ cup (80 g) strawberry jam

6 strawberries, trimmed and sliced lengthwise into ¼-inch-thick (6 mm) slices

1 banana

Maple syrup, to taste, for serving

1 To make the lemon cream: In a medium bowl, using a hand mixer with a whisk attachment, mix the cream cheese and confectioners' sugar on medium speed until creamy and loose in texture. Add the heavy whipping cream and mix on medium speed, gradually increasing the speed to medium-high, until stiff peaks form. Add the lemon zest, vanilla, and salt and combine. Set aside.

2 To make the pastries: Preheat the oven to 400°F (205°C; gas mark 6). Line a baking tray with parchment paper.

3 Carefully roll out the puff pastry sheets with a lightly floured rolling pin onto a floured work surface to remove seams or visible folds. Cut out 12 rounds with the 3½-inch (9 cm) cookie cutter. Transfer the rounds to the prepared baking tray. Use the 3-inch (7.5 cm) cookie cutter to make a slight indent in the middle of these rounds by pressing into the pastry but not all the way through.

4 Brush the beaten egg on the outer rings of each round, then sprinkle the area with the turbinado sugar. Dock the inner circle of each pastry all over with a fork to prevent it from rising.

5 To assemble: Place a dollop of the lemon cream in the inner circles of the rounds and spread to just the edges of this circle.

6 For the strawberry tarts, place a teaspoon of the strawberry jam on the center of the lemon cream of 6 pastries, then cover with sliced strawberries. For the banana tarts, leave the remaining 6 pastries with just the lemon cream; the banana will be added after baking to preserve their color.

7 Bake for 20 minutes, or until the pastry is golden in color. Meanwhile, cut the banana into ¼-inch-thick (6 mm) slices, and when the tarts come out of the oven, top the lemon cream of the banana ones with 4 or 5 banana slices.

8 Serve the fruit tarts hot or cold and drizzle with maple syrup.

"We love by consuming and giving."

—Redcurrant, *The Ancient Magus' Bride*

STARFISH SCONES

ANIME
CLANNAD
SEASON 1 | EPISODE 6
THE OLDER AND YOUNGER SISTER'S FOUNDER'S FESTIVAL

Sanae and Akio are spouses who own a bakery called Furukawa Bread. Sanae, who is known to be a bad baker, fills the entire bakery with starfish pastries that she made herself during Golden Week. Okazaki, the protagonist, refuses to try one, and Sanae's dramatics, falling on the floor crying, are so funny that this easily becomes one of the most memorable scenes from the anime. I adapted the recipe into scones filled with pomegranate jam and clotted cream, which is often served with scones.

YIELD 4 SCONES | PREP 30 MINUTES | COOK 30 MINUTES

SPECIAL TOOLS

3½-inch (9 cm) star-shaped cookie cutter

2-inch (5 cm) star-shaped cookie cutter

SCONES

2 cups (240 g) all-purpose flour, plus more for dusting

1 teaspoon baking powder

¼ cup (50 g) sugar

⅓ cup (75 g) cold salted butter, cut into cubes

1 large egg, beaten

⅓ cup (80 ml) plus 1 teaspoon heavy whipping cream, divided

FILLINGS

1 cup (140 g) pomegranate seeds

1 tablespoon sugar

Pinch salt

½ cup (124 g) clotted cream

1 tablespoon lemon zest

½ tablespoon fresh lemon juice

STEPS

1 To make the scones: Preheat the oven to 350°F (175°C; gas mark 4). Line a baking tray with parchment paper and set aside.

2 In a large bowl, mix the flour, baking powder, and ¼ cup (50 g) sugar until fully incorporated. Add the cold butter and squish the butter and flour together with your fingertips until the mixture resembles sand or bread crumbs. Add the beaten egg and ⅓ cup (80 ml) of the heavy cream and mix until just combined into a dough ball.

CONTINUED

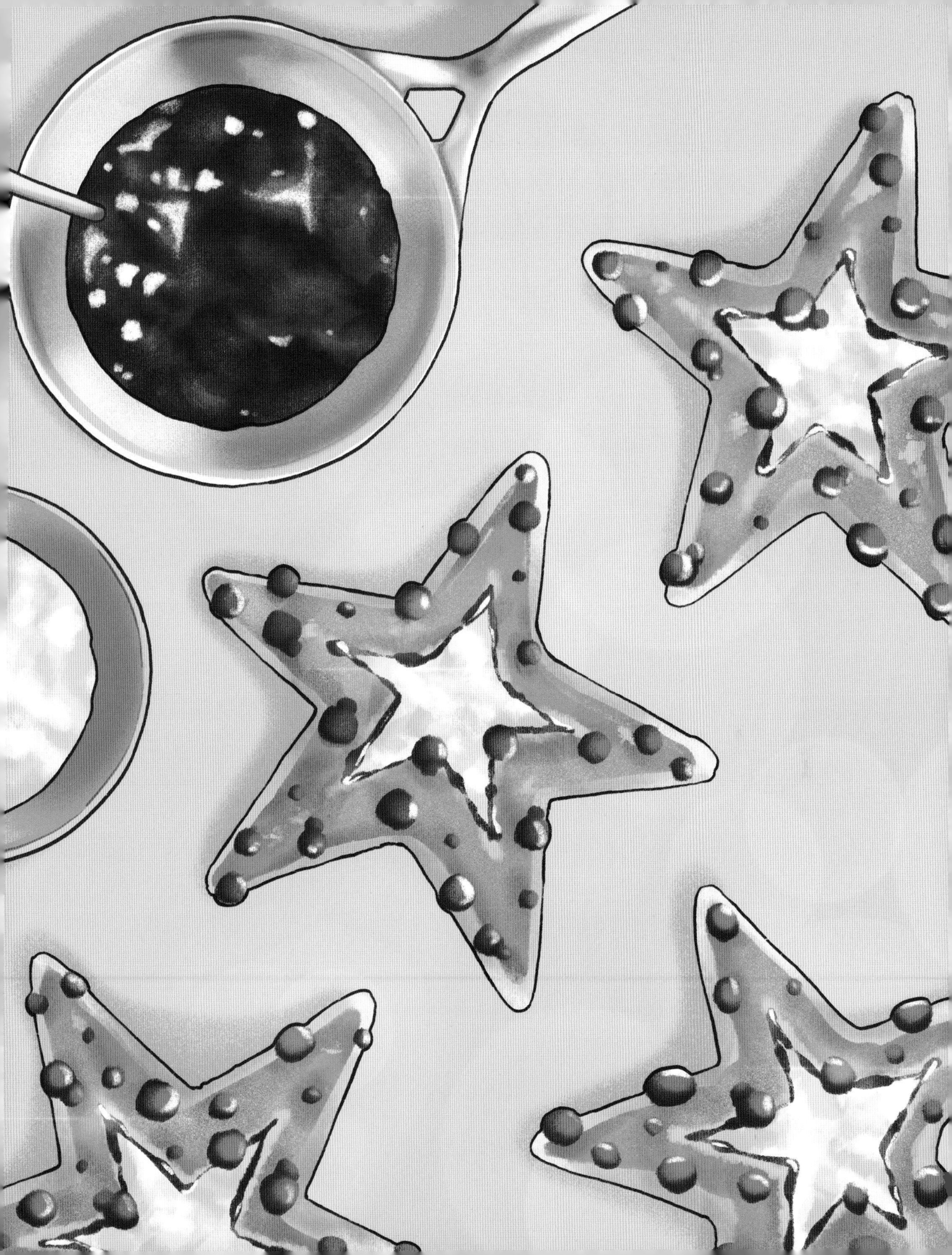

3 Lay down parchment paper on your work surface and place the dough on top. Gently knead the dough less than ten times to bring together loose crumbs. Flatten with a lightly floured rolling pin to ⅛-inch (3 mm) thickness. Cut out 8 stars with the 3½-inch (9 cm) cookie cutter, then cut out 1-inch (2.5 cm) stars from the centers of 4 of these stars.

4 Dip clean fingers or a brush into the remaining 1 teaspoon heavy cream and brush onto the surface of the 4 whole large stars. Place the 4 large stars with the cutouts on top of the stars brushed with cream and lightly press together to adhere, being careful not to squish too hard and flatten the design. Place on the prepared baking tray. (You may reroll the four 1-inch, or 2.5-cm, stars and cut out more star shapes, but these will not come out as perfect when baked as the other stars.)

5 Bake for 20 minutes, or until puffed and slightly browned. Remove from the heat and let cool on the tray.

6 While the scones bake, make the fillings: In a small saucepan, combine the pomegranate seeds, 1 tablespoon sugar, and salt. Cook for 10 minutes over a medium heat, stirring occasionally. Strain the mixture with a fine-mesh strainer into a heatproof bowl, squishing the juice from the pomegranate seeds, being careful not to burn yourself. Let the jam cool.

7 In a small bowl, mix the clotted cream, lemon zest, and lemon juice until well combined.

8 In a separate small bowl, place 1 tablespoon of the clotted cream mixture with 1 teaspoon of the cooled pomegranate jam and stir together to make pink-colored jam.

9 To assemble: Using a brush, spread the pink jam on the surface of the outer star-shaped pastry, then spread the pomegranate jam inside the star-shaped crevice. Spread the clotted cream mixture on top of the pomegranate jam in the crevice.

10 Using a small spoon, add pomegranate jam dots all over the surface of the starfish scones and serve.

"I spent the entire Golden Week developing these yummy pastries. I designed every single one of them from cream-filled to jam-filled!"

—Sanae Furukawa, *Clannad*

SIBERIA SPONGE CAKE

★ ANIME ★
THE WIND RISES

Studio Ghibli's *The Wind Rises* is based on the true story of Japanese warplane designer Jiro Horikoshi. The film takes place in pre–World War II Japan, in the 1920s and 30s when the economy is doing poorly. In one scene, Jiro buys Siberian sponge cake (a layered cake made of Japanese Castella cake and red bean jelly) on his way home from work, the shop owner greeting him like an old friend. He offers the cake to some underprivileged children who seem skeptical and run away, so he takes it home and contemplates with his friend about the current state of Japan.

YIELD 8 SERVINGS · **PREP** 30 MINUTES · **COOK** 3 HOURS · **CHILL** 2 HOURS

SPECIAL TOOLS

2 (7-inch, or 18-cm) square cake pans

RED BEAN PASTE

1 cup (200 g) dried red beans (also called adzuki beans)

½ cup (100 g) sugar

⅛ teaspoon salt

JAPANESE CASTELLA CAKE

1½ tablespoons honey

2 tablespoons canola oil (or any neutral oil)

1 teaspoon vanilla extract

6 large egg yolks

⅔ cup (135 g) sugar, divided

1 cup (130 g) cake flour

Pinch salt

4 large egg whites

Oil, for greasing

RED BEAN JELLY

⅔ cup (165 ml) water

2 teaspoons agar-agar powder

FOR SERVING

Prepared hot green tea

《 CONTINUED 》

SIBERIA SPONGE CAKE STEPS

1 To make the red bean paste: Put the dried red beans into a medium saucepan. Add enough water to submerge the beans, about four times the amount of beans, bring to a boil over medium-high heat, then boil for 5 minutes. Drain the beans, then rinse in the strainer with clean running water. Rinse the saucepan with fresh water and add the beans back in. Add more water to submerge again, about four times their amount. Bring to a boil once more over medium-high heat, then reduce the heat to medium and cover with a lid. Cook the beans until soft, between 1 hour and 30 minutes to 2 hours. Add the ½ cup (100 g) sugar and ⅛ teaspoon salt to the pan, mix, and cook until the water is fully evaporated, about 30 minutes, stirring occasionally. Remove from the heat.

2 Carefully transfer the hot beans to a blender, or use an immersion blender, and blend into a smooth paste. (Optional but recommended: Strain the blended mixture through a fine-mesh strainer to get a more visually appealing jelly filling layer.)

3 While the beans cook, make the Japanese castella cake: Preheat the oven to 350°F (175°C; gas mark 4). (It is essential to preheat the oven for a long time to ensure the oven is hot enough when ready to bake.) Line the sides and bottom of the two 7-inch (18 cm) square cake pans with parchment paper and set aside.

4 In a small heatproof bowl, stir together the honey, canola oil, and vanilla, then microwave until warm, about 30 seconds. In a large bowl, combine the egg yolks and ⅓ cup (67 g) of the sugar. Using a hand mixer with a whisk attachment, mix on high speed until fluffed, doubled in volume, and ribbons are left in the batter while mixing, 5 to 6 minutes. Add the warmed honey mixture to the egg yolk mixture and combine on low speed until fully combined. Add the cake flour and salt and fold in to fully incorporate.

5 Add the egg whites to a separate large bowl. Using the hand mixer with a clean, dry whisk attachment, whip the egg whites and remaining ⅓ cup (68 g) sugar on low speed, gradually increasing to medium high-speed, until stiff peaks form, about 5 minutes.

6 Add one-third of the egg white mixture to the egg yolk mixture and fully combine using the hand mixer with the whisk attachment on low speed until just incorporated. Add another third of the egg whites to the egg yolks and gently combine by folding with a spatula. Add the last third of egg whites and combine again by folding with the spatula. Divide the batter between the prepared baking pans by pouring it from 10 inches (25 cm) above the pans to prevent large air bubbles. Tap the pans a few times on a surface to pop any air bubbles on top.

7 Place the pans in the preheated oven, then reduce the oven temperature to 300°F (150°C; gas mark 2) and bake for 30 to 35, until the tops are golden brown and a toothpick inserted into the centers comes out clean.

8 While the cakes are baking, prepare two pieces of parchment paper that are large enough to cover the tops of the cakes and lightly brush one side of each piece with oil.

SIBERIA SPONGE CAKE STEPS

9 Once the cakes come out of the oven, carefully drop the cakes, in their pans, from 4 inches (10 cm) above a surface onto the surface to deflate them; be careful not to burn yourself. Working with one cake at a time, place an oiled parchment paper on top, with the oiled side touching the cake, and turn over onto a flat surface. Remove the cake pan and leave the cake upside down for 15 minutes to achieve a flat top, then turn over to let completely cool. Once cooled, wrap the cakes separately in plastic wrap, while still on the parchment paper, to keep from drying out.

10 To make the red bean jelly: In a medium pot, combine the water and agar-agar powder and let the agar-agar rehydrate while you prepare the cakes for assembly. Prepare one of the 7-inch (18 cm) cake pans by laying a piece of plastic wrap at least 15 inches (38 cm) long across the pan one way, and another piece of plastic wrap, again, at least 15 inches long (38 cm), across the pan the other way, so they crisscross. Remove the plastic wrap and parchment paper from one of the cakes and place it in the cake pan, top side down, on top of the plastic wrap.

11 Bring the pot with the agar-agar to a boil over medium-high heat. Reduce the heat to medium, then add the red bean paste, mix, and cook for 5 minutes. The consistency should resemble lava. Remove from the heat.

12 To assemble: Pour the red bean jelly filling on top of the cake in the cake pan. Spread evenly, then unwrap the plastic wrap and parchment paper from the second cake and place the cake, top side up, on top of the jelly. Wrap the cakes in the plastic wrap in the pan and gently push down on the surface to adhere the cake and jelly. Place the Siberia cake in the refrigerator for at least 2 hours, or until the red bean jelly filling is set.

13 To serve: Remove the cake from the cake pan and plastic wrap. Place the cake onto a cutting board and slice all the sides for a clean look. Cut the cake into quarters, then slice the quarters diagonally. Enjoy with green tea.

NOTE

The cooking time for the dried red beans can be reduced by 30 minutes to an hour (depending on the beans) if they are soaked in water overnight before cooking.

"Sponge cake? You have some strange eating habits."

—Kiro Honjo, *The Wind Rises*

CARAMEL WAFFLES
WITH APPLES AND PECANS

★ ANIME ★
YOUR LIE IN APRIL

SEASON 1   EPISODE 3
INSIDE SPRING

Kousei Arima, a musical prodigy, stops playing the piano after his mom dies and he suffers a panic attack during a performance. Two years later, he meets Kaori Miyazono, a spirited violinist, who teaches him how to find love in music again. In this episode, Kousei and Kaori go to a café, where Kaori orders caramel waffles with apples and nuts. She mentions how long she's been waiting to try this dessert and takes some photos before eating it and savoring every bite. You'll also want to take a photo of this delicious masterpiece before you dig in!

YIELD 2 SERVINGS · **PREP** 20 MINUTES · **COOK** 20 MINUTES

SPECIAL TOOLS

Waffle iron

SPICED SWEET APPLES AND PECANS

3 Fuji apples, peeled and sliced ¼ inch (6 mm) thick

2 tablespoons unsalted butter

2 pinches salt

½ tablespoon cornstarch

3 tablespoons dark brown sugar

½ teaspoon ground cinnamon

¼ teaspoon grated nutmeg

¼ teaspoon vanilla extract

1 teaspoon lemon juice

¼ cup roasted whole pecans

BUTTERMILK WAFFLES

1 cup (120 g) all-purpose flour

1 tablespoon cornstarch

1½ tablespoons granulated sugar

1 teaspoon baking powder

Pinch salt

1¼ cups (300 ml) buttermilk

2 tablespoons unsalted butter, melted

1 large egg

1 teaspoon vanilla extract

SALTED BUTTERMILK CARAMEL

2 tablespoons water

½ cup (110 g) packed light brown sugar

½ teaspoon baking soda

2 tablespoons cold unsalted butter

½ cup (120 ml) cold buttermilk

2 pinches salt

WHIPPED CREAM

1½ cups (360 ml) heavy whipping cream

½ tablespoon granulated sugar

1 teaspoon vanilla extract

FOR ASSEMBLY

2 sprigs fresh mint

((CONTINUED))

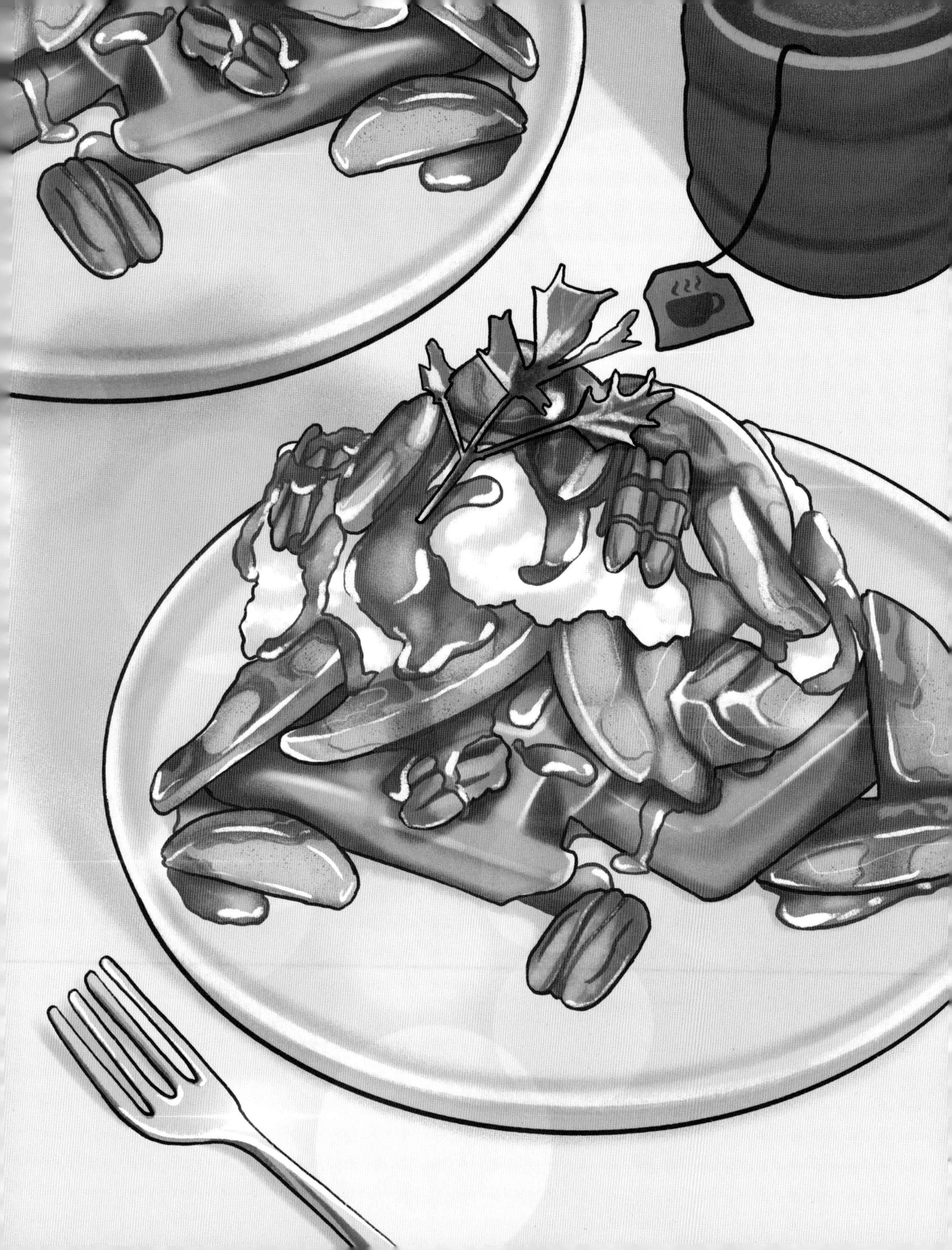

1 To make the spiced sweet apples and pecans: In a medium saucepan, combine all the apple and pecan ingredients over medium heat. Cook, stirring occasionally, until the sauce becomes sticky and the apples are tender, about 8 minutes.

2 To make the buttermilk waffles: In a medium bowl, whisk together the flour, 1 tablespoon cornstarch, 1½ tablespoons granulated sugar, baking powder, and pinch of salt. In a separate medium bowl, whisk together the buttermilk, melted butter, egg, and 1 teaspoon vanilla. Add the dry ingredients to the bowl with the wet ingredients and fully combine.

3 Preheat the waffle iron, then pour about ½ cup (120 ml batter into it and cook for 3 to 4 minutes, or until golden brown on both sides and crisp. Transfer the waffle to a rack to cool. Repeat with the remaining batter. (There should be enough batter for 4 waffles.)

4 Meanwhile, make the salted buttermilk caramel: In a medium saucepan, combine the water and ½ cup (110 g) light brown sugar. Fully saturate the brown sugar with the water by swirling the pan. Turn on the stove to medium and heat the mixture, swirling the pan occasionally, to 320°F (160°C), measuring with a candy thermometer, about 10 minutes.

(At no point should you mix the caramel with any utensils; swirling is the most efficient way to prevent crystallization.) Remove the pan from heat. Carefully add the baking soda and whisk vigorously for 3 seconds (be cautious, as the hot sugar will expand to three times its size). Quickly add the cold butter and cold buttermilk and stir until combined.

5 Place the pan back onto the stove over medium heat and cook, stirring occasionally, for another 6 to 7 minutes, or until the mixture has thickened enough to coat the back of a spoon. Add the 2 pinches of salt, stir to combine, and then remove from heat and transfer to a heatproof container. (The caramel becomes thicker as it cools.)

6 To make the whipped cream: In a medium bowl, combine the heavy whipping cream, ½ tablespoon granulated sugar, and 1 teaspoon vanilla and, using a hand mixer with a whisk attachment, whip on low speed, gradually increasing to high speed, until soft peaks form, about 2 minutes.

7 To assemble: On a large plate, layer some spiced sweet apples and pecans between 2 buttermilk waffles, top with a generous amount of whipped cream, and drizzle with the salted buttermilk caramel. Garnish with a mint sprig. Repeat for the second large plate.

MATCHA MELON PAN TURTLES

★ ANIME ★

YAKITATE!! JAPAN

SEASON 1 EPISODE 16
THE GREEN MARVEL!
IT'S THE MAGICIAN
KAZUMA!

SEASON 1 EPISODE 17
DECISIVE BATTLE!
KOALA'S DRAGON VS
KAZUMA'S TURTLE!

In this exciting two-episode arc, Azuma competes against Koala in the third round of the Pantasia Group's Rookie Competition with a special guest judge. They are tasked to make an animal bread, and Koala's dragon and Azuma's turtle both look impressive. But Azuma's colleagues wonder how Azuma's bread turned out such a vibrant green and not browned after baking. His technique is to use a lower oven temperature with a longer cook time, though that can lead to a dry, tasteless bread. To prevent it from drying out, Azuma brushed on corn syrup before baking. He got this idea from eating a candy apple when he was a child, which was juicy on the inside from the syrup coating. In the end, Azuma's bread was declared the "King of Turtle Breads." I baked these melon pan (melon bread) at the same low temperature of 150°C, or 300°F, but replaced the syrup with granulated sugar.

YIELD **4** MELON PAN · PREP **1** HOUR · CHILL **30** MINUTES · COOK **15** MINUTES · REST **30** MINUTES

SPECIAL TOOLS

Small food-safe paint brush (used only for food) or a toothpick

MATCHA SOFT MILK BREAD

1 recipe Milk Bread from the Chocolate Cornets recipe (page 132; see step 1 on page 184 before making this recipe)

2 tablespoons matcha powder

CRAQUELIN TOPPING

¼ cup (55 g) unsalted butter, at room temperature

½ cup (100 g) sugar, divided

1 tablespoon matcha powder

1 large egg

1 teaspoon vanilla extract

1 cup (120 g) all-purpose flour

1 teaspoon baking powder

Pinch salt

Brown gel food coloring

FOR ASSEMBLY

Brown gel food coloring

«« CONTINUED »»

MATCHA MELON PAN TURTLES STEPS

1 To make the matcha soft milk bread: Follow steps 1 through 3 of the Chocolate Cornets recipe on page 132, adding the 2 tablespoons matcha powder in step 2 with the dry ingredients (flour, milk powder, and salt). Four of the dough pieces will be turned into turtle bodies and the other 2 pieces will be for the turtle heads and feet. Cover the dough pieces with plastic wrap to prevent them from drying out and set aside.

2 To make the craquelin topping: In a medium bowl, using a hand mixer with a beater attachment, cream the butter, ¼ cup (50 g) of the sugar, and 1 tablespoon matcha powder on medium speed until pale and fluffy, 2 to 3 minutes. Add the egg and vanilla and mix on medium-high speed until combined and fluffy, about 4 minutes. In a separate medium bowl, mix the flour, baking powder, and salt together. Add the dry ingredients to the bowl with the wet ingredients and mix on medium speed until the dough comes together, 2 to 3 minutes. Place the cookie dough on plastic wrap, seal, and form into a log. Refrigerate until firm and ready to assemble, about 30 minutes.

3 Once the craquelin is firm, form the turtle bodies by shaping 4 pieces of dough into a ball. Slice the log of craquelin topping into 4 equal-size pieces.

4 For the turtle shells, place a piece of craquelin topping between two pieces of parchment paper and flatten it into a circle ⅛ inch (3 mm) thick. Place the flattened craquelin on top of a prepared dough ball and cover it entirely. Repeat this step with the remaining craquelin pieces and dough balls. Place the remaining ¼ cup (50 g) sugar in a shallow bowl and roll each turtle shell in the sugar to cover it. For the turtle-shell design, use a small knife to score the craquelin topping into a crisscross pattern, or create your own realistic turtle-shell design. Paint the scored areas brown with the brown food coloring. When finished, set the turtle shells aside.

5 For the turtle heads and feet, combine the remaining 2 pieces of dough, then divide into 3 equal-size pieces. One piece will be used for the head and the other two for the feet. For the heads, divide the dough into 4 equal-size pieces and roll each piece into an elongated oval, 1 inch (2.5 cm) wide and narrowing into a neck. For the feet, divide the dough into 16 equal-size pieces. Roll each piece into a ball, then form each ball into a triangle. Flatten one point of each triangle to ⅛-inch (3 mm) thickness for the tip of the foot. With a knife, cut 3 small slits onto the flattened tip to create toes.

6 To assemble: Place the bodies with the shells far apart from one another on a baking tray lined with parchment paper. Lay a head and 4 feet alongside each body. Adhere the head and feet to each body by adding a little bit of water at the seams and then gently pushing the dough together. Cover the melon pan with plastic wrap or a cloth, then let them rise a final time in a warm spot, until doubled in size, about 30 minutes. Preheat the oven to 300°F (150°C; gas mark 2). After they rise, use a small knife to carve a smile into the turtle heads.

7 Bake for 12 to 15 minutes, until slightly browned and crusted. Transfer to a rack to cool completely. Once cooled, draw eyes and color in the smile on each turtle with brown food coloring.

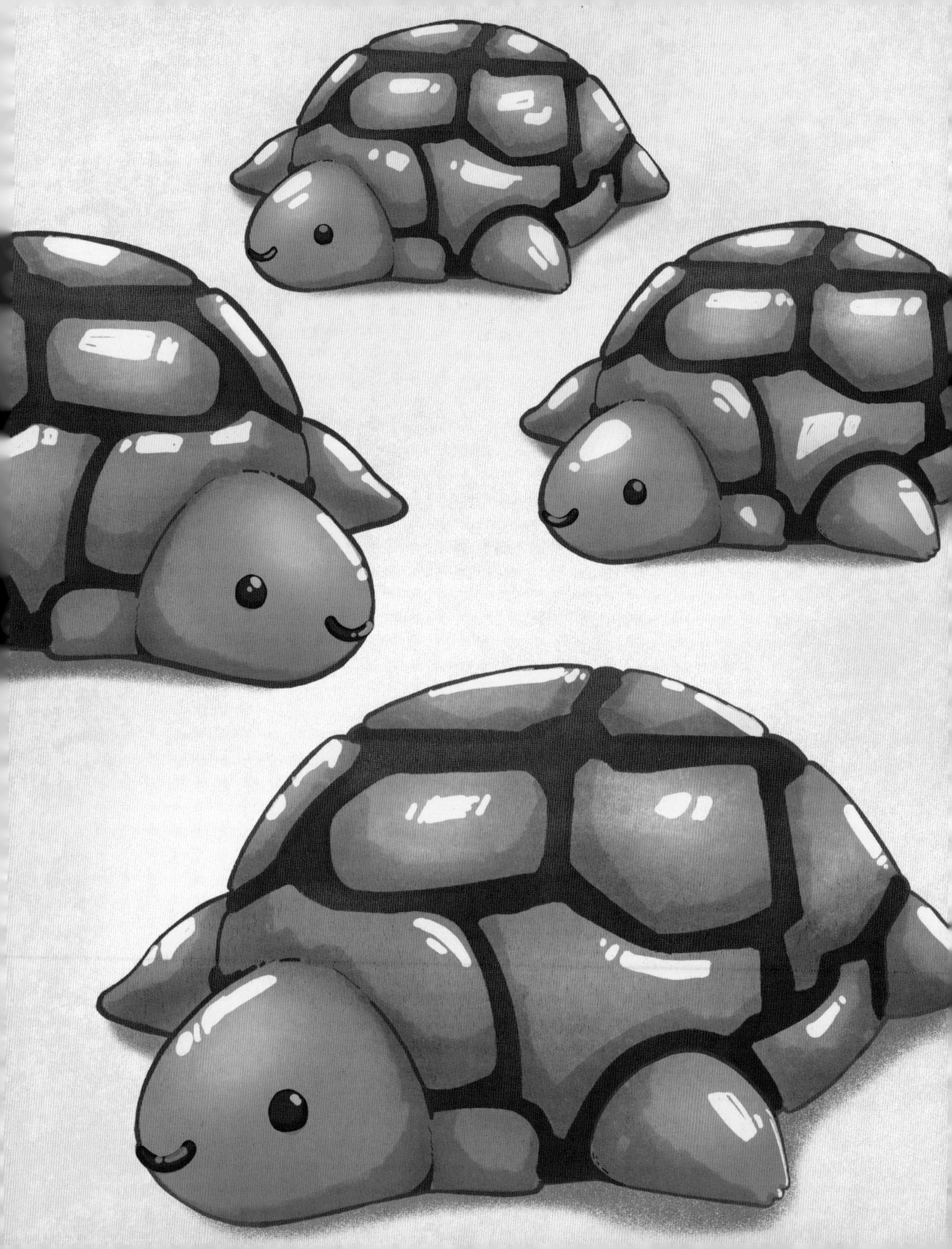

PANNA COTTA WITH RASPBERRY COULIS

★ ANIME ★
CRAYON SHIN-CHAN

MOVIE 21:
BAKAUMA! B-KYUU GOURMET SURVIVAL BATTLE!!

The B-class gourmet festival is opening and featuring traditional, cheap foods. An elitist A-class gourmet association, headed by Don Gourmeto, is tasked to remove all the stalls that don't measure up to their high standards. While Don Gourmeto waits for his team to carry out his plans, he is seen eating A-class panna cotta. Panna cotta is an elegant Italian dessert made with vanilla-flavored cream thickened with gelatin.

YIELD 6 PANNA COTTA · **PREP** 10 MINUTES · **COOK** 20 MINUTES · **CHILL** 4 HOURS · **REST** 10 MINUTES

SPECIAL TOOLS

6 (4-ounce, or 120-ml) ramekins

PANNA COTTA

2 teaspoons gelatin powder

3 tablespoons room-temperature water

2 cups (480 ml) heavy whipping cream

2½ tablespoons sugar

Pinch salt

1 teaspoon vanilla extract

RASPBERRY COULIS

1 cup (125 g) raspberries, plus 12 for serving

Zest and juice of ½ lemon

1 tablespoon sugar

Pinch salt

Fresh mint leaves, to taste, plus 6 small leaves for serving

《 STEPS 》

1 To make the vanilla panna cotta: In a small bowl, add the gelatin powder to the room-temperature water and stir to combine and hydrate the gelatin.

2 In a medium saucepan, bring the heavy cream, 2½ tablespoons sugar, and pinch of salt to a simmer over medium heat. Remove from the heat, add the hydrated gelatin, and stir until dissolved. Strain the mixture with a fine-mesh strainer into a vessel with a spout. Add the vanilla extract and stir.

3 Lay a small cloth towel in a deep baking dish to prevent the ramekins from moving around. Place the ramekins on top of the towel, then pour the mixture into the ramekins, leaving ¼ inch (6 mm) at the top. Let set in the refrigerator until firm, at least 4 hours, or overnight.

4 When the panna cotta is set, make the raspberry coulis: In a small saucepan, mix the raspberries, lemon zest and juice, 1 tablespoon sugar, and pinch of salt together. Turn the heat to medium and crush the raspberries to release their juices. Cook, stirring occasionally, for 10 minutes, or until the raspberries are soft and almost melted.

5 Remove from the heat and carefully transfer to a blender, or use an immersion blender, along with some mint leaves. Once the mixture is cooled, about 10 minutes, pulse until smooth, then press the mixture through a fine-mesh strainer into a bowl.

6 To serve: Place some warm water in a bowl and gently dip the bottom of each ramekin in the water for a few seconds. Wipe off the water with a cloth or paper towel, then hold a serving plate over the top, flip upside down, and remove the ramekin. Draw a line across the top of each panna cotta with the raspberry coulis and top with a small mint leaf. Scatter 2 raspberries on each plate.

"Food is an art. Cooks move synchronized like a metronome, shaping the lines of art on the plate, tasting it as if we are dancing in a ballet."

—Don Gourmeto, *Crayon Shin-chan: Bakauma! B-Kyuu Gourmet Survival Battle!!*

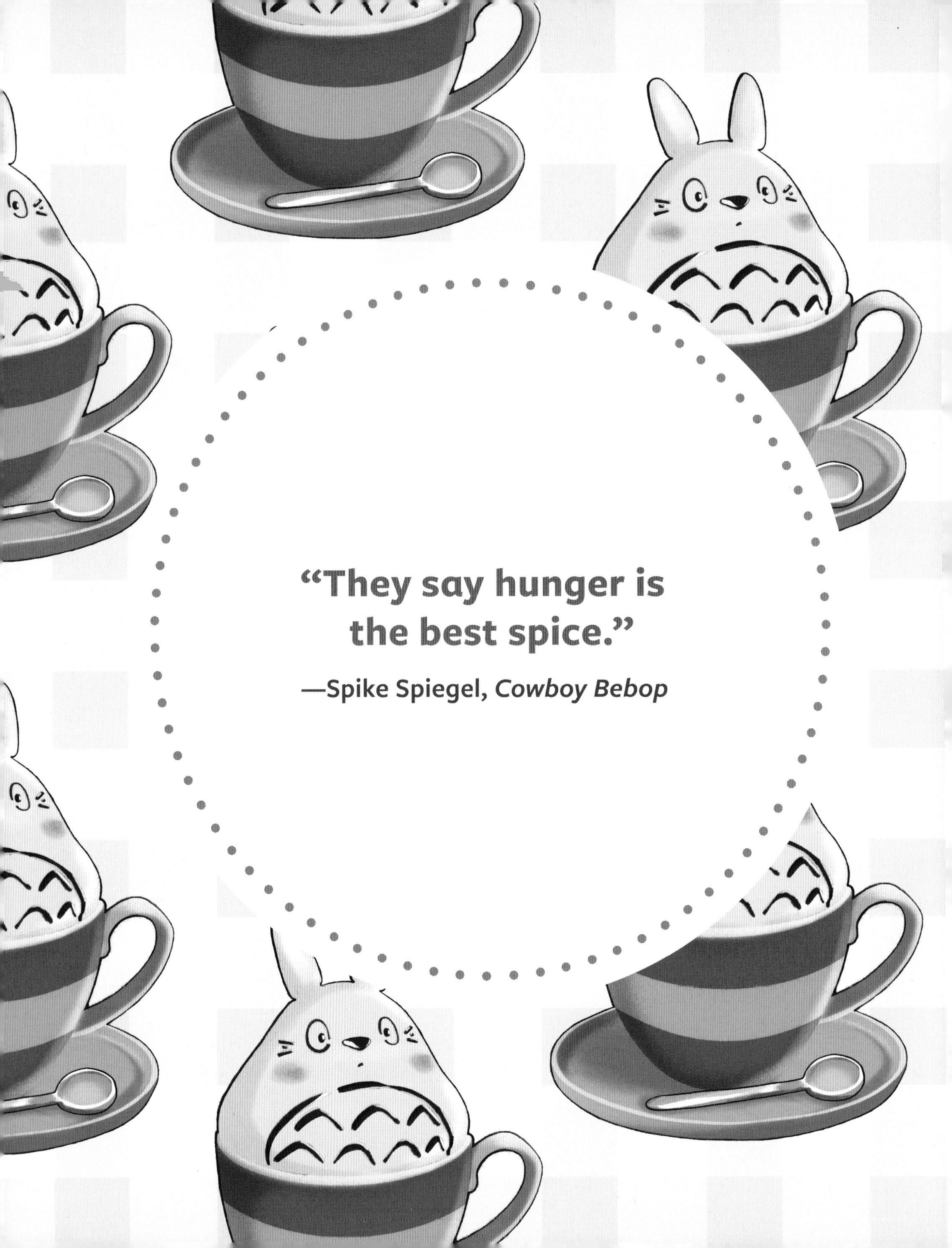

“They say hunger is the best spice.”

—Spike Spiegel, *Cowboy Bebop*

DRINKS

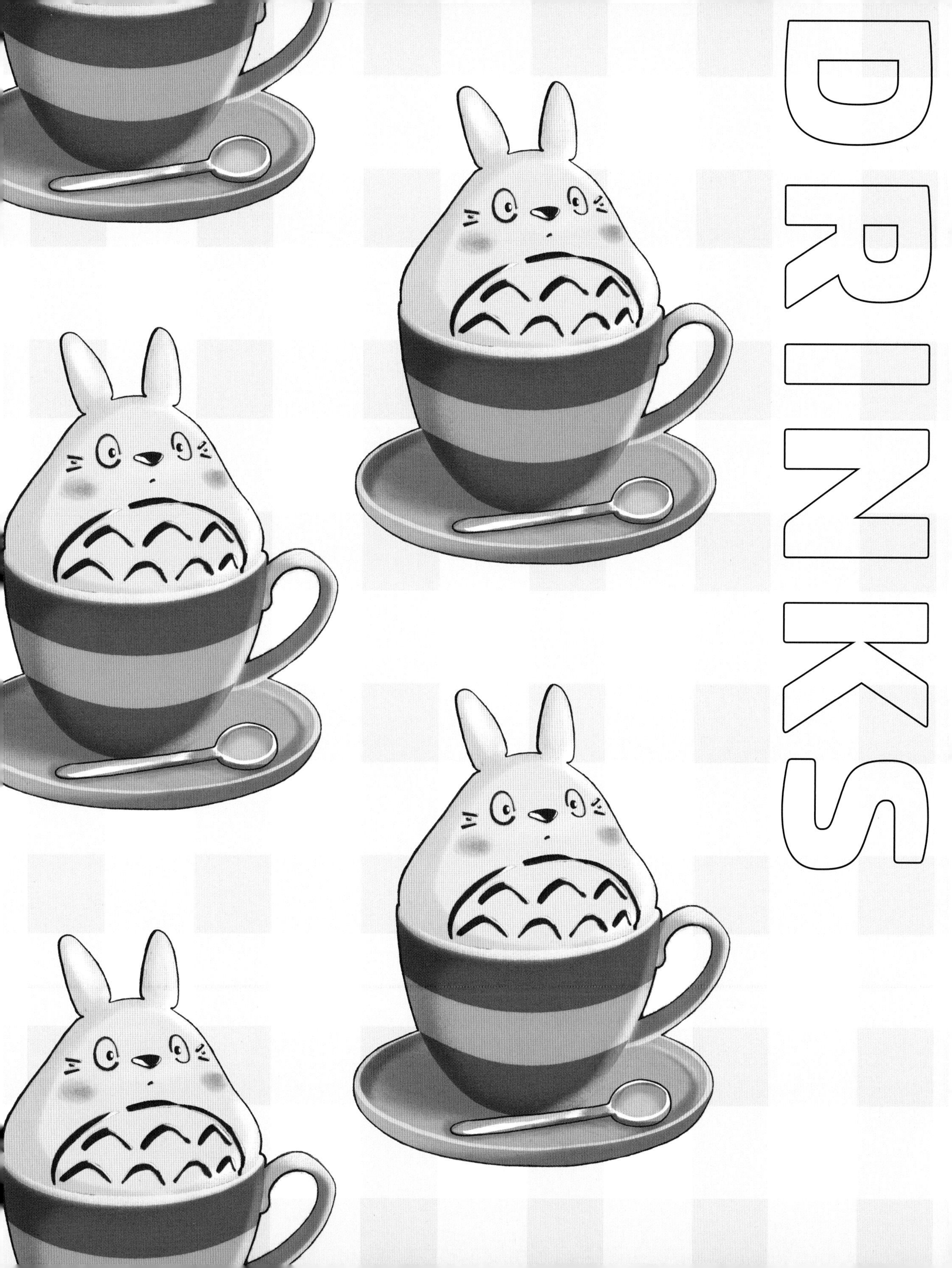

HOT BUTTERED RUM COW

★ ANIME ★

LAID-BACK CAMP

SEASON 2   EPISODE 6

CAPE OHMAMA
IN WINTER

Chiaki, Ena, and Aoi—members of the Outdoor Activities Club—decide to go camping during the wintertime. To warm them up, Chiaki makes a "hot buttered rum cow," a nonalcoholic drink she learned about from working at the liquor store. But don't fret, booze lovers! I have included a substitution for using real rum. This drink would be a nice addition to winter holiday festivities.

YIELD 4 SERVINGS   **PREP** 10 MINUTES   **COOK** 10 MINUTES

INGREDIENTS

¼ cup (55 g) unsalted butter,
plus 1 tablespoon for serving

4 cups (960 ml) dairy or nondairy milk

2 tablespoons dark brown sugar

1 teaspoon ground cinnamon

Pinch freshly grated nutmeg

1 teaspoon vanilla extract

1 teaspoon artificial rum flavoring

4 cinnamon sticks, for serving

‹‹ STEPS ››

1 In a small saucepan, cook the ¼ cup (55 g) butter over medium heat until browned and nutty in aroma, about 6 minutes. Strain the brown butter through a fine-mesh strainer or cheesecloth into a small heatproof bowl.

2 In a medium saucepan, combine the milk, brown sugar, cinnamon, and nutmeg. Bring to a gentle simmer over medium heat, about 8 minutes. Remove from the heat.

3 Add the prepared brown butter, vanilla, and artificial rum flavoring to the pan and stir until well combined.

4 To assemble: Ladle the hot buttered rum cow into four mugs. Add a small slice of the 1 tablespoon butter on top of each drink and drop a cinnamon stick into each mug for stirring.

NOTE

For an alcoholic version, don't add the artificial rum flavoring to the saucepan in step 3, but add 2 ounces (60 ml) of dark rum to each mug before ladling in the hot buttered rum cow.

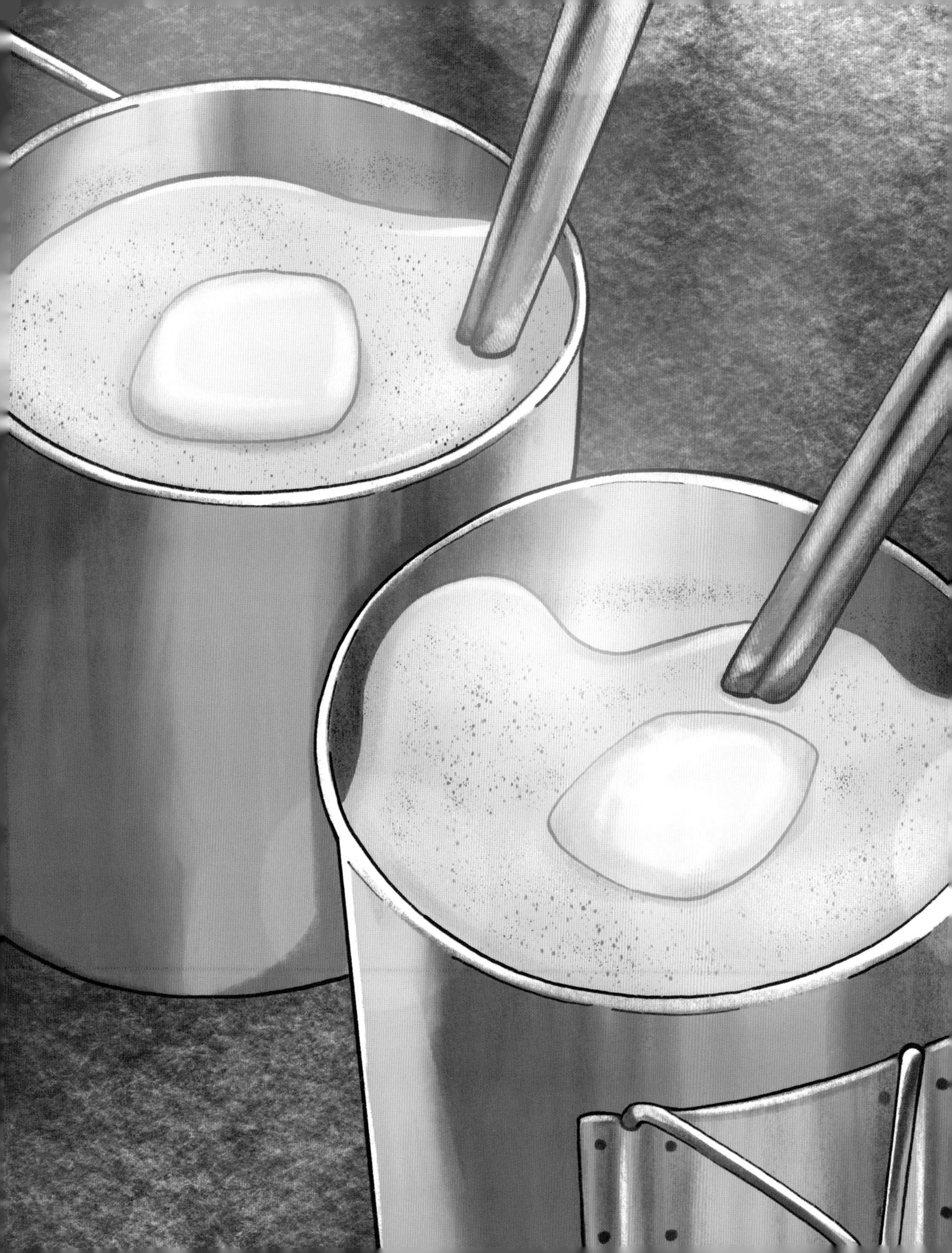

LEMON SOUR

★ ANIME ★
MOB PSYCHO 100 II
SEASON 1 EPISODE 6
POOR, LONELY, WHITEY

When Reigen won't respect Mob's boundaries—calling him on short notice and making him do a lot of the work at their joint business, Spirits and Such Consultation Office—they split up, causing Reigen to become depressed. He realizes that Mob is fine without him and that he's truly lonely when only his mom emails him on his birthday. That night, Reigen goes to the Happy Trails bar and orders a lemon sour, "extra on the sour," and despite the drink having no alcohol, Reigen feels drunk and leaves the bar. A lemon sour is usually made with seltzer and vodka infused with lemon rinds, but without the alcohol, it's just fizzy lemonade!

YIELD 8 SERVINGS · **PREP** 15 MINUTES · **INFUSE** OVERNIGHT

LEMON-INFUSED SYRUP

3 large lemons

1¾ cups (350 g) sugar
(or same weight as lemons)

ICED-LEMON GARNISH

1 large lemon

ASSEMBLY

1 large lemon

Large ice cubes

4 cups (1 L) carbonated water
(seltzer, club soda, mineral water)

)) STEPS ((

1 To make the lemon-infused syrup: Thinly slice the 3 lemons, removing any seeds. Make a layer of lemon slices in a glass container (with a tight-fitting lid) and cover them with a thin layer of sugar. Repeat the layers of lemon slices and sugar until all are used. Cover with the lid and refrigerate overnight; liquid syrup will seep from the lemons and become more flavorful over time. (You can store in the refrigerator for up to 1 week.)

2 To make the iced-lemon garnish: Slice the lemon into 8 wedges, removing any seeds, place them in a single layer on a parchment-lined plate or tray, and freeze.

3 To assemble: Juice the lemon. Add 2 teaspoons of the lemon-infused syrup and ½ tablespoon of the freshly squeezed lemon juice to a tall glass. Add an iced lemon wedge and ice cubes almost to the rim of the glass. Fill the rest of the glass with carbonated water, stir, and serve. Repeat this step for the remaining drinks.

STRAWBERRY MILK

ANIME
GINTAMA
SEASON 1 | EPISODE 11
LOOK, OVERLY STICKY SWEET DUMPLINGS ARE NOT REAL DUMPLINGS, YOU IDIOT!

Gintama **is a wacky, hilarious anime that has a lot of puns and meta-humor. It also is quite random at times, and the fandom has many inside jokes as a result. In this episode, Gin is not only given the nickname "Strawberry Milky," but he also makes his iconic, rousing speech about the importance of strawberry milk, giving the fandom one of its most beloved inside jokes.**

YIELD 4 SERVINGS | PREP 10 MINUTES | COOK 7 MINUTES

INGREDIENTS

1 cup (240 ml) water
¼ cup (50 g) sugar, or to taste
4 cups (580 g) strawberries, finely chopped
4 cups (960 ml) cold dairy or nondairy milk

STEPS

1 In a medium saucepan, combine the water, sugar, and strawberries. Bring to a boil over medium-high heat, then reduce the heat to medium-low and simmer until the mixture is thickened and the strawberries are soft, about 5 minutes.

2 Mash the strawberries and continue cooking for another 2 to 3 minutes. Remove from the heat and let cool to room temperature.

3 Once cooled, add the cold milk to the pan and stir until combined. Strain the mixture with a fine-mesh strainer, if desired, then pour into four mugs.

"I chalk it up to calcium deficiency."

—Gintoki Sakata, *Gintama*

PRAIRIE OYSTER

ANIME
COWBOY BEBOP
SEASON 1 EPISODE 7
HEAVY METAL QUEEN

Cowboy Bebop is set in 2071 and revolves around a band of space bounty hunters who are contracted by the Inter-Solar System Police (ISSP) to catch criminals for them. A common hangover cure for protagonist Spike Spiegel, this drink makes many appearances throughout the series. In the show, it's stated that a prairie oyster is made with gin, a raw egg yolk, hot sauce, and pepper, and while you could use that recipe and get, what I assume is, a good hangover cure, I made a couple of modifications so that it's less of a kick in the face and almost enjoyable.

YIELD **1** SERVING

PREP **2** MINUTES

INGREDIENTS

1 egg yolk (from a pasteurized egg)

2 dashes Worcestershire sauce

2 dashes Tabasco

2 cracks black pepper

Pinch salt

1 ounce (30 ml) dry gin

STEPS

1. Add the egg yolk to a short glass, followed by the rest of the ingredients. (Do not stir in order to keep the egg yolk whole to mimic the texture of an oyster.)

2. Plug your nose, then drink.

NOTE

This recipe calls for a raw egg yolk, which may contain Salmonella (1 in 20,000 pasteurized eggs contain it) and make you ill. Make sure to use only pasteurized eggs and that you understand the risk of eating raw egg yolks.

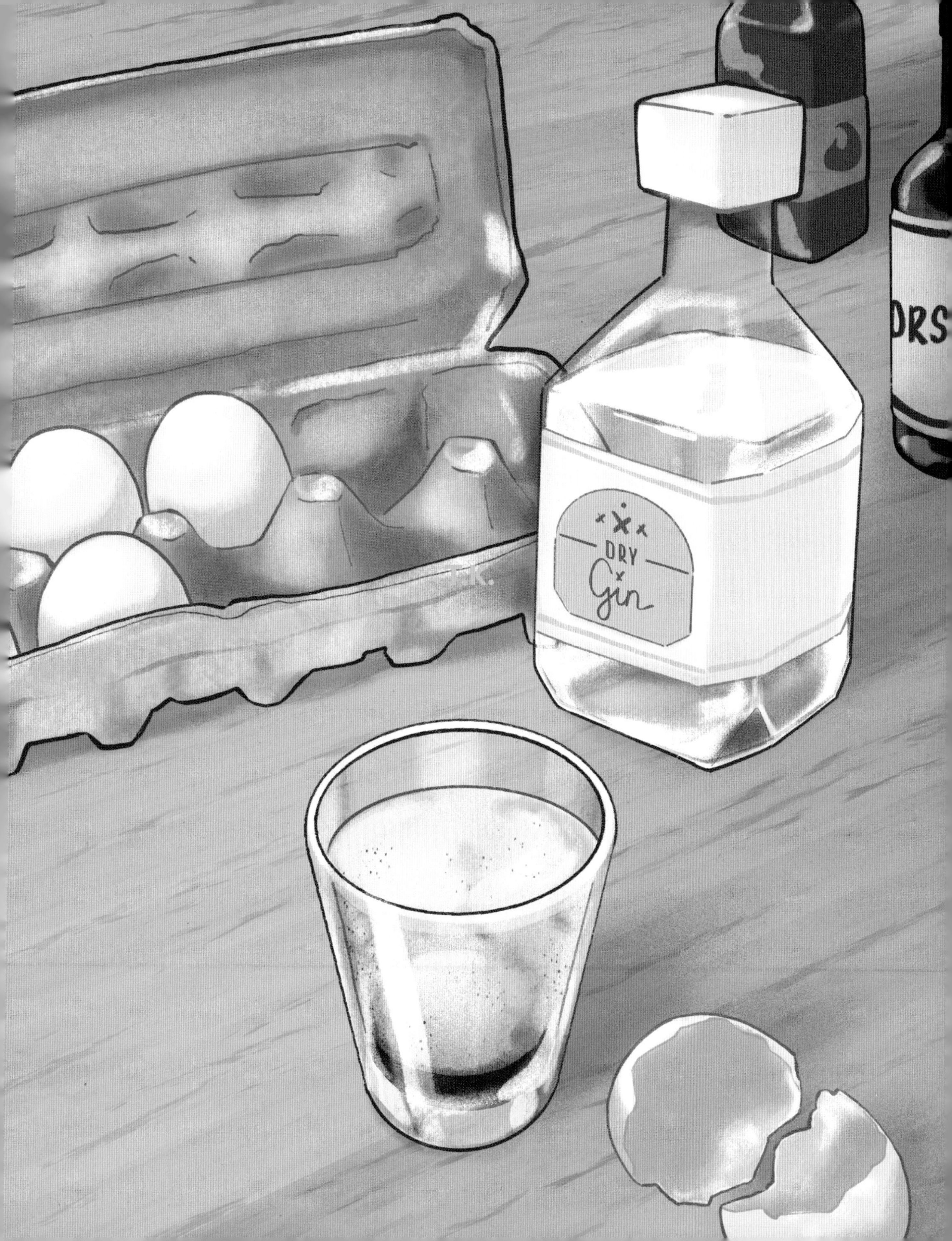
DRY
Gin

TOTORO LATTE ART

★ ANIME
MY NEIGHBOR TOTORO

Unlike the other recipes in this book, this latte art did not appear in the movie but is my own creation to pay homage to one of the most popular Studio Ghibli films of all time! 3-D latte art is a huge trend in Japanese cafés, so I thought it would be fun to include. Totoro is not too hard to replicate, so I hope you give this a try.

YIELD
2
SERVINGS

PREP
10
MINUTES

DECORATE
15
MINUTES

SPECIAL TOOLS

Handheld milk frother

Toothpicks

INGREDIENTS

Prepared coffee drink or hot chocolate

1 cup milk (skim, 1%, 2%, whole, or lactose-free)

Brown gel food coloring, for decorating

《 STEPS 》

1 Place the prepared coffee or hot chocolate into two mugs, leaving some room at the top.

2 In a tall microwave-safe container, microwave the milk until hot, about 1 minute. Remove from the microwave and froth the milk with a handheld frother until the volume has tripled and stopped expanding. Microwave for another 30 seconds, making sure there is space for expansion, to get hard/stiff milk foam.

3 Decorate the drinks by placing large dollops of the milk foam on top of the mug to create Totoro's rotund body. To make an ear, place a small dollop of the milk foam on a spoon and, using another spoon, scoop it back and forth to create a long pointed shape like a bunny ear. Carefully place the ear on top of the body, then smooth out where they connect using the back of the other spoon, gently pressing the seams together. Repeat for the other ear.

4 For the details, place brown gel food coloring on a small plate. Dip a toothpick into the food coloring and draw two ¼-inch (6 mm) circles for eyes and a small dot in each for the pupil; a wide triangular nose in between the eyes; 3 lines on each cheek for the whiskers; and a semicircle outlining the top of the belly, and inside that, 2 rows of upside-down V shapes. For the blush, add a small amount of food coloring to the milk foam and mix using the toothpick for a lighter brown. Gently scoop a small portion and place onto the face. Repeat step 3 and this step for the second mug.

NOTE
Hard milk foam is very forgiving and will not deflate for hours, so take your time if you need to practice and perfect your Totoro characters.

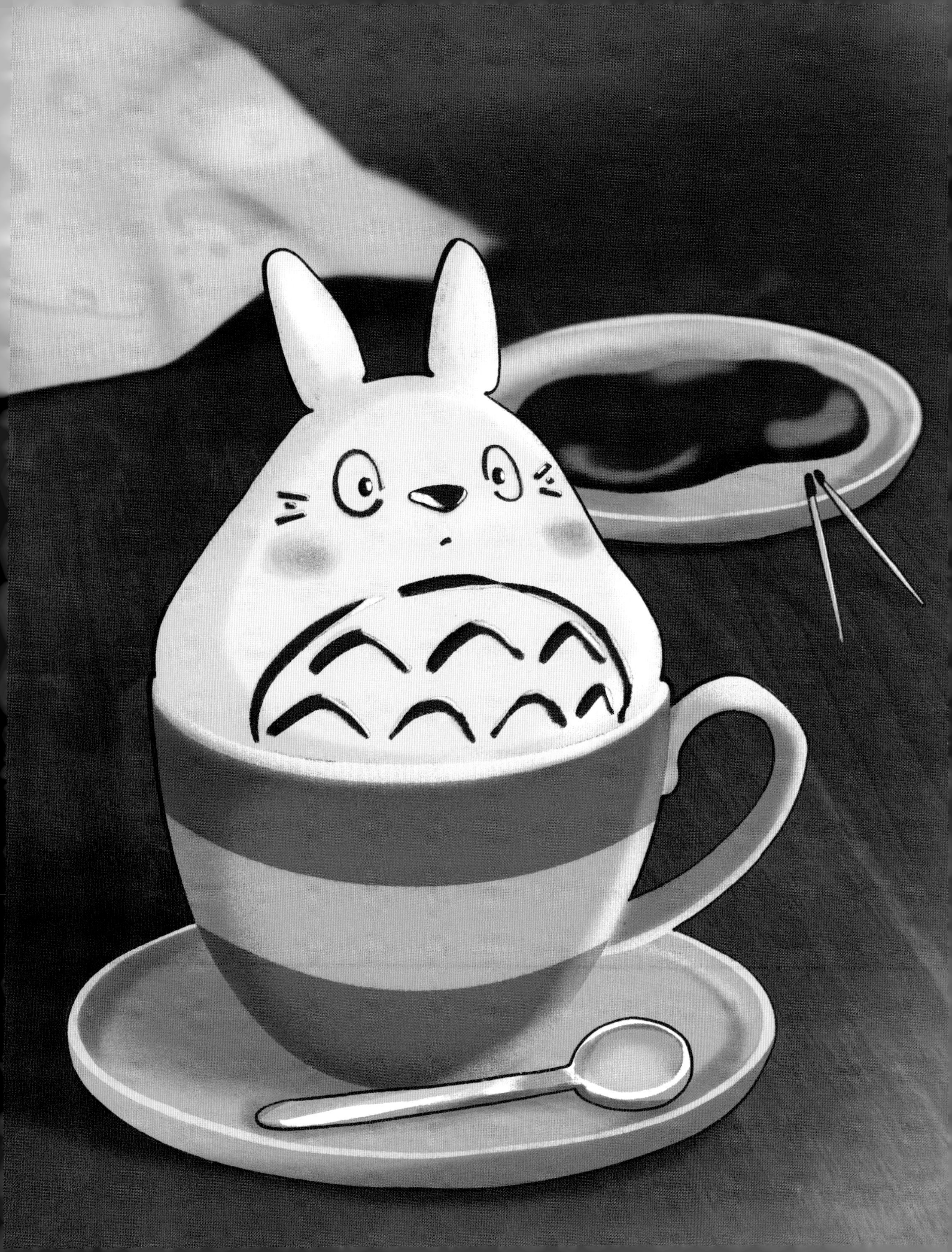

RASPBERRY CITRUS TEA PUNCH

ANIME

WHEN MARNIE WAS THERE

In this Studio Ghibli film, Anna Saski is staying with her foster parents' relatives in a seaside town for the summer. She befriends Marnie, who lives in the abandoned mansion across the salt marsh. Marnie invites Anna to her mansion and tells her about the lavish parties they used to throw there. The inspiration for this punch came from what I imagined was served at those parties, perfect for summertime and a large group!

YIELD 6 SERVING

PREP 20 MINUTES

SPECIAL TOOLS

Glass punch bowl set (optional)

GARNISHES

½ large lemon, thinly sliced and seeded

½ large navel orange, thinly sliced

2 cups (250 g) raspberries

PUNCH

2 cups (250 g) raspberries

4 cups (1 L) boiling water

¼ cup (50 g) sugar, or to taste

2 passion fruit tea bags

Fresh mint leaves, to taste, plus sprigs for serving

Juice of 2 large lemons

Juice of 2 large navel oranges

STEPS

1 To prepare the garnishes: Place the sliced lemons and oranges, along with 2 cups (250 g) raspberries, in the freezer until frozen, at least 15 minutes.

2 Meanwhile, make the punch: Muddle the other 2 cups (250 g) raspberries, then strain through a fine-mesh strainer into a glass punch bowl or large heatproof bowl. Keeping the strainer over the bowl, pour the boiling water over the raspberry pulp. Do not squeeze the raspberry pulp after adding the boiling water; you do not want to burn your hand. Discard the pulp.

3 Add the sugar to the boiling water and stir to dissolve. Add the tea bags and let steep for 2 minutes.

4 Remove and discard the tea bags and let the tea cool to room temperature.

5 Add the mint leaves and lemon and orange juices to the tea and stir to combine. Refrigerate to chill.

6 To serve: Garnish the chilled punch with the frozen fruit and mint sprigs and add a serving ladle to the punch bowl.

FROZEN MANGO COCKTAIL

★ ANIME ★
LOVE IS LIKE A COCKTAIL
SEASON 1   EPISODE 13
THIRTEENTH GLASS: FROZEN MANGO COCKTAIL

Chisato doesn't drink unless her bartending husband, Sora, makes the drink for her. Each episode of this anime highlights a different drink as the two relax after a hard day's work and enjoy dinner together. In this episode, Sora reveals that a long time ago, when he was a full-time bartender, Chisato walked into the bar where he worked and he made her this cocktail, which happened to be her first alcoholic drink. The anime recipe makes this cocktail with 2 ounces (60 ml) each of mango and pineapple juice and 1 ounce (30 ml) of vodka. Though Chisato says that the cocktail tastes like "pineapple shaved ice," I modified the recipe to accentuate the mango flavor and color, since it is a mango cocktail after all!

YIELD **2** SERVINGS   PREP **10** MINUTES   COOK **4** MINUTES

SIMPLE SYRUP

½ cup (120 ml) water

½ cup (100 g) sugar

DRINK

½ cup (70 g) frozen mango chunks

¼ cup (60 g) frozen pineapple chunks

½ tablespoon lemon zest

1 tablespoon fresh lemon juice

½ cup (4 ounces, or 120 ml) vodka (or distilled liquor of choice)

2 sprigs fresh mint, for garnishing

⟨⟨ STEPS ⟩⟩

1 To make the simple syrup: In a small saucepan, bring the water and sugar to a boil over medium heat, then reduce the heat to a simmer until the sugar is dissolved, stirring occasionally, 4 to 5 minutes. Set aside and let cool.

2 To make the drink: Place the frozen mango and pineapple, lemon zest, lemon juice, and vodka in a blender and blend until thick. Taste the mixture, add 2 teaspoons of simple syrup (or to taste), and blend once more.

3 To assemble: Place 2 generous scoops of the mango mixture into each cocktail glass and top with the mint sprigs.

SENKU COLA

ANIME

DR. STONE

SEASON 1 | EPISODE 15

THE CULMINATION OF
TWO MILLION YEARS

A mysterious green flash of light petrifies all of humanity, turning it to stone for over three thousand years. Senku Ishigami, a scientific genius, was one of the first to un-petrify and is now working to rebuild civilization, creating the Kingdom of Science. Opposing him is Tsukasa, head of the Tsukasa Empire, who doesn't believe that the old world should be restored and that they should create the new world as a brutish hierarchy. In order to sway Gen, a smart strategist, from Tsukasa's side to the Kingdom of Science, Senku promises to make him Senku Cola, which requires him to re-create glass as well as carbonated water. Senku mixes the carbonated water with caramelized honey, cilantro, and lime to make the cola and claims that lime zest mixed with crushed cilantro replicates the smell of cola.

YIELD 4 SERVINGS   **PREP** 10 MINUTES   **COOK** 12 MINUTES

INGREDIENTS

½ cup (20 g) finely chopped cilantro

1 tablespoon lime zest

½ tablespoon sugar

¼ cup (60 ml) fresh lime juice

¾ cup (252 g) honey, or to taste

3 tablespoons water

4 cups (1 L) chilled club soda or seltzer

Ice, for serving

((STEPS))

1 Using a mortar and pestle, grind the cilantro, lime zest, and sugar until a paste forms. Add the lime juice and mix until combined.

2 In a medium saucepan, bring the honey and water to a simmer over medium heat. Once the honey turns a dark caramel color, 12 to 14 minutes, turn off the heat.

3 Carefully add the cilantro-lime mixture to the pan. The mixture will bubble up, so quickly whisk it together until combined. Let cool to room temperature, then strain with a fine-mesh strainer.

4 To assemble: Place 2 tablespoons (or to taste) of the honey-cilantro-lime caramel into a glass and add 1 cup (240 ml) of the chilled club soda. Mix with a spoon, then add the ice. Repeat this step with the remaining drinks.

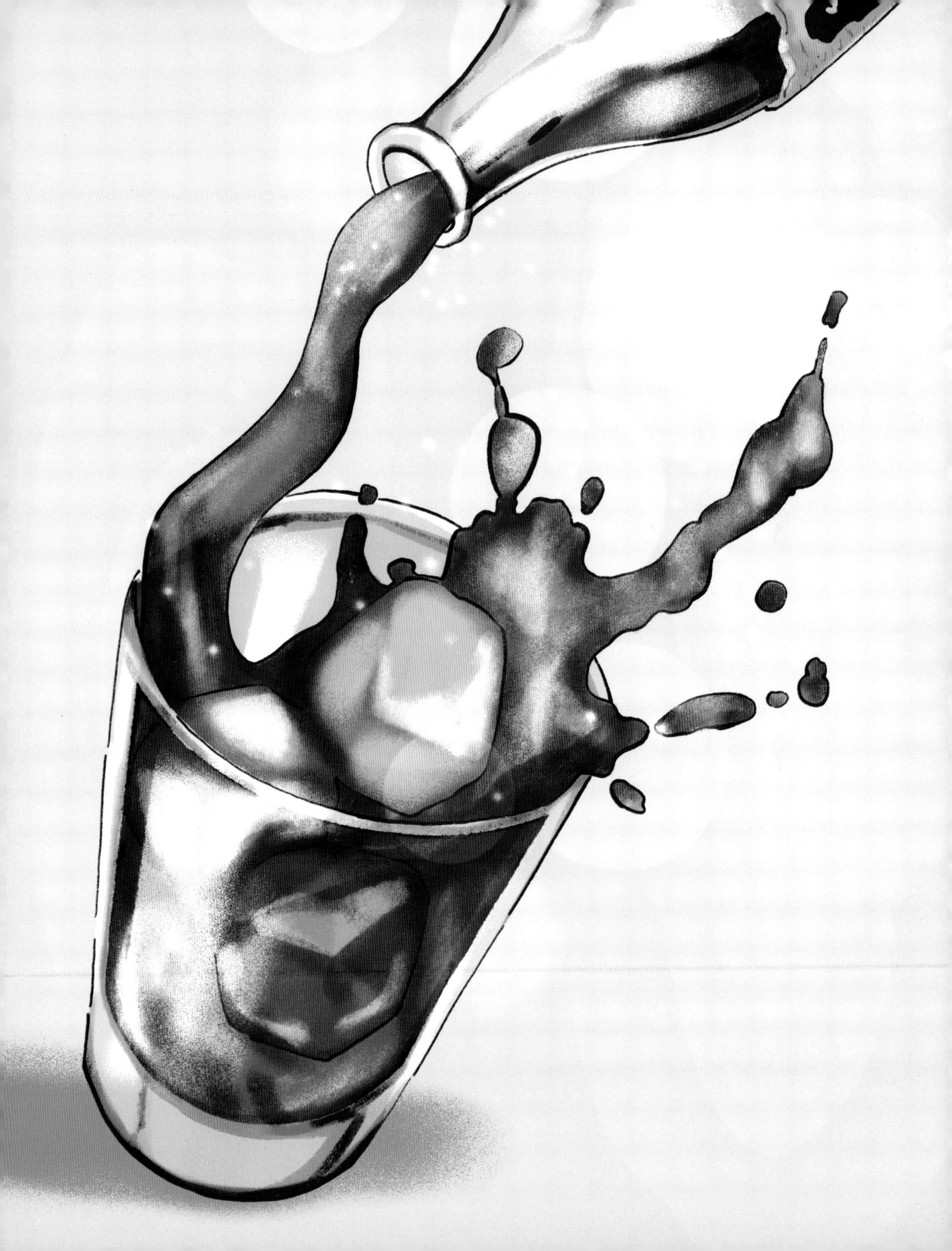

INDEX

R

S

ABOUT THE AUTHOR

Nadine Estero has always loved anime and now combines that interest with her passion for cooking, publicly showcasing her food re-creations on social media (@issagrill). Her works have been featured on numerous entertainment websites and in publications worldwide, including Screen Rant, Dexerto, and the *New York Times*. She also works with companies to make their video game foods come to life from her home in Vancouver, Canada.